175 Best Multifunction Electric Pressure Cooker Recipes

Marilyn Haugen

Robert
ROSE

For complete cataloguing information, see page 224.

Disclaimer
The recipes in this book have been carefully tested by our kitchen and our tasters. To the best of our knowledge, they are safe and nutritious for ordinary use and users. For those people with food or other allergies, or who have special food requirements or health issues, please read the suggested contents of each recipe carefully and determine whether or not they may create a problem for you. All recipes are used at the risk of the consumer. Consumers should always consult their multicooker manufacturer's manual for recommended procedures and cooking times.

We cannot be responsible for any hazards, loss or damage that may occur as a result of any recipe use.

For those with special needs, allergies, requirements or health problems, in the event of any doubt, please contact your medical adviser prior to the use of any recipe.

Design and production: Alicia McCarthy & Kevin Cockburn/PageWave Graphics Inc.
Editor: Sue Sumeraj
Recipe editor: Jennifer MacKenzie
Proofreader: Kelly Jones
Indexer: Gillian Watts
Photography: Tango Photography
Food stylist: Éric Régimbald
Prop stylist: Véronique Gagnon-Lalanne

Cover image: Root Beer Pulled Pork Sandwiches (page 93)

Published by Robert Rose Inc.
120 Eglinton Avenue East, Suite 800, Toronto, Ontario, Canada M4P 1E2
Tel: (416) 322-6552 Fax: (416) 322-6936
www.robertrose.ca

Printed and bound in Canada

1 2 3 4 5 6 7 8 9 FP 25 24 23 22 21 20 19 18 17

Contents

Preface

This is the second cookbook I have been fortunate enough to write using a multifunction electric pressure cooker, also known as a multicooker. My first book included a range of recipes using various multicooker functions, including the pressure cooking function, the slow cooking function and several other functions.

Pressure cooking is the main topic of this book, and for good reason: it makes cooking so much quicker and easier, and the results are mouthwatering. After testing multiple recipes for my first book, I was curious to see how much more this fabulous appliance could do. The answer? A lot! Today's pressure cookers help busy people get a home-cooked meal on the table in record time.

Pressure cooking is the "new" rage in cooking again — just as it was decades ago — and fortunately for today's cook, the safety and ease of use of the newer pressure cookers have been vastly improved. With your electric pressure cooker and this cookbook, you will be able to swiftly put together meals for any time of day. I've provided updated versions of some classic recipes that you are sure to love, and even more recipes for people who are following a paleo, vegetarian or vegan diet. There are even wonderful recipes for make-ahead dishes and one-pot meals, to make cooking even easier.

If you enjoy the recipes and tips in this book, and want to make preparing quick, easy and healthy meals a regular part of your life, stop by my blog, www.FoodThymes.com, to check out some of my other recipes and cookbooks.

Now, let's start cooking!

— *Marilyn Haugen*

Acknowledgments

I cannot begin to thank the many people who made this book possible without first and foremost giving my heartfelt thanks to my mother. Her endless love and encouragement taught me that you can accomplish anything. Without the confidence she instilled in me, this book would not have been possible. I wish she was here now to see it come to life.

My sincere appreciation to Bob Dees, my publisher, who gave me the opportunity to create this cookbook to share with you. My editor, Sue Sumeraj, who is always outstanding to work with, has extraordinary insight into what will make a great experience for our readers. Sue and Jennifer MacKenzie, a recipe developer, editor and author, gave exceptional input for this book, so you can be sure the recipes are easy to understand and will turn out as intended.

Many thanks to Alicia McCarthy and Kevin Cockburn of PageWave Graphics for the wonderful design; to the team at Tango Photography for the stunning photographs; and to all of the outstanding professionals at Robert Rose who made this process a truly enjoyable and successful experience.

Multicooker Basics

If you are looking for an easier and quicker way to get scrumptious meals on your table, then a multifunction electric pressure cooker — or multicooker — is for you. The beauty of this appliance, whether you choose its pressure cooking or slow cooking functions, is that you can prepare a meal with little hands-on time, and the cooker will deliver consistently delicious results. It's perfect for busy people who want to get a nutritious meal on the table with little effort and minimal cleanup.

The recipes in this cookbook take advantage of the pressure cooking capabilities of the multicooker. Pressure cooking is by far the quickest and easiest way to get a fantastic meal on the table. But since there are times when slow cooking is the more convenient option, several recipes offer alternative instructions on preparing the dish using the slow cooking function.

About Multicookers

A multicooker enables you to pressure cook, slow cook, cook rice, make porridge and even make yogurt, all in one small, handy countertop appliance. There are several brands available today at kitchen stores, big-box retailers and online. Many brands and sizes of multicookers can be used to prepare the recipes in this book. I have noted, where appropriate, which recipes should be used only with cookers of a specific size or when you can halve, double or triple a recipe.

The electric multicookers on the market today have several functions that can be used to cook food. This book mainly uses the high and low pressure cooking functions, with occasional optional slow cooking instructions. You can refer to the user manual that came with your appliance for a more detailed explanation of the functions, but in general there are three core processing functions:

- **Pressure:** Your multicooker will offer you options for cooking on high or low pressure.
- **Slow cook:** Your multicooker will offer you options for slow cooking at different temperatures.
- **Sauté:** Depending on what brand of multicooker you are using, this function might be labeled High, Sauté or Brown.

> Pressure cooking preserves the nutrients and moisture of your food while improving flavor and texture.

In addition, there are operation keys that enable you to adjust the cooking time. Each recipe will tell you which functions to use and the cooking time. Keep in mind that it is very important to follow the steps exactly as written to ensure that you get the best results, safely and mess-free.

On the following pages, you'll find some additional tips for success with your multicooker, whether you are following one of the recipes in this book or venturing out on your own.

Pressure Cooking

- The lid must always be closed and locked and the steam release valve closed when you are using a pressure cooking function.

- You must have a minimum of 1 cup (250 mL) liquid in the pot. Check your user manual for your specific cooker for the amount of liquid needed to bring your pot to pressure.

- The cooker must be no more than two-thirds full for any recipe, and no more than half full for ingredients, such as beans and grains, that may foam or expand during cooking.

> The actual cooking time does not start until after working pressure is reached, which can take approximately 10 to 20 minutes, depending on the volume of ingredients in the pot.

Releasing Pressure

- **Quick release:** When the cooking time is done, cancel cooking and quickly open the steam release valve. This immediately releases all of the pressure in the pot and stops the cooking process. (When cooking rice, you may want to partially open and close the valve in short bursts to release the steam.) When the float valve drops down, you will be able to open the lid. Keep your hands and face away from the hole on the top of the steam release valve so you don't get scalded by the escaping steam. You may want to use an oven mitt when opening the valve.

- **10-minute release:** When the cooking time is done, cancel cooking and let the pot stand, covered, for 10 minutes. After 10 minutes, open the steam release valve and remove the lid. This release method is often used for dishes that benefit from an additional 10 minutes in the cooker's steam. (Occasionally, recipes may call for more or less standing time.)

- **Natural release:** When the cooking time is done, cancel cooking and let the pot stand, covered, until the float valve drops down. Open the steam release valve, as a precaution, and remove the lid. This method can take about 15 to 25 minutes, depending on the volume of ingredients and the pressure level. It is used for dishes that foam and could cause clogging of the exhaust valve or spewing of ingredients out through the exhaust valve. It is also used for certain dishes that benefit from the additional standing time.

Soaking Beans

Dried beans can be pressure cooked without soaking, but presoaking them removes some of the indigestible sugars that can cause gas. It also reduces the cooking time and bean breakage. The 8- to 12-hour standard soak is my preferred method, as it does the best job of removing the sugars and decreasing breakage. I offer the other methods as options for those occasions when you don't have time for a long soak (and for certain beans that do not require soaking).

- **8- to 12-hour standard soak:** Rinse and drain the dried beans. Place them in a medium bowl and cover with 4 cups (1 L) cold water for every 1 cup (250 mL) of beans. Let stand for 8 hours or overnight. Drain and rinse the beans.

- **10-minute quick soak:** Rinse and drain the dried beans. Add 4 cups (1 L) cold water and 1 tsp (5 mL) salt for every 1 cup (250 mL) of beans. (Do not fill the pot more than halfway full.) Cook on high pressure for 2 minutes. Let the pot stand, covered, until the float valve drops down before removing the lid.

- **No soaking:** Some beans do not require soaking. If the recipe does not include soaking in the method, no soaking is needed. Even beans for which soaking is recommended *can* be pressure-cooked without soaking, but you'll need to adjust the cooking time (see the chart on page 215).

Slow Cooking

If looking at your slow-cooking dish is something you feel you must do, purchase a clear glass cooking lid that is specifically made to fit your multicooker.

- Unless you are directed by a recipe to leave the lid off, the lid should be closed and locked and the steam release handle opened when you are using the slow cooking function.

- Fill the cooker half to three-quarters full to avoid over- or undercooking.

- Avoid removing the lid during the cooking time. Doing so releases valuable heat, which can alter the amount of cooking time your dish gets at the correct temperature.

- Do not use frozen meats, as the temperature of your dish may never reach a safe temperature.

Sautéing

- The lid must always be kept off when you're sautéing or browning food. Do not even partially cover the pot with the lid, as you might do on the stovetop when simmering sauces, as pressure can build in the pot and be very dangerous.

- The High/Sauté/Brown function may vary in temperature depending on your cooker. When a recipe says "Heat the pressure cooker on High/Sauté/Brown," the highest temperature offered by your cooker is intended, so use the appropriate setting as indicated by your user manual.

- Always cancel cooking when you are done sautéing or browning, before moving on to other steps, such as pressure cooking or slow cooking.

All Functions

- Ingredients should be added in the order listed and as directed in the instructions.

- All ingredients must be added to the inner cooking pot, never directly into the cooker housing.

- Keep the steam release valve free from any obstructions. After each use, make sure to clean the valve and screens.

- Keep your multicooker clear of any cupboards, to prevent damage from the steam released.

- Whenever you are opening the lid after cooking, tilt the cover away from you so you don't get scalded by escaping steam.

At altitudes above 3,000 feet (914 meters), recipes will require a change in cooking time or temperature, or both. Contact your multicooker's manufacturer to learn the adjustments needed for your altitude.

Recommended Accessories

Aside from your multicooker and some standard kitchen utensils, there are a few other kitchen gadgets that you will need (or will find handy) when preparing the recipes in this book.

- **Large chef's knife:** A sharp chef's knife is the best tool for cutting meats and vegetables to fit into your pot.

- **Garlic press:** You can certainly mince garlic by hand, but a press makes this frequent task a snap.

- **Standard measuring cups:** When measuring your ingredients, use the standard liquid and dry measuring cups that you have on hand in your kitchen. The measuring cups that come with many multicookers use a Japanese measuring unit that is about one-fifth smaller than 1 cup (250 mL), at 200 mL.

- **Steamer basket:** You will need a steamer basket to hold vegetables and other ingredients such as meatballs and chicken wings while steaming. Some steamer baskets come with legs that extend their height. While this feature is not necessary, you may find it handy and, in some instances, may find that you do not need to use a steam rack in addition to the basket.

- **Steam rack:** Many cookers come with some type of steam rack. If yours does not, you may want to purchase one separately, as you will find it handy for many recipes.

- **Tall steam rack:** These are useful when you're making a pot-in-pot recipe where you don't want the top layer to touch the bottom ingredients.

- **Ovenproof bakeware:** 4- and 6-oz (125 and 175 mL) ramekins, a 6-cup (1.5 L) round casserole dish, a 4-cup (1 L) round soufflé dish and a 6-inch (15 cm) springform pan are useful for making desserts, egg dishes and rice in your multicooker, or when cooking smaller volumes.

- **Electric mixer:** Either a stand mixer or a handheld mixer can make it much easier to mix ingredients for cakes and puddings.

- **Food processor:** In some recipes, you will need to process ingredients for spreads or sauces.

It's a good idea to keep a pair of kitchen gloves on hand. They are very useful when you're handling hot peppers, certain spices and fruits or vegetables that can stain your hands.

- **Immersion blender or stand blender:** An immersion blender makes puréeing soups, sauces and dips incredibly easy, as you can do it right in the pot. If you don't have an immersion blender, you will find alternative instructions for using a stand blender in a tip accompanying the recipe.
- **Sieve:** A fine-mesh sieve is useful for rinsing rice or beans, and for straining liquids.

The Multicooker Pantry

A multicooker offers many benefits to the home cook, but when it comes to ingredients, two bonuses in particular stand out:

1. You can often use tougher, and therefore less expensive, cuts of meat, and they will become fork-tender in your multicooker.
2. You can prepare beans, rice and stocks from scratch, without any processed ingredients.

The recipes in this book use a wide variety of ingredients, but there are certain staples used in a large number of recipes that you will want to be sure to keep on hand:

Oils

Olive oil is used in many of the recipes in this book. The high quality and superior taste of extra virgin olive oil make it the best choice for salads and other recipes that are not cooked; however, since extra virgin olive oil has a relatively low smoke point, regular olive oil is a better (and less expensive) choice for recipes that are cooked.

Virgin coconut oil, peanut oil, sunflower oil, sesame oil, grapeseed oil and hemp oil are also good options to have on hand.

Vinegars

Vinegar can impact the texture, color, flavor and thickness of dishes, adding acidity and sourness that can increase our enjoyment of our food. There are many types of vinegar, each of which has its own unique flavor. The vinegars used in this book include balsamic vinegar, apple cider vinegar, red wine vinegar, white wine vinegar, rice vinegar and coconut vinegar. If you are unsure which ones to have on hand, start with whichever one is used in a recipe you want to make, then expand your pantry provisions from there.

Where meat is used in the recipes, fresh meat is intended. If necessary, you can use frozen meat, but you will need to increase the cooking time. Also keep in mind that frozen meat cannot be seared before pressure cooking, a difference that can alter the flavor of the finished dish.

Stocks and Broths

Vegetable stock, chicken stock and beef bone broth are used in many recipes to add flavor and as a substitute for water as the liquid. You can use either homemade stock or ready-to-use broth in any of the recipes. You can also use broth prepared from bouillon cubes, but their sodium content is usually quite high, so you may want to reduce the amount of salt in the recipe.

On pages 204–208, you will find recipes for both low-sodium and salt-free homemade stocks and broth. The recipes specify which to use depending on what will create the best flavor balance. You can certainly substitute one for the other, or even use full-sodium ready-to-use broths, but keep in mind that any change will affect the flavor balance of the dish. If you use salt-free stock or broth in a recipe that calls for low-sodium, you may want to add a bit of salt to compensate. (At least in that case you control the amount of added sodium.)

> Using the type of stock or broth specified in the recipe will give you the best balance of flavors in the finished dish.

Sauces

Tomato sauce, pasta sauce and barbecue sauce are used in several recipes. I have included recipes for homemade versions of these sauces (see pages 209–211), to use in my recipes or in any dish you like. But any ready-to-use sauce you enjoy or have on hand can be used in place of the homemade sauces.

Condiments

Versatile condiments that will add zest and flavor to your dishes include Dijon mustard, Sriracha, tamari, soy sauce, Worcestershire sauce and honey. Stock your pantry with a variety of condiments that suit your taste, as they can be used to enhance many dishes.

> If you are confident in your cooking skills and are familiar with a recipe, you may want to adjust the type or amount of an ingredient. Experimentation is fun, but can be a little more risky when you're cooking under pressure. Make sure to alter only one ingredient at a time, and change amounts only in small increments.

Herbs, Seasonings and Flavorings

When adding fresh or dried herbs, seasonings and flavorings, remember that a little goes a long way. Always use the amount specified in the recipe for the best flavor and consistency.

If a recipe calls for fresh ingredients, do not substitute dried; if a recipe calls for dried ingredients, do not substitute fresh. Ingredients behave very differently under pressure or when slow cooking than you may be used to.

Other Staples

Cornstarch, brown sugar, tomato paste and vanilla extract are frequently used in these recipes, as thickeners or flavor enhancers.

Canned or Packaged Substitutions

Whenever possible, these recipes are intended to be from-scratch cooking. In some instances, you may want — or need — to substitute a canned or packaged alternative for the ingredient specified. If you make these types of substitutions, make sure the amount you use is equivalent to the amount of the fresh ingredient specified in the recipe. You may also need to add the ingredient at a different time in the cooking process. Some of the recipes include tips for substituting canned or packaged ingredients in cases where the fresh ingredient may be difficult to find in certain markets or at certain times of year.

The recipes for paleo, vegetarian and vegan diets include only ingredients that are appropriate for those diets; however, when selecting packaged or processed ingredients for these recipes, read labels to make sure they do not contain added ingredients or involve processing methods that conflict with your diet.

Maximizing Your Multicooker's Benefits

Your multicooker's ability to rapidly prepare a delicious meal is bound to make it one of your favorite small kitchen appliances. Here are some tips on how you can make it even more useful:

- Make homemade stocks and sauces (see pages 204–211) for use in other recipes.

- Cook dishes ahead of time and refrigerate or freeze them until ready to serve.

- Prepare an all-in-one meal with several different components using a steam rack and the stacking techniques described in many of the recipes in this book (see page 74 or 176, for example).

- Make a side dish, such as steamed vegetables, to accompany a main dish prepared by other methods.

- When feeding a crowd or any time your oven is filled to capacity, use your multicooker to prepare one of the dishes for your feast.

Always add ingredients in the order listed and according to the recipe directions.

Let's Get Cooking!

Once you have decided on a recipe you want to prepare, scan the ingredient and equipment lists to make sure you have everything you need on hand. For best results, purchase fresh meats, poultry, fish, vegetables and fruits just before you want to use them or, at the most, 2 to 3 days ahead.

You will have the most success with your dishes if you have all of the ingredients prepped and ready to go before you start following the recipe steps (unless otherwise directed in the method).

Quick Tips for Best Results

It's a good idea to measure out your ingredients ahead of time. This is a great way to speed up your cooking and to make sure you have everything ready to use.

- Read the manual included with your multicooker for a complete description of the control panel and all of the functions, operation keys and indicators. The manufacturer is the expert on how to use its equipment for best results and safety.

- Measure ingredients carefully for optimal results.

- Follow the recipe steps exactly and in the order listed.

- Clean the cooker's inner pot, lid and housing according to the manufacturer's directions after each use.

- Clean the anti-block shield on the inside of the lid, the exhaust valve, the condensation collector and the sealing ring regularly to keep your cooker functioning properly.

Safety Note: As with any cooking appliance, parts of the multicooker will become very hot. Be careful when handling the inner pot and any bakeware or steamer inserts used for cooking, and always be very cautious when releasing the steam from the vent and when opening the lid.

Breakfasts

Easy Weekday Creamy Steel-Cut Oatmeal

If you're looking for an easy way to have 5 days of healthy breakfasts ready for you, this recipe is for you. Cook it up on Sunday, then during the work week, in minutes, you can have nutty, creamy oatmeal tailored just for you, with your favorite additions.

MAKES 5 SERVINGS

- Five pint (500 mL) canning jars with lids

1 tbsp	butter or vegetable oil	15 mL
1¼ cups	steel-cut oats	300 mL
5 cups	water	1.25 L
1 tsp	kosher salt	5 mL

1. Pour hot tap water into the canning jars to warm the glass.

2. Heat the pressure cooker on High/Sauté/Brown. Add butter and heat until melted. Add oats and cook, stirring, for 2 to 3 minutes or until lightly toasted and fragrant. Cancel cooking.

3. Add water and salt, stirring well. Close and lock the lid. Cook on high pressure for 5 minutes. Let stand, covered, for 10 minutes, then release any remaining pressure. Stir oatmeal.

4. Empty water from jars. Divide oatmeal evenly among jars. Let stand for 10 minutes or until room temperature. Screw lids on and refrigerate jars for up to 5 days.

5. To reheat, uncover jars and stir oatmeal. Microwave on High for 2 to 3 minutes or until hot. Then choose your stir-ins and toppings from the variations at right.

VARIATIONS (PER JAR)

Pumpkin and Cinnamon Oatmeal: Stir in 3 tbsp (45 mL) pumpkin purée (not pie filling) and sprinkle with cinnamon.

Apples, Raisins and Walnuts Oatmeal: Stir in 3 tbsp (45 mL) raisins and ½ tsp (2 mL) vanilla extract. Top with ½ chopped apple and ¼ cup (60 mL) chopped walnuts.

Pear, Maple and Crème Oatmeal: Top with 1 thinly sliced pear and 3 tbsp (45 mL) crème fraîche. Drizzle with pure maple syrup.

Greek-Inspired Date and Yogurt Oatmeal: Stir in ¼ cup (60 mL) chopped dates. Top with 1 tbsp (15 mL) slivered almonds and a dollop of Greek yogurt.

Coconut and Mango Oatmeal: Stir in 3 tbsp (45 mL) coconut milk. Top with ½ cup (125 mL) diced mango and 3 tbsp (45 mL) toasted coconut flakes.

Strawberry and Flaxseed Oatmeal: Stir in ½ cup (125 mL) sliced strawberries and 1 tbsp (15 mL) ground flax seeds (flaxseed meal).

Blueberry and Lemon Oatmeal: Stir in ½ cup (125 mL) blueberries, 2 tbsp (30 mL) freshly squeezed lemon juice and 2 tsp (10 mL) liquid honey.

Apricot, Sesame and Pistachio Oatmeal: Stir in 1 tbsp (15 mL) apricot marmalade, 1 tbsp (15 mL) orange juice and 2 tsp (10 mL) tahini. Top with 3 tbsp (45 mL) pistachios.

Banana, Date and Pecan Oatmeal: Stir in 3 tbsp (45 mL) chopped dates. Top with 1 sliced banana and 3 tbsp (45 mL) chopped pecans. Drizzle with milk.

Hearty Oatmeal, Apples and Cinnamon

Breakfast is one of the most important meals of the day, and a warm, filling bowl of oatmeal is an excellent way to get your body up and running. The combination of creamy oats, apples and cinnamon is a classic and satisfying breakfast.

MAKES 4 SERVINGS		
1	large apple (such as Gala or Cameo), peeled and diced	1
1 cup	steel-cut oats	250 mL
2 tbsp	packed light brown sugar	30 mL
1 tsp	ground cinnamon	5 mL
1/4 tsp	kosher salt	1 mL
3 1/2 cups	water	875 mL
1 tsp	vanilla extract	5 mL
2 tbsp	butter, softened	30 mL
1/4 cup	slivered almonds, toasted (see tip)	60 mL
	Pure maple syrup (optional)	
	Dried cranberries or cherries (optional)	

1. In the pressure cooker, combine apple, oats, brown sugar, cinnamon, salt, water and vanilla, stirring well. Close and lock the lid. Cook on high pressure for 10 minutes. Let stand, covered, until the float valve drops down. Stir in butter until incorporated.

2. Divide oatmeal among serving bowls and top with almonds. If desired, drizzle with maple syrup and/or sprinkle with cranberries.

TIPS

When preparing oats under pressure, make sure to fill the pot no more than halfway full. If the cooker is more than halfway full, the pressure release device may become clogged as the porridge froths up under pressure.

You can cut this recipe in half, or double or triple it depending upon the size of your pressure cooker.

Toast the almonds in your pressure cooker before beginning step 1. Heat the pressure cooker on High/Sauté/Brown. Add almonds and cook, stirring, for 3 minutes or until fragrant and lightly browned. Transfer almonds to a plate to cool.

Steel-Cut Oats and Farro with Dates and Coconut

I love this warm and hearty breakfast dish, not only because of its inviting textures and sweet and savory combination, but because it helps me get a good balance of grains and fiber first thing in the morning. If you struggle to eat more healthy grains, give this recipe a try — you won't be sorry.

MAKES 2 SERVINGS

2 tsp	butter	10 mL
½ cup	steel-cut oats	125 mL
1 tbsp	farro	15 mL
2 tsp	packed brown sugar	10 mL
¼ tsp	kosher salt	1 mL
⅛ tsp	ground nutmeg	0.5 mL
1½ cups	water	375 mL
2 tbsp	heavy or whipping (35%) cream	30 mL
½ cup	unsweetened shredded coconut	125 mL
⅓ cup	chopped dates	75 mL
	Milk (optional)	
	Brown sugar (optional)	

TIPS

You can double or triple this recipe, as long as you fill the cooker no more than halfway full. If the cooker is more than halfway full, the pressure release device may become clogged as the porridge froths up under pressure.

To reheat any leftovers, cook in a small saucepan over medium heat, stirring, for 5 minutes or until warmed through. You may need to add water, in 1-tbsp (15 mL) increments, if the mixture becomes too dry.

1. Heat the pressure cooker on High/Sauté/Brown. Add butter and heat until melted. Add oats and farrow; cook, stirring, for 2 to 3 minutes or until lightly toasted and fragrant. Cancel cooking.

2. Add brown sugar, salt, nutmeg, water and cream, stirring well. Close and lock the lid. Cook on high pressure for 5 minutes. Let stand, covered, for 10 minutes, then release any remaining pressure.

3. Add coconut and dates, stirring well. Cover and let stand for 7 to 10 minutes or until mixture is your desired consistency. Stir, scraping down the sides of the pot as necessary.

4. Divide oatmeal between serving bowls and, if desired, drizzle with milk and/or sprinkle with brown sugar.

VARIATION

Slow Cooker Oats and Farro: In step 2, close and lock the lid, making sure the steam vent is open. Using your cooker's Slow Cook function, adjust temperature to the lowest level. Cook for 8 hours, then continue with step 3.

Quinoa, Millet and Almond Bowls

Who doesn't want a quick and easy breakfast that is good for you *and* satisfies your sweet and savory cravings? If you need only one serving, you can easily reheat it the next day for a ready-made breakfast.

MAKES 2 SERVINGS

1 tsp	vegetable oil	5 mL
½ cup	quinoa, rinsed and well drained	125 mL
2 tbsp	millet, rinsed	30 mL
Pinch	kosher salt	Pinch
1 cup	water	250 mL
1 tbsp	pure maple syrup	15 mL
½ tsp	vanilla extract	2 mL
⅓ cup	slivered almonds	75 mL

TIPS

You can adjust the serving size of this recipe to fit your cooker, but make sure to fill the pot no more than halfway full.

While some packages say the quinoa is rinsed, I like to rinse it again to remove any bitter taste.

To reheat any leftovers, cook in a small saucepan over medium heat, stirring, for 5 minutes or until warmed through. You may need to add water, in 1-tbsp (15 mL) increments, if the mixture becomes too dry.

1. Heat the pressure cooker on High/Sauté/Brown. Add oil and heat until shimmering. Add quinoa and millet; cook, stirring, for 2 to 3 minutes or until lightly toasted and fragrant. Cancel cooking.

2. Add salt, water, maple syrup and vanilla, stirring well. Close and lock the lid. Cook on high pressure for 2 minutes. Let stand, covered, until the float valve drops down. Stir well, scraping down the sides of the pot as necessary.

3. Divide quinoa mixture between serving bowls and sprinkle with almonds.

Soft-Cooked Eggs and Soldiers

Using the pressure cooker is one of the simplest and most foolproof ways to cook eggs to your ideal degree of doneness. You can soft-cook, medium-cook or hard-cook, whichever you prefer. For this particular recipe, we want soft-cooked eggs so we can dip our "soldiers" in them.

MAKES 2 TO 4 SERVINGS

- Steam rack
- 4 egg cups

4	large eggs	4
4	slices bread	4
	Butter (optional)	

TIP

Follow one of the variations if you prefer your eggs cooked for longer. You can use the hard-cooked eggs to make snacks, salads and deviled eggs. To make them easier to peel, transfer the cooked eggs to cold water. If eating eggs warm, peel them as soon as you can handle them.

1. Add 1 cup (250 mL) water (or the amount required by your cooker to reach pressure) to the pressure cooker and place the steam rack in the pot. Arrange eggs on the rack. Close and lock the lid. Cook on low pressure for 3 minutes for soft-cooked eggs.

2. Meanwhile, toast bread and, if desired, butter toast. Cut toast into 1-inch (2.5 cm) strips.

3. When the cooking time is up, quickly release the pressure. Transfer each egg to an egg cup. Using a spoon, tap around the top portion of the egg (about one-quarter from the top) and remove the shell. Serve with toast strips for dipping in the yolk.

VARIATIONS

Medium-Cooked Eggs: Cook on low pressure for 5 minutes. When the cooking time is up, quickly release the pressure.

Hard-Cooked Eggs: Cook on low pressure for 6 minutes. When the cooking time is up, let stand, covered, until the float valve drops down.

Country Sausage Scotch Eggs

While they're often served as a picnic snack or in a local pub, I also love these eggs for breakfast. Sausage, herbs and a boiled egg all get rolled up into a delightful package that is both satisfying and a unique twist on breakfast.

MAKES 4 SERVINGS

• Steam rack

5	large eggs, divided	5
1 lb	pork sausage (bulk or removed from casings)	500 g
1 tbsp	chopped fresh chives	15 mL
1 tbsp	chopped fresh parsley	15 mL
1 tsp	ground nutmeg	5 mL
2 tsp	grainy mustard	10 mL
	Kosher salt and freshly ground black pepper	
3 tbsp	all-purpose flour	45 mL
¼ cup	panko (approx.)	60 mL
2 tbsp	vegetable oil	30 mL

1. Add 1 cup (250 mL) water (or the amount required by your cooker to reach pressure) to the pressure cooker and place the steam rack in the pot. Arrange 4 eggs on the rack. Close and lock the lid. Cook on low pressure for 6 minutes for hard-cooked. Let stand, covered, until the float valve drops down.

2. Transfer eggs to a bowl of cold water. When cool enough to handle, peel eggs under cold running water and dry with a paper towel.

3. In a medium bowl, combine sausage, chives, parsley, nutmeg and mustard. Season with salt and pepper. Form into 4 oval patties.

4. In a shallow bowl, beat the remaining egg. Place a plate of flour and a plate of panko nearby. Roll a cooked egg in flour and wrap a sausage patty gently around the egg, sealing it completely. Roll sausage-wrapped egg in flour, shaking off any excess, then roll in egg wash and panko. If you prefer a thicker coating, roll in egg wash and panko again. Set aside. Repeat to make 3 more Scotch eggs. Discard any excess egg wash, flour and panko.

5. Heat the pressure cooker on High/Sauté/Brown. Add oil and heat until shimmering. Add eggs and cook, turning, for 4 minutes or until golden brown all over. Transfer to a plate. Cancel cooking.

6. Add 1 cup (250 mL) water (or the amount required by your cooker to reach pressure) to the cooker and place the steam rack in the pot. Arrange Scotch eggs on the rack. Close and lock the lid. Cook on high pressure for 6 minutes. Quickly release the pressure. Transfer eggs to a serving platter and serve warm.

> **TIP**
>
> In step 5, wait until the coating releases itself from the pot before turning the eggs, to avoid breaking apart the sausage.

Ready-to-Go Bacon and Egg Muffins

Some mornings time just seems to get away from us, but that doesn't mean you need to skip breakfast or grab fast food on the run. You can make your own fast breakfast food ahead of time and just grab one of these delightfully tasty breakfast muffins as you're running out the door.

MAKES 4 SERVINGS

- 4 silicone baking cups
- Steam rack

4	large eggs	4
4	slices bacon, cooked and crumbled	4
1	green onion (white part only), sliced	1
¼ cup	shredded Monterey Jack cheese	60 mL
¼ tsp	kosher salt	1 mL
⅛ tsp	freshly ground black pepper	0.5 mL

TIPS

Use a 4-cup (1 L) glass measuring cup with a handle and spout instead of the bowl in step 1. This will make it easier to pour the egg mixture into the muffin cups.

The muffins can be cooled and stored in an airtight container in the refrigerator for up to 5 days. Reheat in the microwave on High for 20 seconds.

Add one of these to the center of a toasted English muffin for a grab-and-go breakfast sandwich.

1. In a medium bowl, whisk eggs. Stir in bacon, green onion, cheese, salt and pepper. Spoon into muffin cups, dividing evenly.

2. Add 1 cup (250 mL) water (or the amount required by your cooker to reach pressure) to the pressure cooker and place the steam rack in the pot. Arrange muffin cups on the rack. Close and lock the lid. Cook on high pressure for 8 minutes. Let stand, covered, for 5 minutes, then release any remaining pressure. Serve hot.

Veggie-Stuffed Bell Peppers

A bounty of mushrooms, onions, spinach, tomatoes and garlic commingles with eggs to create a sensational stuffing for sweet bell peppers. The aromas are so enticing, you'll be sure to make time for breakfast before you dive into your day. This recipe is vegetarian and gluten-free, but you can add meat if you like (see variations).

MAKES 2 SERVINGS

- Steam rack

1 tbsp	butter	15 mL
1	small onion, finely chopped	1
½ cup	sliced mushrooms	125 mL
1	small plum (Roma) tomato, diced	1
1	clove garlic, minced	1
1½ cups	lightly packed baby spinach	375 mL
	Kosher salt and freshly ground black pepper	
2	bell peppers (any color), tops sliced off, ribs and seeds removed	2
4	large eggs, beaten	4

TIPS

If the bottoms of your peppers are uneven and they won't stand upright, cut the bottom tips off the peppers, being careful not to cut through to the center.

When releasing pressure quickly, keep your hands and face away from the hole on top of the steam release handle so you don't get scalded by the escaping steam.

1. Heat the pressure cooker on High/Sauté/Brown. Add butter and heat until melted. Add onion and mushrooms; cook, stirring, for 3 to 5 minutes or until onion is softened and mushrooms have released their liquid. Add tomato and garlic; cook, stirring, for 2 minutes or until fragrant. Add spinach and cook, stirring, for 1 to 2 minutes or until wilted. Season with salt and pepper. Cancel cooking.

2. Divide veggie mixture evenly between bell peppers. Pour in eggs, dividing evenly. Rinse and dry the cooker's inner pot.

3. Add 1 cup (250 mL) water (or the amount required by your cooker to reach pressure) to the cooker and place the steam rack in the pot. Arrange filled peppers on the rack. Close and lock the lid. Cook on high pressure for 7 minutes. Quickly release the pressure. Using silicone tongs, transfer peppers to serving plates. Serve immediately.

VARIATIONS

Meaty Stuffed Bell Peppers: Stir in 6 slices bacon, cooked and crumbled, or ⅓ cup (75 mL) diced cooked ham after canceling cooking in step 1.

Sausage and Veggie–Stuffed Bell Peppers: Add ½ cup (125 mL) bulk pork sausage (or meat removed from casings) with the onion and mushrooms; cook until no longer pink before continuing with step 1.

Mushroom, Spinach and Red Pepper Crustless Quiche

A savory combination of vegetables adds inviting texture and flavor to this warm quiche. Not only is this mouthwatering quiche a satisfying start to your morning, but it's gluten-free and vegetarian.

MAKES 4 SERVINGS

- Steam rack
- Steamer basket
- 4-cup (1 L) round soufflé dish, bottom and sides buttered

3 cups	loosely packed baby spinach	750 mL
1 tbsp	butter	15 mL
8 oz	sliced mushrooms	250 g
½	red bell pepper, chopped	½
6	large eggs	6
1 cup	shredded Swiss cheese	250 mL
½ tsp	kosher salt	2 mL
¼ tsp	freshly ground black pepper	1 mL
1 cup	milk	250 mL

1. Add 1 cup (250 mL) water (or the amount required by your cooker to reach pressure) to the pressure cooker and place the steam rack in the pot. Arrange spinach in the steamer basket and place basket on the rack. Close and lock the lid. Cook on high pressure for 1 minute. Quickly release the pressure. Drain spinach and squeeze dry. Set aside. Rinse and dry the cooker's inner pot.

2. Heat the cooker on High/Sauté/Brown. Add butter and heat until melted. Add mushrooms and red pepper; cook, stirring frequently, for 5 minutes or until liquid from mushrooms has evaporated. Cancel cooking.

3. In a large bowl, whisk eggs. Stir in mushroom mixture, cheese, salt, pepper and milk. Pour into prepared soufflé dish and cover loosely with foil.

4. Add 1 cup (250 mL) water (or the amount required by your cooker to reach pressure) to the cooker and place the steam rack in the pot. Place the soufflé dish on the rack. Close and lock the lid. Cook on high pressure for 10 minutes. Let stand, covered, for 10 minutes, then release any remaining pressure. Check to make sure a knife inserted in the center of the quiche comes out clean; if more cooking time is needed, reset to high pressure for 2 minutes. Open the lid and let quiche stand for 5 minutes, then remove soufflé dish from cooker. Cut into 4 wedges and serve immediately.

VARIATION

Add 3 slices bacon, cooked and chopped, to the top of the quiche in step 3 before covering with foil.

TIPS

You can use a 10-oz (300 g) package of frozen chopped spinach, thawed and drained, in place of the steamed fresh baby spinach and skip step 1.

If you are avoiding gluten, make sure your shredded cheese does not have any added flour and is processed in a gluten-free facility.

Cheesy Ham and Broccoli Quiche

This crustless quiche is an inviting and delicious addition to breakfast or lunch. I have made variations of this dish for years, and it continues to be an all-time favorite for family and guests. Serve it up with a dish of fruit and berries for a mouthwatering pairing.

MAKES 4 SERVINGS

- Steam rack
- Steamer basket
- 4-cup (1 L) round soufflé dish, bottom and sides buttered

2 cups	broccoli florets	500 mL
6	large eggs	6
2 tsp	dry mustard	10 mL
¼ tsp	kosher salt	1 mL
Pinch	freshly ground black pepper	Pinch
½ cup	milk	125 mL
1 cup	diced cooked ham	250 mL
1 cup	shredded Swiss cheese	250 mL
1 tbsp	dried onion flakes	15 mL

TIPS

You can use a 10-oz (300 g) package of frozen chopped broccoli, thawed and drained, in place of the steamed fresh broccoli and skip step 1.

Add ½ cup (125 mL) finely chopped onion in place of the onion flakes.

1. Add 1 cup (250 mL) water (or the amount required by your cooker to reach pressure) to the pressure cooker and place the steam rack in the pot. Arrange broccoli in the steamer basket and place basket on the rack. Close and lock the lid. Cook on high pressure for 3 minutes. Quickly release the pressure. Immediately plunge broccoli into a bowl of cold water; drain. Chop broccoli and set aside. Rinse and dry the cooker's inner pot.

2. In a large bowl, whisk eggs. Whisk in mustard, salt, pepper and milk. Stir in broccoli, ham, cheese and onion flakes. Pour into prepared soufflé dish and cover loosely with foil.

3. Add 1 cup (250 mL) water (or the amount required by your cooker to reach pressure) to the cooker and place the steam rack in the pot. Place the soufflé dish on the rack. Close and lock the lid. Cook on high pressure for 10 minutes. Let stand, covered, for 10 minutes, then release any remaining pressure. Check to make sure a knife inserted in the center of the quiche comes out clean; if more cooking time is needed, reset to high pressure for 2 minutes. Open the lid and let quiche stand for 5 minutes, then remove soufflé dish from cooker. Cut into 4 wedges and serve immediately.

Ham, Pepper and Egg Casserole

Rise and shine! This yummy egg casserole is a splendid alternative to the same-old boiled, fried or poached eggs. You can mix it up with different vegetables or meats, or even go meatless.

MAKES 4 SERVINGS

- 4-cup (1 L) round soufflé dish, bottom and sides buttered
- Steam rack

6	slices day-old bread, crusts trimmed off and bread cubed (about 5 cups/1.25 L)	6
1	roasted red bell pepper, drained and diced	1
¾ cup	diced cooked ham	175 mL
¾ cup	shredded sharp (old) Cheddar cheese	175 mL
3	large eggs, beaten	3
1 cup	milk	250 mL
½ tsp	kosher salt	2 mL
¼ tsp	freshly ground black pepper	1 mL

TIP

Hearty breads, such as country-style, sourdough or French, work best in this recipe because they retain their shape better.

1. Layer half of the bread cubes in prepared soufflé dish. Sprinkle evenly with red pepper, ham and cheese. Layer the remaining bread cubes on top.

2. In a small bowl, whisk eggs, then whisk in milk, salt and pepper; pour over bread cubes.

3. Add 1 cup (250 mL) water (or the amount required by your cooker to reach pressure) to the pressure cooker and place the steam rack in the pot. Place the soufflé dish on the rack. Close and lock the lid. Cook on high pressure for 10 minutes. Check to make sure a knife inserted in the center of the casserole comes out clean; if more cooking time is needed, reset to high pressure for 2 minutes. Quickly release the pressure.

4. Meanwhile, preheat broiler, with the top rack about 5 inches (12.5 cm) from the heat source. Carefully transfer casserole to oven and broil for 5 minutes or until top is golden brown and bubbly. Let stand for 5 minutes, then cut into 4 wedges and serve immediately.

VARIATION

Substitute 6 slices bacon, cooked and coarsely chopped, for the ham.

Pancetta, Cheese and Egg Bake

While not a traditional "bake," this pressure-steamed egg dish is just like the real deal, but even better. Pressure cooking is faster and much more efficient than heating up the oven for a single serving.

MAKES 1 SERVING

- 6-oz (175 mL) ramekin, buttered
- Steam rack

1 tsp	virgin olive oil	5 mL
2 tbsp	diced pancetta	30 mL
4	baby spinach leaves, stems removed	4
1½ tbsp	shredded fontina or freshly grated Parmesan cheese, divided	22 mL
2	large eggs	2
	Kosher salt and freshly ground black pepper	

TIPS

If you prefer your eggs softer and runnier and your pressure cooker has a low setting, use that setting in step 3. If your cooker does not have a low setting, you can get a similar result by covering the ramekin with heavy-duty foil.

Serve with a bowl of fresh berries and a slice of toast, for a pleasing breakfast.

1. Heat the pressure cooker on High/Sauté/Brown. Add oil and heat until shimmering. Add pancetta and cook, stirring, for 3 to 5 minutes or until browned. Cancel cooking.

2. Layer spinach, pancetta and 1 tbsp (15 mL) cheese in prepared ramekin. Crack eggs next to each other on top and sprinkle with the remaining cheese.

3. Add 1 cup (250 mL) water (or the amount required by your cooker to reach pressure) to the pressure cooker and place the steam rack in the pot. Place the ramekin on the rack. Close and lock the lid. Cook on high pressure for 5 minutes. Quickly release the pressure. Carefully remove ramekin and season to taste with salt and pepper. Serve immediately.

Huevos Rancheros

These incredibly tasty rancher's-style eggs are a Mexican favorite, and understandably so. Don't be intimidated by the long list of ingredients — I've included a recipe for homemade salsa. Once you have that prepared, it really is just a quick assembly in your pressure cooker. Plus, the salsa is good for other uses.

MAKES 1 SERVING

- Food processor or blender
- 6-oz (175 mL) ramekin, sprayed with nonstick cooking spray
- 4-oz (125 mL) ramekin
- 18- by 12-inch (45 by 30 cm) sheet heavy-duty foil
- Steam rack

Salsa

2	cloves garlic, minced	2
1	small jalapeño pepper, seeded	1
1	small onion, chopped	1
¼ cup	lightly packed fresh cilantro leaves	60 mL
1 tsp	granulated sugar	5 mL
1 tsp	ground cumin	5 mL
1 tsp	smoked paprika (optional)	5 mL
½ tsp	ground oregano	2 mL
½ tsp	kosher salt	2 mL
1	can (14½ oz/411 mL) diced fire-roasted tomatoes, drained and juice reserved	1
1	can (4 oz/114 mL) diced green chiles	1
2 tbsp	freshly squeezed lime juice	30 mL

Eggs

2	large eggs	2
½ cup	refried beans	125 mL
2	taco-size (6-inch/15 cm) flour tortillas	2
2 tbsp	shredded cotija, Oaxaca or Monterey Jack cheese	30 mL
	Torn fresh cilantro leaves	

1. *Salsa:* In food processor, combine garlic, jalapeño, onion, cilantro, sugar, cumin, paprika (if using), oregano, salt, tomatoes (without juice), chiles and lime juice; process to desired consistency. For more liquid in your salsa, add drained tomato juice, in 1-tbsp (15 mL) increments, and process.

2. *Eggs:* Add 2 tbsp (30 mL) salsa to the prepared 6-oz (175 mL) ramekin. Crack eggs side by side on top.

3. Place beans in the 4-oz (125 mL) ramekin. Wrap tortillas in foil.

4. Add 1 cup (250 mL) water (or the amount required by your cooker to reach pressure) to the pressure cooker and place the steam rack in the pot. Place both ramekins on the rack. Place foil-wrapped tortillas on top of the ramekins. Close and lock the lid. Cook on high pressure for 10 minutes. Quickly release the pressure.

5. Using silicone tongs, remove tortillas from pot, open foil carefully and transfer tortillas to a serving plate. Carefully remove the ramekins from the pot and, using a large spoon, divide eggs evenly between tortillas. Pour salsa over top, leaving the yolks exposed. Sprinkle with cheese and cilantro. Serve with beans on the side.

TIP

This recipe makes 2 cups (500 mL) of salsa. Refrigerate the remainder for up to 3 days.

Blueberry, Maple and Pecan French Toast

Let me share a little secret: this French toast is suspiciously similar to a decadent bread pudding. But I just combined berries, bread, eggs and milk — now doesn't that sound like breakfast? When you fall in love with this recipe, you will want to have it for both breakfast and dessert.

MAKES 6 SERVINGS

- 6-cup (1.5 L) round soufflé dish, bottom and sides buttered
- Steam rack

3	large eggs	3
¼ tsp	kosher salt	1 mL
¼ tsp	ground cinnamon	1 mL
2 cups	milk	500 mL
3 tbsp	pure maple syrup	45 mL
6	slices challah bread or Texas toast, crusts trimmed off and bread cubed (about 5 cups/1.25 L)	6
½ cup	dried blueberries	125 mL
½ cup	chopped pecans	125 mL
	Grated zest of ½ orange	

TIP

If you like a crustier topping on your French toast, when the cooking time is up in step 4, preheat the broiler. After removing the soufflé dish from the cooker, transfer it to the oven and broil for 3 minutes or until the top is browned and crusty.

1. In a medium bowl, whisk eggs. Add salt, cinnamon, milk and maple syrup, stirring well. Set aside.

2. In a large bowl, combine bread cubes, blueberries, pecans and orange zest. Pour egg mixture over bread. Let stand for 30 minutes or until bread has absorbed liquid.

3. Pour bread mixture into prepared soufflé dish and cover with foil.

4. Add 1 cup (250 mL) water (or the amount required by your cooker to reach pressure) to the pressure cooker and place the steam rack in the pot. Place the soufflé dish on the rack. Close and lock the lid. Cook on high pressure for 25 minutes. Let stand, covered, for 10 minutes, then release any remaining pressure. Check to make sure a knife inserted in the center of the French toast comes out clean; if more cooking time is needed, reset to high pressure for 4 minutes. Remove soufflé dish from cooker and let stand for 5 minutes before serving.

VARIATION

Slow Cooker Blueberry, Maple and Pecan French Toast: Complete steps 1 and 2, combining in the inner pot instead of a bowl and let stand as directed. Close and lock the lid, making sure the steam vent is open. Using your cooker's Slow Cook function on the lowest level, cook for 3½ to 4 hours or until a knife inserted into the center of the dish comes out clean.

Country-Style Breakfast Hash

Talk about a whopper, this breakfast has it all. If you have a hungry, hardworking crew at your house and want to give them a great-tasting breakfast that will stay with them, this is your dish. Send them out the door happy and ready to start the day.

MAKES 6 SERVINGS

1 tbsp	virgin olive oil	15 mL
1 lb	ground pork or turkey sausage (bulk or removed from casings)	500 g
1	small onion, chopped	1
1	roasted red bell pepper, drained and chopped	1
1 tsp	paprika	5 mL
½ tsp	dried sage	2 mL
½ tsp	kosher salt	2 mL
⅛ tsp	cayenne pepper	0.5 mL
1	package (28 oz/750 g) frozen cubed hash brown potatoes	1
¾ cup	low-sodium chicken stock (page 206) or ready-to-use chicken broth (see tip)	175 mL

TIPS

The stock in this recipe does not meet the minimum 1 cup (250 mL) liquid required by most cookers. However, additional liquid will be released from the frozen potatoes and other ingredients. If your cooker requires more than 1 cup (250 mL) liquid, you will need to add more stock, up to the required amount.

When releasing pressure quickly, keep your hands and face away from the hole on top of the steam release handle so you don't get scalded by the escaping steam.

1. Heat the pressure cooker on High/Sauté/Brown. Add oil and heat until shimmering. Add pork and onion; cook, breaking pork up with a spoon, for 5 to 7 minutes or until pork is no longer pink and onion is softened. Add roasted pepper, paprika, sage, salt and cayenne; cook, stirring, for 1 minute or until fragrant. Cancel cooking.

2. Stir in hash browns and stock. Close and lock the lid. Cook on high pressure for 8 minutes. Quickly release the pressure and open the lid.

3. Heat the cooker on High/Sauté/Brown. Cook, stirring gently, for 3 to 5 minutes or until liquid has evaporated and potatoes are slightly crispy. Serve immediately.

VARIATIONS

Cheesy Breakfast Hash: Sprinkle 1 cup (250 mL) shredded Monterey Jack or pepper Jack cheese over the hash browns in step 3, just before serving. Cover and let stand for 5 minutes. Serve immediately.

Pepper Gravy over Hash: Pepper gravy is the perfect complement to this hearty breakfast. In a small saucepan, melt 1 tbsp (15 mL) butter over medium heat. Whisk in 1 tbsp (15 mL) all-purpose flour. Gradually stir in ¼ cup (60 mL) milk. Season with ½ tsp (2 mL) freshly ground black pepper and ¼ tsp (1 mL) kosher salt. Bring to a boil, then reduce heat to low and cook, stirring, for 3 minutes or until thickened. Drizzle gravy over individual servings of hash.

Soups, Stews and Chilis

Carrot and Coriander Soup

This is a lusciously silky and sweet soup with nutty hints of coriander. A bit of baking soda helps the onions and carrots develop rich caramel undertones.

MAKES 4 SERVINGS

- Immersion blender (see tip)

6 tbsp	butter, divided	90 mL
1¼ cups	finely chopped onions (about 2 medium)	300 mL
3	cloves garlic, minced	3
½ tsp	baking soda	2 mL
2½ cups	low-sodium vegetable stock (page 204) or ready-to-use vegetable broth, divided	625 mL
1 lb	medium carrots (about 6 to 8), cut into 2-inch (5 cm) pieces	500 g
1 tsp	ground coriander	5 mL
1½ cups	heavy or whipping (35%) cream	375 mL
	Kosher salt and freshly ground black pepper	

TIPS

In step 3, instead of using an immersion blender, you can transfer the soup, in batches, to a blender. After blending, return soup to the cooker. Be very careful when transferring soup, as it is very hot. Do not fill your blender more than half full, to prevent hot soup from spewing out the top.

Top each serving with a dollop of plain Greek yogurt or sour cream with a pinch of curry powder mixed in.

1. Heat the pressure cooker on High/Sauté/Brown. Add 3 tbsp (45 mL) butter and heat until melted. Add onions and cook, stirring, for 3 to 5 minutes or until translucent. Add garlic and cook, stirring, for 1 minute or until fragrant. Cancel cooking.

2. In a small bowl, whisk together baking soda and ¼ cup (60 mL) stock. Add carrots, soda mixture and the remaining stock to the cooker, stirring well. Close and lock the lid. Cook on high pressure for 8 minutes. Quickly release the pressure.

3. Using the immersion blender, blend soup until smooth. Blend in the remaining butter.

4. Heat the cooker on High/Sauté/Brown. Add coriander and cream; cook, stirring often, for 5 minutes or until heated through and thickened. Season to taste with salt and pepper.

VARIATIONS

To ramp up the carrot flavor, substitute carrot juice for the vegetable stock and add 1½ tsp (7 mL) kosher salt.

You can substitute coconut milk for the cream, if you prefer.

Add 1 tbsp (15 mL) minced gingerroot with the garlic in step 1.

Creamy Curried Carrot Soup

In this soup, luscious sweet carrots receive a flavor infusion from ginger, curry and a savory combination of vegetables. The pressure cooker not only makes the carrots tender, it infuses the flavors into a truly delectable soup.

MAKES 8 SERVINGS

- Immersion blender (see tip)

3 tbsp	butter	45 mL
2	onions, finely chopped	2
2	stalks celery, chopped	2
2	cloves garlic, minced	2
2 tbsp	apple cider vinegar	30 mL
4	carrots, cut into 1-inch (2.5 cm) pieces	4
1	small yellow-fleshed potato, chopped	1
2 tbsp	grated gingerroot (about a 2-inch/5 cm piece)	30 mL
2 tsp	curry powder, divided	10 mL
5 cups	low-sodium vegetable stock (page 204) or ready-to-use vegetable broth	1.25 L
1 cup	coconut milk	250 mL
	Kosher salt and freshly ground black pepper	
1 cup	plain Greek yogurt	250 mL
3 tbsp	chopped fresh chives	45 mL
	Hot pepper flakes (optional)	

1. Heat the pressure cooker on High/Sauté/Brown. Add butter and heat until melted. Add onions and celery; cook, stirring, for 3 to 5 minutes or until onions are translucent. Add garlic and cook, stirring, for 1 minute or until fragrant. Add vinegar and cook, scraping up any browned bits from the bottom of the pot, for 2 minutes or until vinegar is reduced by half. Cancel cooking.

2. Add carrots, potato, ginger, 1 tsp (5 mL) curry powder and stock, stirring well. Close and lock the lid. Cook on high pressure for 5 minutes. Quickly release the pressure.

3. Using the immersion blender, blend soup until smooth.

4. Heat the cooker on High/Sauté/Brown. Add coconut milk and the remaining curry powder; cook, stirring, for 3 to 5 minutes or until soup is your desired consistency. Season to taste with salt and pepper.

5. Ladle into individual serving bowls. Serve dolloped with yogurt and garnished with chives and, if desired, hot pepper flakes.

VARIATION

You can substitute heavy or whipping (35%) cream for the coconut milk, if you prefer.

TIPS

Use thinner carrots whenever possible. Carrots' inner cores can add a slightly bitter taste if they are too predominant.

In step 3, instead of using an immersion blender, you can transfer the soup, in batches, to a blender. After blending, return soup to the cooker. Be very careful when transferring soup, as it is very hot. Do not fill your blender more than half full, to prevent hot soup from spewing out the top.

Farmers' Market Corn Chowder

In this creamy and buttery soup, delectable sweet corn gets infused with herbs and cooked to mouthwatering tenderness. I've topped it off with bacon and Cheddar cheese for a hearty chowder that will keep you coming back for more.

MAKES 6 SERVINGS		
⅓ cup	butter, divided	75 mL
2	onions, finely chopped	2
6	ears sweet corn (preferably bicolor), kernels cut off	6
2 tsp	dried parsley	10 mL
1 tsp	dried thyme	5 mL
½ tsp	garlic powder	2 mL
Pinch	granulated sugar	Pinch
3 cups	low-sodium chicken stock (page 206) or ready-to-use chicken broth	750 mL
2 tbsp	cornstarch	30 mL
1½ cups	half-and-half (10%) cream	375 mL
4	slices bacon, cooked crisp and crumbled	4
1 cup	shredded Cheddar cheese	250 mL
	Kosher salt and freshly ground black pepper	

1. Heat the pressure cooker on High/Sauté/Brown. Add 2 tbsp (30 mL) butter and heat until melted. Add onions and cook, stirring, for 3 to 5 minutes or until translucent. Cancel cooking.

2. Add corn, parsley, thyme, garlic powder, sugar, stock and the remaining butter, stirring well. Close and lock the lid. Cook on high pressure for 2 minutes. Quickly release the pressure. Check to make sure the corn is tender; if more cooking time is needed, close the lid and let stand for 2 minutes or until done to your liking.

3. In a small bowl, whisk together cornstarch and cream.

4. Heat the cooker on High/Sauté/Brown. Stir in cornstarch mixture and cook, stirring, for 3 minutes or until thickened. Stir in bacon and cheese. Season to taste with salt and pepper.

TIPS

I like to use early-season bicolor corn, as I find it to be much sweeter and more tender. If you cannot find bicolor corn, use 3 ears each of yellow and white corn, or 6 ears of any sweet corn variety. If fresh corn is not available, you can use 4½ cups (1.125 L) thawed frozen corn kernels instead.

When using the quick release method to release pressure, keep your hands and face away from the hole on the top of the steam release handle so you don't get scalded by the escaping steam.

French Onion Soup

This is one of the most inviting soups, with its bubbling broiled cheese floating atop caramelized onions bursting with umami. Instead of toiling over the stove to caramelize the onions and simmer the soup, you can make this dish more quickly and with hands-off cooking time.

- 4 ovenproof soup bowls
- Rimmed baking sheet

6 tbsp	butter, divided	90 mL
1 tbsp	vegetable oil	15 mL
5	large onions (about 3 lbs/1.5 kg total), cut into 1/8-inch (3 mm) thick slices	5
1/2 tsp	baking soda	2 mL
	Kosher salt and freshly ground black pepper	
1/2 cup	dry white wine	125 mL
1 tsp	balsamic vinegar	5 mL
2	sprigs fresh thyme	2
1	bay leaf	1
1	clove garlic, minced	1
8 cups	low-sodium chicken stock (page 206) or ready-to-use chicken broth	2 L
8	slices French baguette	8
8 oz	Gruyère cheese, shredded	250 g

TIP

You may need more or fewer than 8 baguette slices, depending upon the diameter of your loaf. You will want to cover as much of the surface of the soup as possible.

1. Heat the pressure cooker on High/Sauté/Brown. Add 5 tbsp (75 mL) butter and the oil; heat until butter has melted. Stir in onions and baking soda, season with salt and pepper, and cook, stirring, for 3 minutes or until onions are slightly softened. Cancel cooking.

2. Close and lock the lid. Cook on high pressure for 20 minutes. Quickly release the pressure and open the lid.

3. Heat the cooker on High/Sauté/Brown. Cook, stirring, for 5 minutes or until liquid is evaporated and onions are deep brown. Add wine and vinegar, scraping up any browned bits from the bottom of the pot. Cook, stirring, for 3 minutes or until wine smell is diminished. Add thyme, bay leaf, garlic and stock; cook, stirring occasionally, for 10 minutes. Cancel cooking. Discard thyme sprigs and bay leaf.

4. Meanwhile, preheat broiler. Arrange baguette slices on baking sheet and broil until toasted. Spread the remaining butter over toast.

5. Spoon one-quarter of the soup into each soup bowl. Arrange toast on top of soup, without overlapping. Sprinkle cheese over toast, dividing evenly. Place bowls on baking sheet. Broil until cheese is melted and browned in spots. Serve immediately.

VARIATIONS

You can substitute additional chicken stock for the wine, stirring until the stock is slightly reduced.

Substitute provolone or Swiss cheese for the Gruyère.

Hearty Potato and Celery Root Soup

The beauty of this soup is that it tastes just as good hot or cold, giving you a variety of serving possibilities — it can be a starter or a main, in any season and for any occasion. The celery root gives an added dimension of flavor that makes this soup even more delightful.

MAKES 6 SERVINGS

- Immersion blender (see tip)

3	slices bacon, cut into 1-inch (2.5 cm) pieces	3
2	leeks (white part only), thinly sliced and separated	2
3	yellow-fleshed potatoes, peeled and chopped	3
1	celery root, peeled and chopped	1
4 cups	low-sodium chicken stock (page 206) or ready-to-use chicken broth	1 L
1 tbsp	chopped fresh dill	15 mL
1 tbsp	chopped fresh parsley	15 mL
1½ cups	heavy or whipping (35%) cream	375 mL
	Kosher salt and freshly ground black pepper	

TIPS

Leeks should be carefully washed before use, as they can be very sandy in between their rings. Pat dry with a paper towel after washing.

In step 4, instead of using an immersion blender, you can transfer the soup, in batches, to a blender. After blending, return soup to the cooker. Be very careful when transferring soup, as it is very hot. Do not fill your blender more than half full, to prevent hot soup from spewing out the top.

1. Heat the pressure cooker on High/ Sauté/Brown. Add bacon and cook, stirring occasionally, for 5 minutes or until browned but not crispy. Transfer bacon to a plate lined with paper towels.

2. Add leeks to the bacon fat in the cooker and cook, stirring, for 4 minutes or until softened and lightly browned. Cancel cooking.

3. Add potatoes, celery root and stock, stirring well. Close and lock the lid. Cook on high pressure for 5 minutes. Let stand, covered, until the float valve drops down. Check to make sure the potatoes and celery root are fork-tender; if more cooking time is needed, reset to high pressure for 1 minute.

4. Using the immersion blender, blend soup to your desired consistency.

5. Heat the cooker on High/Sauté/Brown. Stir in dill, parsley and cream; cook, stirring, for 3 to 5 minutes or until soup is your desired consistency. Season to taste with salt and pepper. Serve hot or chilled.

VARIATION

Vegetarian Potato and Celery Root Soup: Omit the bacon and skip step 1. In step 2, cook the leeks in 1 tbsp (15 mL) virgin olive oil. Use vegetable stock or broth in place of chicken stock.

Roasted Tomato and Basil Soup

While roasting the tomatoes for this recipe takes more effort, the depth of flavor it adds is well worth it — plus, it's mostly hands-off. Pressure cooking this classic soup more than makes up the time, while giving it a rich flavor.

MAKES 6 SERVINGS

- Preheat oven to 400°F (200°C)
- Baking sheet, lined with heavy-duty foil
- Immersion blender (see tip)

3 lbs	plum (Roma) tomatoes, cut in half lengthwise	1.5 kg
6 tbsp	virgin olive oil, divided	90 mL
	Kosher salt and freshly ground black pepper	
2	onions, chopped	2
6	cloves garlic, minced	6
2 cups	loosely packed fresh basil leaves, chopped	500 mL
1 tsp	granulated sugar	5 mL
4 cups	water	1 L
1	can (28 oz/796 mL) diced tomatoes, with juice	1
1 cup	heavy or whipping (35%) cream	250 mL

1. Place tomatoes in a large bowl and add 4 tbsp (60 mL) oil, 1 tsp (5 mL) salt and ½ tsp (2 mL) pepper, tossing gently to combine. Arrange tomatoes, cut side up, on prepared baking sheet. Bake in preheated oven for 45 minutes.

2. Meanwhile, heat the pressure cooker on High/Sauté/Brown. Add the remaining oil and heat until shimmering. Add onions and cook, stirring, for 7 minutes or until starting to brown. Add garlic and cook, stirring, for 1 minute or until fragrant. Cancel cooking.

3. Add basil, sugar, water, canned tomatoes and roasted tomatoes. Do not stir (see tip). Close and lock the lid. Cook on high pressure for 7 minutes. Let stand, covered, for 10 minutes, then release any remaining pressure.

4. Using the immersion blender, blend soup until smooth.

5. Heat the cooker on High/Sauté/Brown. Stir in whipping cream and cook until warmed through. Season to taste with salt and pepper.

TIPS

If you prefer not to roast your own tomatoes, you can omit the plum tomatoes and skip step 1. In step 2, use 2 tbsp (30 mL) oil. In step 3, add a drained 28-oz (796 mL) can of fire-roasted tomatoes with the diced tomatoes and cook on high pressure for 6 minutes.

Do not be tempted to add the tomatoes first to your pressure cooker pot or to mix the ingredients. Tomatoes can scorch on the bottom of the cooker if added first.

In step 4, instead of using an immersion blender, you can transfer the soup, in batches, to a blender. After blending, return soup to the cooker. Be very careful when transferring soup, as it is very hot. Do not fill your blender more than half full, to prevent hot soup from spewing out the top.

Chipotle Black Bean Soup

This spicy and smoky black bean soup gets its trademark flavor from chipotle peppers in adobo sauce and bell peppers. To add even more interest, hints of cocoa powder and lime contribute to a mole-style taste. Topped with red and green onions and cooling avocado, this soup has a wonderful finish.

MAKES 8 SERVINGS

2 cups	dried black beans	500 mL
	Water	
2 tbsp	virgin olive oil	30 mL
3	red onions (about 10 oz/300 g total), chopped, divided	3
1	red bell pepper, chopped	1
1	green bell pepper, chopped	1
5	cloves garlic, minced	5
1 tbsp	dried oregano	15 mL
1 tbsp	ground cumin	15 mL
2	bay leaves	2
2	chipotle peppers, chopped, with 2 tbsp (30 mL) adobo sauce	2
1 tbsp	unsweetened cocoa powder	15 mL
6	green onions (white and light green parts only), sliced, divided	6
3 tbsp	freshly squeezed lime juice	45 mL
	Kosher salt	
1	avocado, chopped	1

1. Place beans in a large bowl, add 8 cups (2 L) cold water and let soak at room temperature for 8 hours or overnight. Drain and rinse beans. Set aside.

2. Heat the pressure cooker on High/Sauté/Brown. Add oil and heat until shimmering. Set aside ¼ cup (60 mL) of the red onions and add the remainder to the cooker, along with the red and green peppers; cook, stirring often, for 3 to 5 minutes or until onions are translucent. Add garlic and cook, stirring, for 1 minute or until fragrant. Cancel cooking.

3. Add oregano, cumin, bay leaves, chipotles with adobo sauce and 6 cups (1.5 L) water, stirring well. Stir in beans. Close and lock the lid. Cook on high pressure for 9 minutes. Let stand, covered, until the float valve drops down. Check to make sure the beans are tender; if more cooking time is needed, reset to high pressure for 1 minute or until done to your liking. Discard bay leaves.

4. In a small bowl, combine cocoa and 3 tbsp (45 mL) water.

5. Heat the cooker on High/Sauté/Brown. Stir in 5 green onions, cocoa mixture and lime juice. Season to taste with salt. Cook, stirring, for 5 minutes or until soup is your desired consistency. For a thinner soup, add more water, ¼ cup (60 mL) at a time.

6. Ladle into individual serving bowls. Serve garnished with avocado, the remaining green onions and the reserved red onions.

VARIATION

Add 8 oz (250 g) diced cured chorizo sausage with the chipotles.

TIPS

This recipe is meant for pressure cookers that are 6 quarts (6 L) or larger. If you are using a smaller cooker, cut the recipe in half.

Serve with cornbread, for a delightful balance of flavors.

Homestyle Minestrone

Pure and simple minestrone is the kind of soup that warms you to the core and just screams comfort food on a cold, wintery day. However, the flavor of this soup is anything but simple, with its combination of fresh vegetables graced with rosemary and sage.

MAKES 6 SERVINGS

1 cup	dried cannellini (white kidney) beans	250 mL
4 cups	cold water	1 L
1 tbsp	virgin olive oil	15 mL
1	onion, chopped	1
1	carrot, chopped	1
1	stalk celery, chopped	1
2	small tomatoes, chopped	2
1	sprig fresh rosemary	1
1	bay leaf	1
2 tsp	chopped fresh sage	10 mL
4 cups	salt-free vegetable stock (page 205) or ready-to-use vegetable broth	1 L
1 cup	ditalini pasta	250 mL
	Kosher salt and freshly ground black pepper	
2 tbsp	extra virgin olive oil (optional)	30 mL
	Grated Parmigiano-Reggiano cheese	

TIPS

You can replace the cannellini beans with Great Northern beans, red kidney beans or lima beans without changing the cooking time.

This recipe can be doubled as long as the ingredients (through step 3) do not fill the pot more than halfway.

1. Place beans in a large bowl, add cold water and let soak at room temperature for 8 hours or overnight. Drain and rinse beans. Set aside.

2. Heat the pressure cooker on High/ Sauté/Brown. Add virgin olive oil and heat until shimmering. Add onion, carrot and celery; cook, stirring occasionally, for 3 to 5 minutes or until onion is translucent. Cancel cooking.

3. Add beans, tomatoes, rosemary, bay leaf, sage and stock, stirring well. Close and lock the lid. Cook on high pressure for 17 minutes. Let stand, covered, for 10 minutes, then release any remaining pressure. Check to make sure the beans are tender; if more cooking time is needed, reset to high pressure for 2 minutes or until done to your liking. Discard rosemary sprig and bay leaf.

4. Heat the cooker on High/Sauté/Brown. Stir in pasta and bring to a boil; cook, stirring occasionally, for the time recommended on the pasta package for al dente. Season to taste with salt and pepper.

5. Stir soup and ladle into individual serving bowls. Serve drizzled with extra virgin olive oil (if using) and sprinkled with cheese.

Southwestern Bean and Barley Soup

This lively bean and barley soup is not just tasty, it's vegan and gluten-free. But for you carnivores out there, it's so easy to add some shredded rotisserie chicken and make it your own.

MAKES 6 SERVINGS		
$\frac{1}{3}$ cup	dried black beans	75 mL
$\frac{1}{3}$ cup	dried Great Northern beans	75 mL
$\frac{1}{3}$ cup	dried red kidney beans	75 mL
4 cups	cold water	1 L
1 tbsp	virgin olive oil	15 mL
1	onion, chopped	1
1	carrot, chopped	1
1	stalk celery, chopped	1
$\frac{1}{2}$ cup	pearl barley	125 mL
1 tbsp	chili powder	15 mL
1 tsp	ground cumin	5 mL
$\frac{1}{2}$ tsp	dried oregano	2 mL
4 cups	low-sodium vegetable stock (page 204) or ready-to-use vegetable broth	1 L
	Kosher salt	

TIP

You can make this soup ahead of time — actually, the flavors meld and it's even tastier — and reheat it on another day. Once the soup cools, transfer it to airtight containers and refrigerate for up to 5 days. The soup will thicken up considerably, so when reheating it, you may want to add water, stock or broth, up to $\frac{1}{4}$ cup (60 mL) at a time, until it reaches your desired consistency.

1. Place black, Great Northern and kidney beans in a large bowl, add cold water and let soak at room temperature for 8 hours or overnight. Drain and rinse beans. Set aside.

2. Heat the pressure cooker on High/ Sauté/Brown. Add oil and heat until shimmering. Add onion, carrot and celery; cook, stirring, for 3 to 5 minutes or until onion is translucent. Cancel cooking.

3. Add beans, barley, chili powder, cumin, oregano and stock, stirring well. Close and lock the lid. Cook on high pressure for 7 minutes. Let stand, covered, until the float valve drops down. Check to make sure the beans are tender; if more cooking time is needed, reset to high pressure for 1 minute or until done to your liking. Season to taste with salt.

4. Ladle into individual serving bowls and serve immediately.

VARIATION

Southwestern Chicken, Bean and Barley Soup: Substitute chicken stock or broth for the vegetable stock. Add $1\frac{1}{2}$ cups (375 mL) shredded rotisserie chicken (or leftover shredded cooked chicken) at the beginning of step 3.

Shrimp Bisque

Any type of a seafood bisque says New Year's Eve to me. Of course, you can enjoy it anytime, but a wonderful shrimp bisque is the perfect way to start off your new year. What I especially like about preparing it in the pressure cooker is that it frees up my time for making hors d'oeuvres and visiting with friends and family. You can even make the shrimp broth ahead of time and add it when you are ready to cook your bisque.

MAKES 6 SERVINGS

2 lbs	cooked shell-on large shrimp (31/35 count)	1 kg
3 tbsp	butter	45 mL
½ cup	dry white wine (such as Chardonnay)	125 mL
1	carrot, cut into 3-inch (7.5 cm) pieces	1
1	stalk celery, with green leafy parts, cut into thirds	1
1	sweet onion (such as Vidalia), sliced	1
3	sprigs fresh tarragon	3
2	sprigs fresh thyme	2
1	bay leaf	1
	Water	
1 tsp	paprika	5 mL
½ cup	heavy or whipping (35%) cream	125 mL
3 tbsp	dry sherry	45 mL
2 tbsp	tomato paste	30 mL
	Kosher salt and freshly ground black pepper	

TIP

You can prepare the shrimp broth through step 4 ahead of time. Let it cool, transfer it to an airtight container and refrigerate for up to 3 days or freeze for up to 3 months.

1. Peel shrimp, reserving shells and tails. Cover and refrigerate shrimp.

2. Heat the pressure cooker on High/Sauté/Brown. Add butter and heat until melted. Stir in shells and tails; cook, stirring, for 3 to 4 minutes or until aromatic. Add wine and scrape up any browned bits from the bottom of the pot. Cancel cooking.

3. Add carrot, celery, onion, tarragon, thyme and bay leaf. Add enough cold water to cover ingredients by 1 inch (2.5 cm). Close and lock the lid. Cook on high pressure for 7 minutes. Let stand, covered, until the float valve drops down. Check to make sure the carrots are fork-tender; if more cooking time is needed, reset to high pressure for 1 minute.

4. Using a fine-mesh sieve, carefully strain broth into a 4-cup (1 L) glass measuring cup, discarding solids. Add enough water to the broth to measure 4 cups (1 L). Rinse and dry the cooker's inner pot.

5. Return broth to the cooker and stir in paprika, cream, sherry and tomato paste. Heat the cooker on High/Sauté/Brown and cook, stirring, for 4 to 5 minutes or until broth is reduced and slightly thickened.

6. Add shrimp and cook, stirring, for 2 minutes or until warmed through. Season to taste with salt and pepper. Serve immediately.

Bouillabaisse

You don't have to be in the Mediterranean to enjoy one of the region's best dishes: fresh seafood steeped in an herb-infused broth, paired with crusty French bread that is spread with a garlicky, spicy rouille — a truly divine meal.

MAKES 6 SERVINGS

• Food processor

Rouille

1	roasted red bell pepper, drained	1
1	clove garlic, peeled	1
1/3 cup	almonds	75 mL
1/4 cup	fresh parsley leaves	60 mL
1/2 tsp	kosher salt	2 mL
Pinch	cayenne pepper	Pinch
1 tbsp	freshly squeezed lemon juice	15 mL
1/3 cup	extra virgin olive oil	75 mL
	French bread, sliced and toasted	

Bouillabaisse

2 tbsp	virgin olive oil	30 mL
1	onion, chopped	1
1	leek (white and light green parts only), sliced	1
2	cloves garlic, chopped	2
10	sprigs fresh parsley (about 1/4 bunch)	10
10	sprigs fresh thyme (about 1/4 bunch)	10
2	bay leaves	2
	Fronds of 1 fennel bulb, divided	
Pinch	saffron threads	Pinch
1 1/2 cups	chopped tomatoes	375 mL
8 cups	water	2 L
1 1/2 lbs	mussels, scrubbed and debearded	750 g
1 1/2 lbs	jumbo shrimp (21/25 count), peeled and deveined	750 g
1 1/2 lbs	skinless halibut fillet, cut into 2-inch (5 cm) chunks	750 g
1 1/2 lbs	skinless cod fillets, cut into 2-inch (5 cm) chunks	750 g

1. *Rouille:* In food processor, combine roasted pepper, garlic, almonds, parsley, salt, cayenne and lemon juice; process until smooth. With the motor running, through the feed tube, gradually add oil, processing until a paste forms. Set aside.

2. *Bouillabaisse:* Heat the pressure cooker on High/Sauté/Brown. Add oil and heat until shimmering. Add onion and leek; cook, stirring, for 3 to 5 minutes or until translucent. Add garlic and cook, stirring, for 1 minute or until fragrant. Cancel cooking.

3. Add parsley, thyme, bay leaves, half the fennel fronds, saffron, tomatoes and water, stirring well. Close and lock the lid. Cook on high pressure for 5 minutes. Quickly release the pressure.

4. Strain liquid from cooker into a bowl and discard solids. Return liquid to the cooker and add mussels and shrimp. Heat the cooker on High/Sauté/Brown, cover and cook for 2 minutes.

5. Add halibut and cod, cover and cook for 2 to 3 minutes or until mussels are opened, shrimp are pink, firm and opaque and fish flakes easily when tested with a fork. Discard any mussels that did not open.

6. Ladle bouillabaisse into bowls and garnish with the remaining fennel fronds. Spread rouille on French bread and serve with bouillabaisse.

TIP

If you are using a pressure cooker that is smaller than 6 quarts (6 L), cut this recipe in half.

Easy Weeknight Clam Chowder

This creamy chowder is made with fresh clams, a sampling of aromatics, salty bacon and melt-in-your-mouth potatoes, for the perfect coastal delicacy. If you are far from the coast or just want to use canned or frozen clams, this recipe has you covered too.

MAKES 4 TO 6 SERVINGS

• Steamer basket

2½ lbs	cherrystone clams, rinsed well	1.25 kg
	Bottled clam juice or water	
6	slices bacon, cut into 1-inch (2.5 cm) pieces	6
1	onion, finely chopped	1
1 tsp	celery salt	5 mL
½ tsp	freshly ground black pepper	2 mL
2	cloves garlic, minced	2
½ cup	dry white wine	125 mL
2	yellow-fleshed potatoes, diced	2
1	sprig fresh thyme	1
1	bay leaf	1
2 tbsp	butter	30 mL
2 tbsp	all-purpose flour	30 mL
½ cup	milk	125 mL
1½ cups	heavy or whipping (35%) cream	375 mL
	Soup crackers	

1. Tap clam shells with your finger and discard any that do not snap closed.

2. Add 1 cup (250 mL) water (or the amount required by your cooker to reach pressure) to the pressure cooker and place the steamer basket in the pot. Arrange clams inside basket. Close and lock the lid. Cook on low pressure for 5 minutes. Quickly release the pressure. Tip the clam shells into the cooker to retain any juices. Remove clam meat, chop into smaller pieces and set aside. Discard shells and any unopened clams.

3. Strain liquid from the pot into a 2-cup (500 mL) or larger glass measuring cup. Add enough bottled clam juice to measure 2 cups (500 mL); set aside. Rinse and dry the cooker's inner pot.

4. Heat the cooker on High/Sauté/Brown. Add bacon and cook, turning occasionally, for 3 minutes or until bacon begins to render its fat and starts to sizzle. Add onion, celery salt and pepper; cook, stirring occasionally, for 3 to 5 minutes or until onion is translucent. Add garlic and cook, stirring, for 1 minute or until fragrant. Add wine and cook, scraping up any browned bits from the bottom of the pot, for 3 minutes or until wine is almost evaporated. Cancel cooking.

5. Add potatoes, thyme, bay leaf and clam juice, stirring well. Close and lock the lid. Cook on high pressure for 5 minutes. Quickly release the pressure. Check to make sure the potatoes are fork-tender; if more cooking time is needed, close the lid and let stand for 2 minutes or until done to your liking. Discard thyme and bay leaf.

6. Meanwhile, in a small saucepan, melt butter over low heat. Whisk in flour until blended and cook, stirring, for 2 minutes. Whisk in milk to make a slurry.

7. Heat the cooker on High/Sauté/Brown. Return clam meat to the cooker and add slurry and cream; cook, stirring often, for 5 minutes or until thickened to your liking.

8. Ladle chowder into individual serving bowls. Serve garnished with soup crackers.

Chicken Noodle Soup

Sometimes the simplest things are the best, and that was never more true than for a bowl of chicken noodle soup. This soup is downhome goodness and — don't tell Grandma — outstandingly delicious.

MAKES 4 SERVINGS

1 tbsp	virgin olive oil	15 mL
1 tbsp	butter	15 mL
1	onion, finely chopped	1
2	cloves garlic, minced	2
2	carrots, chopped	2
2	stalks celery, with green leafy parts from 1 stalk, chopped	2
1	bay leaf	1
2 tsp	fresh thyme leaves	10 mL
5 cups	low-sodium chicken stock (page 206) or ready-to-use chicken broth, divided	1.25 L
2	bone-in skin-on chicken breasts	2
8 oz	wide egg noodles	250 g
3 tbsp	finely chopped fresh parsley	45 mL
	Kosher salt and freshly ground black pepper	

TIP

I prefer using bone-in, skin-on chicken breasts because of the rich flavor the bones and skin add to the soup. You can use boneless skinless breasts if you prefer, but reduce the pressure cooking time in step 2 to 5 minutes.

1. Heat the pressure cooker on High/Sauté/Brown. Add oil and butter; heat until oil is shimmering and butter has melted. Add onion and cook, stirring often, for 3 to 5 minutes or until translucent. Add garlic and cook, stirring, for 1 minute or until fragrant. Cancel cooking.

2. Add carrots, celery, celery greens, bay leaf, thyme and 2 cups (500 mL) stock, stirring well. Add chicken. Close and lock the lid. Cook on high pressure for 11 minutes. Quickly release the pressure. Check to make sure the chicken is no longer pink inside; if more cooking time is needed, reset to high pressure for 2 minutes. Discard bay leaf.

3. Using tongs, transfer chicken to a cutting board. Shred chicken and discard bones and skin.

4. Return chicken to the cooker and add the remaining stock. Heat the cooker on High/Sauté/Brown. When soup begins to boil, stir in noodles and cook for the time recommended on the noodle package or until noodles are done to your liking. Stir in parsley. Season to taste with salt and pepper. Serve immediately.

Creamy Chicken and Wild Rice Soup

What I really love about this soup is that the tenderness of the chicken combines with a little bit of chewiness from the wild rice in a creamy, warming bit of bliss. Plus, it tastes fabulous!

MAKES 6 SERVINGS

2 tbsp	butter	30 mL
1 cup	chopped onion	250 mL
1 cup	diced carrots	250 mL
1 cup	diced celery	250 mL
2	boneless skinless chicken breasts, cut into cubes	2
½ cup	long-grain brown rice	125 mL
½ cup	wild rice	125 mL
1 tbsp	chopped fresh thyme	15 mL
1 tsp	kosher salt	5 mL
½ tsp	freshly ground black pepper	2 mL
4¾ cups	low-sodium chicken stock (page 206) or ready-to-use chicken broth	1.175 L
1 tbsp	cornstarch	15 mL
2 tbsp	cold water	30 mL
4 oz	brick-style cream cheese, cubed	125 g
1 cup	milk	250 mL
1 cup	half-and-half (10%) cream	250 mL

1. Heat the pressure cooker on High/Sauté/Brown. Add butter and heat until melted. Add onion, carrots and celery; cook, stirring, for 4 to 5 minutes or until tender. Cancel cooking.

2. Add chicken, long-grain rice, wild rice, thyme, salt, pepper and stock, stirring well. Close and lock the lid. Cook on high pressure for 7 minutes. Let stand, covered, for 5 minutes, then quickly release the pressure. Check to make sure the chicken is no longer pink inside; if more cooking time is needed, reset to high pressure for 1 minute.

3. In a small bowl, whisk together cornstarch and cold water.

4. Heat the cooker on High/Sauté/Brown. Stir in cornstarch mixture. Add cream cheese and stir until melted. Add milk and cream; cook, stirring, until heated through (do not let boil).

TIP

You can substitute a 6-oz (170 g) package of long-grain and wild rice mix for the bulk long-grain rice and wild rice. When adding the rice to the soup, do not add the seasoning packet if it's included in the rice package.

Filipino Chicken and Rice Soup

This warm and inviting soup is a style of congee, a hearty and deeply flavored dish made with rice and seasonings that is a popular staple throughout Asia. The Filipino version is also called *arroz caldo*. Indeed, an Asian comfort food dish with a Spanish name — have I sparked your interest? If you have never tried congee, get ready to be delighted. And don't forget to try some of the variations I've included, too.

MAKES 4 SERVINGS

2 tbsp	vegetable oil	30 mL
1	onion, thinly sliced	1
4	cloves garlic, minced	4
1 tbsp	minced gingerroot	15 mL
6 cups	low-sodium chicken stock (page 206) or ready-to-use chicken broth	1.5 L
1 tbsp	fish sauce	15 mL
6	boneless skinless chicken thighs	6
1 cup	jasmine rice	250 mL
	Kosher salt and freshly ground black pepper	
1 tbsp	freshly squeezed lime juice	15 mL
4	green onions (white and light green parts only), thinly sliced	4
	Chili or sesame oil (optional)	

1. Heat the pressure cooker on High/Sauté/Brown. Add vegetable oil and heat until shimmering. Add onion and cook, stirring often, for 3 to 5 minutes or until translucent. Add garlic and ginger; cook, stirring, for 1 minute or until fragrant. Cancel cooking.

2. Add stock and fish sauce, stirring well. Add chicken. Close and lock the lid. Cook on high pressure for 11 minutes. Quickly release the pressure. Check to make sure the juices run clear when chicken is pierced; if more cooking time is needed, reset to high pressure for 2 minutes.

3. Using tongs, transfer chicken to a cutting board and cut into bite-size pieces. Return chicken to the cooker.

4. Add rice, stirring well. Reset cooker to high pressure for 1 minute. Let stand, covered, for 10 minutes, then release any remaining pressure. Season to taste with salt and pepper. Stir in lime juice.

5. Ladle soup into individual serving bowls. Garnish with green onions and drizzle with chili oil (if using).

VARIATIONS

Vegetarian Chinese Congee: Use vegetable stock or broth in place of the chicken stock. Omit the fish sauce and chicken. In step 2, add 3 stalks celery, diced, 2 cups (500 mL) broccoli florets and 1 carrot, peeled and diced; decrease the cooking time to 3 minutes. Skip step 3.

Spicy Pork Congee: In place of the chicken, add 1 lb (500 g) boneless pork shoulder blade roast, trimmed and cut into ½-inch (1 cm) cubes. In step 2, decrease the cooking time to 10 minutes. Pork should be tender and no longer pink inside. In step 4, substitute 2 tbsp (30 mL) chili garlic sauce for the lime juice. Serve garnished with chopped fresh cilantro.

Bacon and Egg Congee: Omit the oil, garlic, ginger, chicken and lime juice. In step 1, heat the pressure cooker on High/Sauté/Brown. Add 8 slices of bacon, cut into 1-inch (2.5 cm) pieces, and cook, stirring often, for 5 minutes or until slightly crispy and fat is rendered. Transfer bacon to a plate lined with paper towels. Add onion to the cooker and cook, stirring often, for 3 to 5 minutes or until translucent. Add 1 cup (250 mL) stock, scraping up browned bits. Cancel cooking. Stir in the remaining stock and fish sauce. Skip the remainder of step 2 and step 3. Follow step 4 as directed, but without adding the lime juice. Serve garnished with bacon and 2 chopped hard-cooked eggs.

TIPS

Prepare and measure out all of your ingredients ahead of time and have them ready to quickly add to the pressure cooker. This helpful style of food preparation is called *mise en place,* meaning "everything in its place."

When releasing pressure quickly, keep your hands and face away from the hole on top of the steam release handle so you don't get scalded by the escaping steam.

Curried Chicken and Coconut Soup

This fragrant Thai-style soup has a delightful commingling of flavors from the coconut milk, green onions, curry, ginger and lime. The chicken and spinach make it hearty and satisfying.

MAKES 4 SERVINGS		
³⁄₄ cup	sliced green onions (white and light green parts only)	175 mL
1 tbsp	minced gingerroot	15 mL
	Grated zest and juice of 2 limes, divided	
3 cups	low-sodium chicken stock (page 206) or ready-to-use chicken broth	750 mL
1³⁄₄ cups	unsweetened coconut milk	425 mL
2 tbsp	Thai curry paste, divided	30 mL
4	bone-in skin-on chicken thighs (about 1¹⁄₂ lbs/750 g)	4
5 cups	packed baby spinach	1.25 L
	Kosher salt and freshly ground black pepper	
¹⁄₄ cup	chopped fresh cilantro	60 mL

1. In the pressure cooker, combine green onions, ginger, zest of 1¹⁄₂ limes, juice of 1 lime, stock, coconut milk and 1 tbsp (15 mL) curry paste, stirring well. Add chicken. Close and lock the lid. Cook on high pressure for 10 minutes. Let stand, covered, for 5 minutes, then release any remaining pressure. Check to make sure the juices run clear when chicken is pierced; if more cooking time is needed, reset to high pressure for 2 minutes.

2. Using tongs, transfer chicken to a cutting board and let cool slightly. Remove and discard skin and bones. Cut chicken into ³⁄₄-inch (2 cm) cubes.

3. Return chicken to the cooker. Heat the cooker on High/Sauté/Brown. Add spinach and cook, stirring, for 1 minute or until wilted. Stir in the remaining curry paste, lime zest and lime juice. Season to taste with salt and pepper.

4. Ladle soup into individual serving bowls and garnish with cilantro. Serve immediately.

TIPS

A 14-oz (400 mL) can of coconut milk will yield about the right amount for this recipe. Tetra Paks are another option and come in various sizes.

Thai curry paste comes in green, yellow and red. Different brands vary in spiciness and sweetness. Check the ingredient list for an indication of the flavors. Experiment with different brands and types to find your favorite. You can add more or less curry paste in step 3, as desired.

If you are using a 4-quart (4 L) pressure cooker, cut this recipe in half.

Mulligatawny

This full-flavored chicken, lentil and tomato soup brings together British and Indian ingredients for an interesting combination of sweet and spicy flavors. When cooked under pressure, the powerful symphony of spices, herbs and vegetables melds into a highly satisfying soup.

MAKES 4 SERVINGS		
3 tbsp	vegetable oil	45 mL
3	large bone-in skin-on chicken thighs (about 1 lb/500 g)	3
	Kosher salt and freshly ground black pepper	
1	onion, finely chopped	1
1	carrot, finely chopped	1
1	stalk celery, finely chopped	
3	cloves garlic, finely chopped	3
1	apple, peeled and cut into 1/4-inch (0.5 cm) pieces	1
1	sweet potato, peeled and cut into 1/4-inch (0.5 cm) pieces	1
1	plum (Roma) tomato, cut into 1/4-inch (0.5 cm) pieces	1
1	1-inch (2.5 cm) piece gingerroot, grated	1
1 1/2 tbsp	garam masala	22 mL
1 tsp	ground coriander	5 mL
1 tsp	ground cumin	5 mL
1 tsp	ground turmeric	5 mL
1 tsp	curry powder	5 mL
2	bay leaves	2
1 cup	dried red lentils, rinsed	250 mL
6 cups	low-sodium chicken stock (page 206) or ready-to-use chicken broth	1.5 L
2/3 cup	plain Greek yogurt	150 mL
	Hot pepper flakes	

1. Heat the pressure cooker on High/Sauté/Brown. Add oil and heat until shimmering. Season chicken with salt and pepper. Add to the cooker, skin side down, and cook, turning once, for 9 minutes or until skin is golden and bottom is brown. Using tongs, transfer chicken to a plate and set aside.

2. Add onion, carrot and celery to the cooker and cook, stirring often, for 3 to 5 minutes or until onion is translucent. Add garlic and cook, stirring, for 1 minute or until fragrant. Add apple, sweet potato, tomato, ginger, garam masala, coriander, cumin, turmeric and curry powder, stirring until vegetables are evenly coated with spices. Cancel cooking.

3. Add bay leaves, lentils and stock, stirring well. Return chicken and any accumulated juices to the cooker. Close and lock the lid. Cook on high pressure for 12 minutes. Let stand, covered, for 10 minutes, then release any remaining pressure. Check to make sure the potatoes and lentils are tender and the juices run clear when chicken is pierced; if more cooking time is needed, reset to high pressure for 2 minutes. Discard bay leaves.

4. Using tongs, transfer chicken to a cutting board. Shred meat and discard skin and bones. Return chicken to the cooker, stirring to combine. Season to taste with salt and pepper.

5. Ladle soup into individual serving bowls. Dollop with yogurt and garnish with hot pepper flakes.

Split Pea and Ham Soup

What could take hours on the stovetop is completed, start to finish, in under 30 minutes with your pressure cooker. The result is a deeply flavorful, rich and creamy soup. You can also make it using the slow cooker function, for an equally flavorful soup that is almost entirely hands-off.

MAKES 6 SERVINGS

3 tbsp	butter	45 mL
1	onion, finely chopped	1
1	stalk celery, diced	1
2	cloves garlic, minced	2
3	carrots, thinly sliced	3
2	bay leaves	2
1 tsp	dried oregano	5 mL
1 lb	dried green split peas, rinsed	500 g
8 oz	diced cooked ham	250 g
6 cups	low-sodium chicken stock (page 206) or ready-to-use chicken broth	1.5 L
	Water (optional)	
	Kosher salt and freshly ground black pepper	

TIP

Do not fill your pressure cooker more than halfway full when cooking legumes; they tend to foam and could clog the steam release valve. Always clean the steam release valve after cooking legumes to clear it of any obstructions for your next use.

1. Heat the pressure cooker on High/Sauté/Brown. Add butter and heat until melted. Add onion and celery; cook, stirring, for 3 to 5 minutes or until onion is translucent. Add garlic and cook, stirring, for 1 minute or until fragrant. Cancel cooking.

2. Add carrots, bay leaves, oregano, split peas, ham and stock, stirring well. Close and lock the lid. Cook on high pressure for 18 minutes. Let stand, covered, until the float valve drops down. Check to make sure the peas and carrots are tender; if more cooking time is needed, reset to high pressure for 3 minutes. Discard bay leaves.

3. If you prefer a thinner soup, add water, a little bit at a time, and cook, stirring, on High/Sauté/Brown until soup is your desired consistency. Season to taste with salt and pepper. Serve immediately.

VARIATION

Slow Cooker Split Pea and Ham Soup: In step 2, add 2 cups (500 mL) water with the stock. Close and lock the lid, making sure the steam vent is open. Press Slow Cook and adjust the temperature to the lowest setting. Cook for 9 hours. (Or adjust the temperature to the highest setting and cook for $4\frac{1}{2}$ hours.)

Navy Bean and Ham Soup

This classic bean soup is simple in its style and ingredients, yet it's an ever-popular soup. It's also known by many as Senate bean soup because a version of it has been served in the U.S. Senate every day except one (when beans were rationed during the Second World War) since the early 1900s. The recipe once called for potatoes, but this version has since become the favorite.

MAKES 6 SERVINGS

1 lb	dried navy (white pea) beans (about 3 cups/750 mL)	500 g
	Water	
2 tbsp	butter	30 mL
1	onion, finely chopped	1
2	cloves garlic, coarsely chopped	2
2 cups	diced cooked ham	500 mL
	Kosher salt and freshly ground black pepper	
	Fresh parsley, minced	

TIPS

When preparing legumes of any type, make sure to fill the pot no more than halfway full. Do not attempt to double or triple the recipe unless you are using a large-capacity cooker; otherwise, the exhaust valve may become clogged as the beans froth up under pressure. Adding butter or oil with the legumes will help to reduce the amount of froth.

Beans can be presoaked, drained and frozen up to 3 months in advance. If you are using your beans for various recipes, measure the dry and soaked weight of the beans and mark it on the container before freezing.

1. Place beans in a large bowl, add 12 cups (3 L) cold water and let soak at room temperature for 8 hours or overnight. Drain and rinse beans. Set aside.

2. Heat the pressure cooker on High/Sauté/Brown. Add butter and heat until melted. Add onion and cook, stirring, for 7 minutes or until lightly browned. Add garlic and cook, stirring, for 1 minute or until fragrant. Cancel cooking.

3. Add beans, ham, $\frac{1}{2}$ tsp (2 mL) salt and 8 cups (2 L) water, stirring well. Close and lock the lid. Cook on high pressure for 12 minutes. Let stand, covered, until the float valve drops down. Check to make sure the beans are tender; if more cooking time is needed, reset to high pressure for 3 minutes. Season to taste with salt and pepper.

4. Spoon into individual serving bowls and garnish with parsley. Serve immediately.

Smoky Seven-Bean and Ham Soup

This recipe contains a cornucopia of beans and a smoky ham hock that are cooked under pressure to yield a soup that is tender, juicy and richly flavored. While only a short amount of cooking time is needed, this soup tastes like it has been simmering all day.

MAKES 6 SERVINGS

½ cup	dried split chickpeas	125 mL
½ cup	dried navy (white pea) beans	125 mL
½ cup	dried pinto beans	125 mL
½ cup	dried large lima beans	125 mL
½ cup	dried Great Northern beans	125 mL
½ cup	dried red kidney beans	125 mL
	Water	
2 tbsp	virgin olive oil	30 mL
1	large onion, finely chopped	1
1	carrot, diced	1
1	stalk celery, diced	1
3	cloves garlic, minced	3
1½ tsp	smoked paprika	7 mL
1 tsp	ground cumin	5 mL
½ cup	dried yellow split peas, rinsed	125 mL
1 tsp	granulated sugar	5 mL
2	bay leaves	2
1	small meaty smoked ham hock	1
1	can (28 oz/796 mL) diced fire-roasted tomatoes, with juice	1
3 cups	low-sodium chicken stock or ready-to-use chicken broth	750 mL
	Kosher salt and freshly ground black pepper	

1. Place chickpeas and navy, pinto, lima, Great Northern and kidney beans in a large bowl, add 12 cups (3 L) cold water and let soak at room temperature for 8 hours or overnight. Drain and rinse beans. Set aside.

2. Heat the pressure cooker on High/Sauté/Brown. Add oil and heat until shimmering. Add onion, carrot and celery; cook, stirring, for 3 to 5 minutes or until onion is translucent. Add garlic, paprika and cumin; cook, stirring, for 1 minute or until fragrant. Cancel cooking.

3. Add bean mixture, split peas, sugar, bay leaves, ham hock, tomatoes, stock and 3 cups (750 mL) water, stirring well. Close and lock the lid. Cook on high pressure for 18 minutes. Let stand, covered, until the float valve drops down. Check to make sure the peas and beans are tender; if more cooking time is needed, reset to high pressure for 4 minutes. Discard bay leaves.

4. Transfer ham hock to a cutting board and let cool slightly. Trim meat from bone, shred meat and discard bone, gristle, fat and skin.

5. Return ham to the cooker and season to taste with salt and pepper. Heat the cooker on High/Sauté/Brown. Cook, stirring occasionally, for 3 to 5 minutes or until soup is your desired consistency.

TIP

This recipe is intended for 6-quart (6 L) or larger pressure cookers. Do not double it. When cooking legumes, you should never fill your cooker more than half full.

Bacon and Beer Cheese Soup

This creamy, deeply flavored cheese soup is perfect for crisp fall and winter days and makes a great complement to game day snacks. If you aren't feeding a crowd, it reheats very well, for an easy weekday meal.

MAKES 8 SERVINGS		
6	slices thick-cut bacon	6
1	large sweet onion (such as Vidalia), finely chopped	1
1	small red or green bell pepper, finely chopped	1
3	cloves garlic, minced	3
2	carrots, grated	2
1	stalk celery, finely chopped	1
2 tsp	dry mustard	10 mL
1/8 tsp	cayenne pepper	0.5 mL
3	cans or bottles (each 12 oz/ 341 mL) lager-style beer, at room temperature	3
2 cups	low-sodium chicken stock (page 206) or ready-to-use chicken broth	500 mL
2 tsp	Worcestershire sauce	10 mL
4 oz	brick-style cream cheese, softened	125 g
4 cups	shredded sharp (old) Cheddar cheese (16 oz/500 g)	1 L
2 cups	shredded Monterey Jack cheese (8 oz/250 g)	500 mL
2½ cups	half-and-half (10%) cream	625 mL
3 tbsp	all-purpose flour (optional)	45 mL
	Kosher salt and freshly ground black pepper	
	Popcorn	

1. Heat the pressure cooker on High/Sauté/ Brown. Add bacon and cook, turning, for 5 minutes or until just crisp. Using tongs, transfer bacon to a plate lined with paper towels; let cool, then crumble.

2. Add onion and bell pepper to the bacon fat in the cooker; cook, stirring, for 3 to 5 minutes or until onion is translucent. Cancel cooking.

3. Add garlic, carrots, celery, mustard, cayenne, beer, stock and Worcestershire sauce, stirring well. Close and lock the lid. Cook on high pressure for 4 minutes. Quickly release the pressure.

4. Stir in cream cheese, Cheddar, Monterey Jack and cream. Heat the cooker on High/Sauté/Brown. Cook, stirring, for 5 minutes or until cheese is melted and soup is thickened to your liking (do not let boil). If more thickening is needed, sprinkle in flour, 1 tbsp (15 mL) at a time, stirring until thickened to your liking. Stir in bacon. Season to taste with salt and pepper. Serve garnished with popcorn.

TIPS

If adding flour to the soup in step 4, sprinkle it through a fine-mesh sieve to avoid clumping.

This soup can be stored in an airtight container in the refrigerator for up to 3 days. When reheating, cook on low heat, stirring, and add milk as necessary to achieve your desired consistency. Be careful to not overheat the soup, as the dairy can separate or scorch on the bottom.

Creamy Baked Potato Soup with Bacon and Chives

What could be better than a loaded baked potato with all the fixings? A creamy soup, of course, with potatoes, garlic and bacon all in one handy bowl. Sprinkle with Cheddar cheese and chives, and add a dollop of sour cream, and you have a soup that is otherworldly. I have offered up two versions — one you can make quickly in your pressure cooker and one that you can start in your slow cooker and have ready later in the day.

MAKES 6 SERVINGS

6	slices bacon	6
1	large shallot, finely chopped	1
1	clove garlic, minced	1
3 cups	chopped new potatoes (about 1 lb/500 g)	750 mL
3 cups	low-sodium chicken stock (page 206) or ready-to-use chicken broth	750 mL
3/4 cup	heavy or whipping (35%) cream	175 mL
1 tbsp	butter, softened	15 mL
1 cup	shredded sharp (old) Cheddar cheese, divided	250 mL
	Kosher salt and freshly ground black pepper	
1/2 cup	sour cream	125 mL
3 tbsp	snipped fresh chives	45 mL

1. Heat the pressure cooker on High/Sauté/Brown. Add bacon and cook, turning, for 5 minutes or until just crisp. Using tongs, transfer bacon to a plate lined with paper towels; let cool, then crumble.

2. Add shallot and cook, stirring, for 2 to 3 minutes or until translucent. Add garlic and cook, stirring, for 30 seconds or until fragrant. Cancel cooking.

3. Add potatoes and stock, stirring well. Close and lock the lid. Cook on high pressure for 7 minutes. Let stand, covered, until the float valve drops down.

4. Using a potato masher, coarsely mash potatoes so that some chunks remain. Stir in bacon, cream and butter. Heat the cooker on High/Sauté/Brown. Cook, stirring occasionally, for 5 to 7 minutes or until soup is thickened to your liking. Stir in 1/2 cup (125 mL) cheese. Season to taste with salt and pepper.

5. Ladle soup into individual serving bowls. Sprinkle with the remaining cheese, dollop with sour cream and garnish with chives.

VARIATION

Slow Cooker Baked Potato Soup: In step 3, close and lock the lid, making sure the steam vent is open. Press Slow Cook and adjust the temperature to the lowest setting. Cook for 8 hours. (Or adjust the temperature to the highest setting and cook for 4 hours.) Continue with step 4.

Hearty Beef Barley Soup

This wonderfully rich and hearty soup is so full-flavored, yet it takes less than one-third of the time as the traditional stovetop method. I use beef chuck roast, for more tender chunks of meat with a beefier flavor. Browning the vegetables and then adding them near the end of cooking also enhances the flavors.

MAKES 8 SERVINGS

1 lb	boneless beef chuck roast, cut into 1½-inch (4 cm) thick slices	500 g
	Kosher salt and freshly ground black pepper	
1 tbsp	vegetable oil (approx.)	15 mL
2 tbsp	butter	30 mL
3	carrots, diced	3
2	stalks celery, diced	2
1	onion, finely chopped	1
3	cloves garlic, minced	3
½ cup	pearl barley	125 mL
2	sprigs fresh thyme	2
1	bay leaf	1
½ tsp	dried parsley	2 mL
4 cups	low-sodium beef bone broth (page 208) or ready-to-use beef broth	1 L
1 cup	water (approx.)	250 mL

TIP

When releasing the pressure in step 3, begin by slowly turning the pressure release knob. There may be some initial spewing of foam from the valve. Close the knob. Continue to open and close the knob in short spurts until no foam remains.

1. Season beef with salt and pepper. Heat the pressure cooker on High/Sauté/Brown. Add oil and heat until shimmering. Working in batches, add beef and cook, turning once, for 5 minutes per side or until browned on both sides, adding more oil as needed between batches. Transfer beef to a cutting board. Let rest for 7 minutes, then cut into 1-inch (2.5 cm) chunks.

2. Meanwhile, add butter to the cooker and heat until melted. Add carrots, celery and onion; cook, stirring, for 7 minutes or until lightly browned. Add garlic and cook, stirring, for 1 minute or until fragrant. Using a slotted spoon, transfer vegetables to a plate and set aside. Cancel cooking.

3. Return beef and any accumulated juices to the cooker. Add barley, thyme, bay leaf, parsley, broth and water, stirring well. Close and lock the lid. Cook on high pressure for 15 minutes. Quickly release the pressure (see tip). Check to make sure the beef is fork-tender; if more cooking time is needed, reset to high pressure for 4 minutes. Discard thyme sprigs and bay leaf.

4. Add browned vegetables to the cooker. Close and lock the lid. Cook on high pressure for 7 minutes. Quickly release the pressure.

5. If soup is too thick, add water, ¼ cup (60 mL) at a time, until soup is your desired consistency. Reheat on High/Sauté/Brown, if needed. Season to taste with salt and pepper. Serve immediately.

Beef, Tomato and Orzo Soup

Tiny, delicate rice-shaped pasta, known as orzo, swirl through this full-flavored soup. The ground beef and tomatoes complement the orzo nicely, but the real bonus comes from the veggies and herbs that meld with the soup.

MAKES 8 SERVINGS

1 tbsp	virgin olive oil	15 mL
1 lb	ground beef	500 g
1	onion, finely chopped	1
4	cloves garlic, minced	4
6	tomatoes, diced (about 3 cups/ 750 mL)	6
2 tbsp	dried parsley	30 mL
2 tsp	ground cumin	10 mL
1/4 tsp	hot pepper flakes	1 mL
4 cups	low-sodium beef bone broth (page 208) or ready-to-use beef broth	1 L
1/2 cup	orzo	125 mL
2 cups	coarsely chopped baby spinach	500 mL
	Kosher salt and freshly ground black pepper	

TIPS

You can substitute a 28-oz (796 mL) can of diced tomatoes, with juice, for the fresh tomatoes in this recipe.

If you prefer more hot pepper flakes, stir them in with the spinach in step 3. Do not add more in step 2. Hot pepper flakes intensify in flavor when cooked under pressure.

1. Heat the pressure cooker on High/ Sauté/Brown. Add oil and heat until shimmering. Add beef and cook, breaking it up with a spoon, for 7 minutes or until no longer pink. Add onion and cook, stirring, for 3 to 5 minutes or until translucent. Add garlic and cook, stirring, for 1 minute or until fragrant. Cancel cooking.

2. Add tomatoes (with any juice collected while chopping), parsley, cumin, hot pepper flakes and stock, stirring well. Close and lock the lid. Cook on high pressure for 25 minutes. Quickly release the pressure.

3. Heat the cooker on High/Sauté/ Brown. Stir in orzo and cook, stirring occasionally, for the time recommended on the pasta package for al dente. Stir in spinach and cook, stirring, for 1 minute or until wilted. Season to taste with salt and pepper. Serve immediately.

Pork and Hominy Stew

You may know this stew as pork posole, an inviting Mexican dish. The combination of textures and flavors is exceptional. The pork is melt-in-your-mouth tender, the hominy adds a chewy bite, and the chiles combine for a spicy undertone.

MAKES 8 SERVINGS

2 cups	dry hominy kernels, soaked overnight, rinsed and drained	500 mL
4 cups	low-sodium chicken stock (page 206) or ready-to-use chicken broth	1 L
4 cups	water	1 L
2 lbs	boneless pork shoulder blade roast, trimmed and cut into 2-inch (5 cm) cubes	1 kg
	Kosher salt and freshly ground black pepper	
4	cloves garlic, minced	4
2	bay leaves	2
2 tbsp	ancho chile powder	30 mL
1 tbsp	dried Mexican oregano (see tip)	15 mL
1 tsp	ground cumin	5 mL
1	can (4 oz/114 mL) diced green chiles	1
2	radishes, thinly sliced	2
1	avocado, cubed	1
½ cup	lightly packed fresh cilantro leaves	125 mL
1	lime, cut into wedges	1

1. In the pressure cooker, combine hominy, stock and water. Close and lock the lid. Cook on high pressure for 12 minutes. Let stand, covered, until the float valve drops down.

2. Season pork with salt and pepper. Add pork, garlic, bay leaves, chile powder, oregano and cumin to the cooker, stirring well. Close and lock the lid. Cook on high pressure for 10 minutes. Let stand, covered, until the float valve drops down. Check to make sure the hominy is soft and chewy and the pork is fork-tender, with just a hint of pink inside; if more cooking time is needed, reset to high pressure for 2 minutes. Discard bay leaves.

3. Stir in chiles. Heat the cooker on High/Sauté/Brown. Cook, stirring occasionally, for 7 to 10 minutes or until stew is your desired consistency.

4. Ladle stew into individual serving bowls. Garnish with radishes, avocado and cilantro. Serve with lime wedges.

TIP

Mexican oregano has more citrus notes than its Mediterranean counterpart and goes especially well with chile peppers and cumin. In my opinion, these differences make it well worthwhile to have it on hand.

Homestyle Beef Stew

If you're in the mood for a bowl of comfort food, this homey stew should be at the top of your list. There is good reason it is an all-time classic. Tender chunks of beef mingle with carrots, potatoes and seasonings to create a mouthwatering, tummy-warming dish.

MAKES 6 SERVINGS		
3 lbs	boneless beef chuck roast, cut into 1½-inch (4 cm) chunks	1.5 kg
	Kosher salt and freshly ground black pepper	
2 tbsp	vegetable oil (approx.)	30 mL
2	onions, finely chopped	2
2	stalks celery, chopped	2
3	cloves garlic, minced	3
1 cup	dry red wine	250 mL
1 lb	small yellow-fleshed potatoes, quartered	500 g
3	carrots, cut into 2-inch (5 cm) pieces	3
3	sprigs fresh thyme	3
2	bay leaves	2
2 tsp	paprika	10 mL
2 cups	low-sodium beef bone broth (page 208) or ready-to-use beef broth	500 mL
2 tbsp	tomato paste	30 mL
1 tbsp	Worcestershire sauce	15 mL

1. Generously season beef with salt and pepper. Heat the pressure cooker on High/Sauté/Brown. Add 1 tbsp (15 mL) oil and heat until shimmering. Working in batches, add beef and cook, turning occasionally, for 5 minutes or until browned on all sides, adding more oil as needed between batches. Using a slotted spoon, transfer beef to a plate.

2. Add any remaining oil to the cooker, if needed. Add onions and celery; cook, stirring, for 3 to 5 minutes or until onions are translucent. Add garlic and cook, stirring, for 1 minute or until fragrant. Add wine and cook, stirring and scraping up any browned bits from the bottom of the pot, for 3 minutes or until reduced by half. Cancel cooking.

3. Return beef and any accumulated juices to the cooker. Add potatoes, carrots, thyme, bay leaves, paprika, broth, tomato paste and Worcestershire sauce, stirring well. Close and lock the lid. Cook on high pressure for 20 minutes. Quickly release the pressure. Check to make sure the beef is fork-tender; if more cooking time is needed, reset to high pressure for 5 minutes. Discard thyme sprigs and bay leaves. Season to taste with salt and pepper. Serve immediately.

TIPS

You can substitute beef stew meat for the roast in this recipe. Look for cuts that are well marbled, for maximum flavor.

You can double this recipe, provided you do not fill your cooker above the maximum fill line.

For cookers that are smaller than 6 quarts (6 L), cut this recipe in half.

Leftover beef stew can be stored in an airtight container in the refrigerator for up to 3 days.

Beef, Bean and Tomato Chili

This is my favorite style of chili — pure and simple comfort food. At the start of fall, when the weather gets crisp and cool, I know it's time for a hearty bowl of chili. I've sped up the long and slow cooking process by using the pressure cooker, but that hasn't affected the taste.

MAKES 8 SERVINGS

3 cups	dried red kidney beans (about 1 lb/500 g)	750 mL
	Water	
1 tbsp	vegetable oil	15 mL
1	onion, finely chopped	1
1	green bell pepper, finely chopped	1
3	cloves garlic, minced	3
¼ cup	chili powder	60 mL
1 tbsp	dried oregano	15 mL
1 tsp	ground cumin	5 mL
½ tsp	ground cloves	2 mL
2 lbs	ground beef	1 kg
1	can (28 oz/796 mL) crushed tomatoes	1
2 cups	low-sodium beef bone broth (page 208) or ready-to-use beef broth	500 mL
	Kosher salt	

TIP

There are many ways to jazz up the chili to suit your tastes. Some of my favorites are sprinkling shredded Cheddar cheese and sliced green onions over top. You may also want to add a dollop of sour cream, sliced jalapeños or hot pepper sauce.

1. Place beans in a large bowl, add 12 cups (3 L) cold water and let soak at room temperature for 8 hours or overnight. Drain and rinse beans. Set aside.

2. Heat the pressure cooker on High/Sauté/Brown. Add oil and heat until shimmering. Add onion and green pepper; cook, stirring, for 3 to 5 minutes or until onion is translucent. Add garlic, chili powder, oregano, cumin and cloves; cook, stirring, for 1 minute or until fragrant. Add beef and cook, breaking it up with a spoon, for 5 minutes or until no longer pink. Cancel cooking.

3. Add beans, tomatoes, broth and 1 cup (250 mL) water, stirring well. Close and lock the lid. Cook on high pressure for 15 minutes. Let stand, covered, until the float valve drops down. Check to make sure beans are tender and flavors are melded; if more cooking time is needed, reset to high pressure for 5 minutes or until done to your liking. Season to taste with salt. Serve immediately.

VARIATIONS

Substitute 1 lb (500 g) ground pork for half the beef.

Slow Cooker Beef, Bean and Tomato Chili: Substitute 5 cans (each 14 to 15 oz/398 to 425 mL) red kidney beans for the dried beans and skip step 1. Add the beans with the tomatoes. Close and lock the lid, making sure the steam vent is open. Press Slow Cook and adjust the temperature to the lowest setting. Cook for 6 to 8 hours or until done to your liking. Season to taste with salt.

Rancher's Hearty Beef Chili

One of the best things about chili is that there are almost as many variations as there are people who love it. This version is made for those hungry ranchers from Texas and the Southwest. It contains loads of chunky beef and just the right amount of kick to get your taste buds in high gear.

MAKES 4 SERVINGS		
2 lbs	beef stew meat, cut into 1-inch (2.5 cm) cubes	1 kg
1 tsp	kosher salt	5 mL
2 tbsp	virgin olive oil (approx.)	30 mL
1	onion, chopped	1
2	cloves garlic, minced	2
1	can or bottle (12 oz/341 mL) ale or lager beer	1
3	large tomatoes, chopped	3
2	chipotle peppers, chopped, with 1 tbsp (15 mL) adobo sauce	2
1	green bell pepper, chopped	1
1 tbsp	chili powder	15 mL
2 tsp	ground cumin	10 mL
1 tsp	granulated sugar	5 mL
1 tbsp	tomato paste	15 mL
1/2	small red onion, finely chopped	1/2

TIPS

Cut your beef into pieces of a similar size, so they cook evenly.

Give your ranchers some tasty toppings to add to their chili; sour cream, guacamole, shredded Cheddar cheese, shredded pepper Jack cheese and sliced jalapeños are all great choices.

Leftover red onion can be refrigerated in an airtight container for up to 7 days. Do not wrap onions in plastic wrap. Use leftover onion on salads, sandwiches, burgers and tacos.

1. Season beef with salt. Heat the pressure cooker on High/Sauté/Brown. Add oil and heat until shimmering. Working in batches, add beef and cook, stirring, for 2 to 3 minutes or until browned on all sides, adding more oil as needed between batches. Using a slotted spoon, transfer beef to a plate.

2. Add any remaining oil to the cooker, if needed. Add onion and cook, stirring, for 3 to 5 minutes or until translucent. Add garlic and cook, stirring, for 1 minute or until fragrant. Add ale and cook for 2 minutes, scraping up any browned bits from the bottom of the pot. Cancel cooking.

3. Return beef and any accumulated juices to the cooker. Add tomatoes, chipotles with adobo sauce, green pepper, chili powder, cumin, sugar and tomato paste, stirring well. Close and lock the lid. Cook on high pressure for 12 minutes. Quickly release the pressure. Check to make sure the beef is fork-tender; if more cooking time is needed, reset to high pressure for 3 minutes.

4. Ladle chili into individual serving bowls. Garnish with red onion.

VARIATION

If you prefer not to use beer, you can replace it with 1½ cups (375 mL) low-sodium beef bone broth (page 208) or ready-to-use beef broth. (If you use full-sodium broth, reduce the salt in the recipe to ½ tsp/2 mL.)

Main Courses

All-Time Favorite Macaroni and Cheese

My oh my, how we love our mac and cheese. We loved it as children, survived college on it, served it to our smiling children and even "adulted" it with variations galore. Now it's time to pressurize this favorite to pure perfection. To make it even more delightful — if that's possible — I've included some variations to tease your taste buds.

MAKES 4 SERVINGS

2 cups	elbow macaroni	500 mL
1 tsp	granulated sugar	5 mL
1/8 tsp	ground nutmeg	0.5 mL
2 cups	low-sodium chicken stock (page 206) or ready-to-use chicken broth	500 mL
1	can (12 oz or 370 mL) evaporated milk	1
1½ cups	shredded sharp (old) Cheddar cheese	375 mL
1 cup	shredded Gruyère cheese	250 mL

1. In the pressure cooker, combine macaroni, sugar, nutmeg and stock. Close and lock the lid. Cook on high pressure for 5 minutes. Quickly release the pressure.

2. Stir in milk. Heat the cooker on High/Sauté/Brown. Cook, stirring, for 2 to 3 minutes or until sauce has thickened and pasta is done to your liking. Cancel cooking.

3. Add Cheddar and Gruyère, ½ cup (125 mL) at a time, stirring until cheese is melted and combined before adding more. Serve immediately.

VARIATIONS

Zesty Macaroni and Cheese: Replace the sugar with dry mustard, and replace the nutmeg with cayenne pepper.

Lobster Mac: Preheat broiler. Replace the Gruyère with more Cheddar. In step 3, stir in 2 cups (500 mL) Cheddar as directed, then stir in 12 oz (375 g) chopped cooked lobster. Transfer mixture to an oven-safe casserole dish and top with the remaining Cheddar. In a small bowl, combine ½ cup (125 mL) panko, ¼ cup (60 mL) chopped fresh chives and 1 tbsp (15 mL) melted butter. Sprinkle over casserole. Broil until top is golden brown. Serve immediately.

Broccoli Mac: Steam 3 cups (750 mL) broccoli florets in your pressure cooker on high pressure for 3 minutes, then quickly release the pressure. Set aside. Replace the nutmeg with dry mustard. Follow steps 1 to 3 and stir in broccoli just before serving.

TIPS

Two cups (500 mL) elbow macaroni is about half of a 16-oz (500 g) package.

You can double this recipe, provided you do not fill your pressure cooker above the maximum fill line.

White Fish with Tomatoes and Spinach

This simple and light dish can be made with a wide selection of white fish, depending upon availability and your preferences. Fresh herbs impart a tantalizing flavor, and the tomatoes and spinach not only add flavor but make for an inviting side dish.

MAKES 2 SERVINGS

- Steamer basket
- Steam rack

8 oz	baby spinach	250 g
3	tomatoes, thickly sliced, divided	3
10 oz	skinless white fish fillet (see tip), cut in half	300 g
3	cloves garlic, minced	3
1 tbsp	virgin olive oil	15 mL
1 tsp	kosher salt	5 mL
1 tsp	freshly ground black pepper	5 mL
2	sprigs fresh thyme	2
2 tsp	drained capers	10 mL

TIPS

For the fish, use tilapia, grouper, halibut, flounder, cod or sole.

When quickly releasing pressure, remove the lid carefully, allowing steam to escape away from you.

1. Layer spinach in the steamer basket. Arrange half the tomatoes on top. Carefully place fish on top of tomatoes.

2. In a small bowl, combine garlic and oil. Brush top of fish with garlic oil. Season with salt and pepper. Lay 1 thyme sprig on each fillet. Arrange the remaining tomatoes on top.

3. Add 1 cup (250 mL) water (or the amount required by your cooker to reach pressure) to the pressure cooker and place the steam rack in the pot. Place the steamer basket on the rack. Close and lock the lid. Cook on high pressure for 5 minutes. Quickly release the pressure. Check to make sure the fish is opaque and flakes easily when tested with a fork; if more cooking time is needed, close the lid and let stand for 1 to 2 minutes. Discard thyme sprigs.

4. Using a spatula, carefully transfer fish with spinach and tomatoes to individual serving plates. Serve garnished with capers.

Bibimbap with Salmon and Spinach

Bibimbap is one of the better known and most-loved Korean dishes. Simply stated, it is a mixture of rice, meat and vegetables. However, the combination of flavors and inspired ingredients make it anything but simple. Give this recipe a try, then use it as a base for mixing and matching an array of ingredients. Creating a bibimbap concoction is a great way to use up leftover vegetable odds and ends that might otherwise go to waste.

MAKES 4 SERVINGS

- Steam rack
- Steamer basket
- Sheet of heavy-duty foil, sprayed with nonstick cooking spray

2 tbsp	unseasoned rice vinegar	30 mL
2 tsp	granulated sugar	10 mL
	Kosher salt	
½	small daikon radish, julienned (about 1 cup/250 mL)	½
6 cups	lightly packed spinach leaves (about 6 oz/175 g)	1.5 L
	Toasted sesame oil	
8 oz	skin-on salmon fillet	250 g
	Freshly ground black pepper	
1 tbsp	vegetable oil	15 mL
2	carrots, julienned	2
1 cup	short-grain white rice, rinsed	250 mL
1½ cups	low-sodium chicken stock (page 206) or ready-to-use chicken broth	375 mL
2	large eggs	2
1 tsp	Asian chili paste (such as gochujang or sambal)	5 mL
	Sesame seeds	
	Thinly sliced green onions (white and light green parts only)	

1. In a medium bowl, combine vinegar, sugar and ¼ tsp (1 mL) salt. Add radish and toss to coat. Set aside.

2. Add 1 cup (250 mL) water (or the amount required by your cooker to reach pressure) to the pressure cooker and place the steam rack in the pot. Arrange spinach in the steamer basket and place basket on the rack. Close and lock the lid. Cook on high pressure for 1 minute. Quickly release the pressure. Remove the basket (leaving the rack and water in the pot), drain spinach and squeeze dry. Drizzle with sesame oil. Set aside.

3. Place salmon, skin side down, in center of prepared foil sheet. Season with salt and pepper. Fold foil into a flat packet around the fish and seal edges tightly. Place packet on steam rack. Close and lock the lid. Cook on low pressure for 5 minutes. Quickly release the pressure. Transfer packet to a plate, carefully open foil and check to make sure salmon is opaque and flakes easily when tested with a fork; if more cooking time is needed, reseal packet and reset to low pressure for 2 minutes.

4. Open packet and let stand until slightly cooled. Break salmon into large flakes and discard skin. Set aside. Rinse cooking pot and wipe dry.

5. Heat the cooker on High/Sauté/ Brown. Add vegetable oil and heat until shimmering. Add carrots and cook, stirring, for 1 minute. Cancel cooking. Transfer carrots to a bowl and set aside.

6. Add rice and stock to the cooker, stirring well. Close and lock the lid. Cook on high pressure for 8 minutes. Quickly release the pressure and set the cooker to Warm/Keep Warm.

7. Drain radish and squeeze dry. Add radish and carrots to rice, stirring gently and scraping up any bits from the bottom of the pot, until combined. Smooth top of rice mixture. Drizzle 2 tsp (10 mL) sesame oil over rice. Break eggs, side by side, on top of rice. Heat the cooker on High/Sauté/Brown. Cover and cook for 5 minutes.

8. Set the cooker to Warm/Keep Warm. Arrange salmon and spinach next to eggs. Cover and steam until egg whites are opaque and yolks are runny. Add chili paste to center top.

9. Gently stir rice mixture, scraping up any crusty bits from the bottom of the pot. Spoon into individual serving bowls. Sprinkle with sesame seeds and green onions.

TIPS

To julienne vegetables, cut off the ends and sides to form a rectangular block. Cut the block into 3-inch (7.5 cm) long sections. Cut the sections into 1/4-inch (0.5 cm) thick slabs. Keeping the slabs in a stack, cut them into 1/4-inch (0.5 cm) matchsticks.

Prepare and measure out all of your ingredients ahead of time and have them ready to quickly add to the pressure cooker. This helpful style of food preparation is called *mise en place*, meaning "everything in its place."

When releasing pressure quickly, keep your hands and face away from the hole on top of the steam release handle so you don't get scalded by the escaping steam.

Serve with additional sesame oil or chili paste for seasoning to taste.

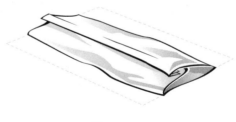

How to fold a flat foil packet

Braised Salmon with Fennel

The delicate and aromatic addition of fennel to this braised salmon has a subtle, yet flavorful impact. Top the salmon with steamed asparagus, and you have a complete meal in no time.

- Steam rack
- 4 pieces parchment paper, cut to fit fillets

1 cup	dry white wine (see tip)	250 mL
1 tbsp	Pernod (optional)	15 mL
1½ lb	skin-on salmon fillet, cut into 4 equal pieces	750 g
	Virgin olive oil	
½	fennel bulb, cored and thickly sliced, fronds chopped and reserved	½
8 oz	asparagus spears, tough ends trimmed and spears halved	250 g
	Kosher salt and freshly ground black pepper	

TIPS

Use more wine, or add water, if required by your cooker to reach pressure.

You can substitute low-sodium chicken stock (page 206) or ready-to-use chicken broth for the wine.

If you are not using Pernod, you may want to add 1 tsp (5 mL) anise extract and 1 tsp (5 mL) lemon juice to the wine, for more flavor.

Using your fingers, carefully check each salmon fillet for tiny pin bones. Remove any bones with tweezers or needle-nose pliers.

1. Add wine and Pernod (if using) to the pressure cooker. Place the steam rack in the cooker. Brush salmon on both sides with oil and place 1 piece, skin side down, on each prepared piece of parchment paper. Arrange all 4 pieces on steam rack, without overlapping. Scatter fennel slices and asparagus on top of salmon. Drizzle with a little oil. Season with salt and pepper.

2. Close and lock the lid. Cook on high pressure for 5 minutes. Quickly release the pressure. Check to make sure the fish is opaque and flakes easily when tested with a fork; if more cooking time is needed, reset to high pressure for 1 minute.

3. Transfer salmon to individual serving plates. Arrange fennel slices and asparagus on top and around salmon. Garnish with fennel fronds. Serve immediately.

Grandma's Chicken and Dumplings

When I am yearning for a comforting, feel-good dish, I reach for my grandmother's chicken and dumplings. It makes me feel like everything is going to be just fine.

MAKES 6 SERVINGS

Chicken

1	whole chicken (about 3½ lbs/ 1.75 kg), cut into 10 pieces (see tip)	1
1 cup	low-sodium chicken stock or ready-to-use chicken broth	250 mL
4	carrots, chopped	4
3	stalks celery, chopped	3
2	small onions, chopped	2
2 tbsp	chopped fresh parsley	30 mL
1 tbsp	chopped fresh thyme	15 mL
1 tsp	dried sage	5 mL
	Kosher salt and freshly ground black pepper	

Dumplings

1½ cups	all-purpose baking mix (such as Bisquick)	375 mL
2 tsp	chopped fresh chives	10 mL
⅔ cup	milk	150 mL
2 tbsp	butter, melted	30 mL

TIPS

For 10 pieces, cut the chicken into wings, legs, thighs, ribs and breast halves.

You can use a whole chicken without cutting it up if it fits well in your pressure cooker. In step 1, cook on high pressure for 27 minutes, then continue as directed.

1. *Chicken:* Add chicken pieces and stock to the pressure cooker. Close and lock the lid. Cook on high pressure for 12 minutes. Check to make sure an instant-read thermometer inserted in the thickest part of a leg registers 165°F (74°C); if more cooking time is needed, reset to high pressure for 2 minutes. Quickly release the pressure.

2. Transfer chicken to a plate and let stand until cool enough to handle. Remove and discard skin and bones. Cut chicken into 2-inch (5 cm) pieces and set aside. Reserve 1½ cups (375 mL) liquid from the pot. Discard or save the remaining liquid for another use (see tip).

3. Add carrots, celery, onions, parsley, thyme, sage and the reserved liquid to the cooker. Close and lock the lid. Cook on high pressure for 5 minutes. Quickly release the pressure.

4. Heat the cooker on High/Sauté/Brown. Return chicken and any accumulated juices to the cooker and heat until simmering. Season to taste with salt and pepper.

5. *Dumplings:* Meanwhile, in a medium bowl, stir together baking mix, chives, milk and butter until just combined. Drop dough by rounded spoonfuls, spacing them apart, on top of chicken mixture. Cook for 9 to 12 minutes or until dumplings are plump and a tester inserted in the center comes out clean.

Coq au Vin

In the 1970s, Julia Child brought French cooking to the North American masses with her easy-to-make versions of traditional French cuisine. Her coq au vin was one of the first classics to become popular. Give this pressure cooker version a try, and you will quickly see why it is such a favorite.

MAKES 4 SERVINGS

8 oz	slab or thick-cut bacon, diced	250 g
1 tbsp	virgin olive oil (if needed)	15 mL
1	whole frying chicken (about 2½ lbs/1.25 kg), cut into 10 pieces (see tip)	1
	Kosher salt and freshly ground black pepper	
1 lb	mushrooms, trimmed and quartered	500 g
16	pearl onions	16
2	cloves garlic, minced	2
1 cup	dry red wine (such as Burgundy or Pinot Noir)	250 mL
1	bay leaf	1
1 tbsp	fresh thyme leaves	15 mL
1 cup	salt-free chicken stock (page 207) or ready-to-use chicken broth	250 mL
1 tbsp	tomato paste	15 mL
2 tbsp	cornstarch	30 mL
2 tbsp	cold water	30 mL
2 tbsp	chopped fresh parsley	30 mL

1. Heat the pressure cooker on High/Sauté/Brown. Add bacon and cook, stirring often, for 5 to 7 minutes or until crisp. Transfer bacon to a plate lined with paper towels. Discard all but 2 tbsp (30 mL) bacon drippings from the pot. (Add oil, if necessary, to measure 2 tbsp/30 mL.)

2. Season chicken with salt and pepper. Working in batches, add chicken to the cooker and cook, turning once, for 5 to 7 minutes or until browned on both sides. Using tongs, transfer chicken to a plate.

3. Add mushrooms and onions to the cooker and cook, stirring often, for 5 to 7 minutes or until golden brown. Using a slotted spoon, transfer mushrooms and onions to another plate.

4. Add garlic to the cooker and cook, stirring, for 1 minute or until fragrant. Add wine and boil, scraping up any browned bits from the bottom of the pot, for 3 minutes or until wine is reduced by half. Cancel cooking.

5. Add bay leaf, thyme, stock and tomato paste, stirring well. Return chicken and any accumulated juices to the cooker. Close and lock the lid. Cook on high pressure for 10 minutes. Quickly release the pressure. Check to make sure an instant-read thermometer inserted in the thickest part of a leg registers 165°F (74°C); if more cooking time is needed, reset to high pressure for 2 minutes. Discard bay leaf. Using tongs, transfer chicken to a serving bowl and tent with foil to keep warm.

6. In a small bowl, whisk together cornstarch and cold water.

7. Heat the cooker on High/Sauté/Brown. Stir in cornstarch mixture and cook, stirring, for 3 minutes or until sauce is thickened. Stir in bacon, mushrooms and onions; cook until heated through. Season to taste with salt.

8. Pour sauce over chicken. Serve garnished with parsley.

TIPS

For 10 pieces, cut the chicken into wings, legs, thighs, ribs and breast halves.

This dish is easily made a day ahead of time, cooled and refrigerated, and then reheated in a Dutch oven over medium-low heat, stirring gently and turning chicken pieces over, before serving. In fact, many would insist that it *should* be made ahead, to deepen the flavors. But if you don't have time for that, pressure cooking does a wonderful job of enhancing the flavors.

To really deepen the flavor, pour the wine over the chicken, cover and refrigerate for 8 to 12 hours. Pat the chicken dry before seasoning, and use the wine in the recipe. The chicken will have a reddish color when you begin cooking it.

Honey Bourbon Chicken Leg Quarters

I love the zesty taste of bourbon chicken, but when I find myself wanting chicken that's a little more tender, with a little less sauce, this take on honey bourbon chicken hits the spot.

MAKES 2 SERVINGS		
1	clove garlic, minced	1
2 tbsp	dried onion flakes	30 mL
½ cup	liquid honey	125 mL
¼ cup	bourbon (see tip)	60 mL
¼ cup	soy sauce	60 mL
¼ cup	ketchup	60 mL
1 tbsp	vegetable oil	15 mL
1 tbsp	Worcestershire sauce	15 mL
2	chicken leg quarters	2
1 tbsp	cornstarch	15 mL
1 tbsp	cold water	15 mL

TIPS

If you prefer not to use bourbon, use 2½ tbsp (37 mL) water plus 1½ tbsp (22 mL) balsamic vinegar in its place.

The measures here are for 6-quart (6 L) or smaller pressure cookers. Many larger cookers require more than 1 cup (250 mL) of liquid and would not be suitable for this recipe.

1. In the pressure cooker, combine garlic, onion flakes, honey, bourbon, soy sauce, ketchup, oil and Worcestershire sauce, stirring well. Using tongs, add chicken, turning to coat. Arrange chicken, skin side up, evenly in the bottom of the pot (see tip).

2. Close and lock the lid. Cook on high pressure for 13 minutes. Quickly release the pressure. Check to make sure an instant-read thermometer inserted in the thickest part of a leg registers 165°F (74°C); if more cooking time is needed, reset to high pressure for 2 minutes. Using tongs, transfer chicken to a plate and tent with foil to keep warm.

3. In a small bowl, whisk together cornstarch and cold water.

4. Heat the cooker on High/Sauté/Brown. Stir in cornstarch mixture and cook, stirring often, for 3 to 5 minutes or until sauce is thickened to a glaze. Return chicken to the cooker, turning to coat in glaze.

5. Transfer chicken to individual serving plates. Serve drizzled with remaining glaze.

Chicken Cacciatore

Cacciatore is a dish made "hunter-style" and quite often includes pheasant, rabbit or whatever was caught in the daily hunt. But the most common version of this classic Italian dish is made with chicken, plus the standard base ingredients of tomatoes, vegetables and a bit of wine. While there are many variations of this dish, it is always hearty and satisfying.

MAKES 6 SERVINGS

3 lbs	bone-in chicken thighs and legs	1.5 kg
	Kosher salt and freshly ground black pepper	
1/4 cup	virgin olive oil	60 mL
1 lb	cremini mushrooms, trimmed and quartered	500 g
1	small onion, thinly sliced	1
4	cloves garlic, minced	4
3/4 cup	dry white wine	175 mL
1	can (28 oz/796 mL) whole tomatoes, with juice	1
2	sprigs fresh rosemary	2
1	bay leaf	1
1 tsp	dried oregano	5 mL
1/2 cup	black Italian olives (preferably Gaeta), pitted and lightly smashed	125 mL
1/4 cup	drained capers, patted dry	60 mL
2 tbsp	finely chopped fresh parsley	30 mL

TIP

If your cooker requires more than 1¼ cups (300 mL) liquid to reach pressure, add as much water in step 3 as is required. In step 5, you may want to thicken your sauce; to do so, whisk together 1 tbsp (15 mL) each cornstarch and cold water, stir the mixture into the sauce and cook for 7 to 10 minutes or until thickened. Do not cook longer, or the sauce may scorch on the bottom.

1. Season chicken with salt and pepper. Heat the pressure cooker on High/Sauté/Brown. Add oil and heat until shimmering. Working in batches, add chicken and cook, turning, for 5 minutes or until browned on all sides. Using tongs, transfer chicken to a plate.

2. Add mushrooms to the cooker and cook, stirring often, for 7 minutes or until browned. Add onion and cook, stirring often, for 3 to 5 minutes or until translucent. Add garlic and cook, stirring, for 1 minute or until fragrant. Add wine and cook, scraping up any browned bits from the bottom of the pot, for 1 minute or until combined. Cancel cooking.

3. Return chicken and any accumulated juices to the cooker. Crush tomatoes by hand into the pot. Add ½ cup (125 mL) tomato juice from can; discard remainder (see tip). Add rosemary, bay leaf and oregano.

4. Close and lock the lid. Cook on high pressure for 12 minutes. Quickly release the pressure. Check to make sure an instant-read thermometer inserted in the thickest part of a thigh registers 165°F (74°C); if more cooking time is needed, reset to high pressure for 3 minutes. Discard rosemary sprigs and bay leaf. Using tongs, transfer chicken to a serving platter and tent with foil to keep warm.

5. Heat the cooker on High/Sauté/Brown. Cook, stirring often, for 5 minutes or until sauce is thickened to your liking.

6. Spoon sauce over chicken. Serve garnished with olives, capers and parsley.

One-Pot BBQ Chicken and Rice

This dish explodes with umami and, because it's prepared in the pressure cooker, you can have dinner on the table quickly, easily and with minimal cleanup. The brown rice pilaf has a wonderful balance of flavors that nicely complement the rich and tangy barbecue sauce.

MAKES 6 SERVINGS

- 4-cup (1 L) round casserole dish
- Tall steam rack

Rice Pilaf

1½ cups	long-grain brown rice	375 mL
2¼ cups	water	550 mL
1 tbsp	virgin olive oil	15 mL
8 oz	mushrooms, coarsely chopped	250 g
1	onion, finely chopped	1
1	stalk celery, finely chopped	1
¼ cup	slivered almonds	60 mL
2 tbsp	chopped fresh parsley	30 mL

BBQ Chicken

12	bone-in skin-on chicken thighs (about 4¼ lbs/2.125 g total)	12
2 tsp	paprika	10 mL
	Kosher salt	
2 tbsp	virgin olive oil	30 mL
2	tart apples (such as Granny Smith), finely chopped	2
1	onion, finely chopped	1
1	clove garlic, minced	1
½ cup	packed light brown sugar	125 mL
1 tsp	onion powder	5 mL
¾ cup	water (see tip)	175 mL
½ cup	chili sauce	125 mL
¼ cup	apple cider vinegar	60 mL
2 tbsp	tomato paste	30 mL
1 tbsp	Dijon mustard	15 mL
1 tbsp	pure maple syrup	15 mL
2 tsp	Worcestershire sauce	10 mL

1. *Rice Pilaf:* Add brown rice and water to casserole dish. Set aside.

2. Heat the pressure cooker on High/Sauté/Brown. Add oil and heat until shimmering. Add mushrooms, onion and celery; cook, stirring often, for 3 to 5 minutes or until mushrooms have released their liquid and onion is translucent. Transfer mixture to casserole dish.

3. *BBQ Chicken:* Sprinkle chicken with paprika and season with salt.

4. Add oil to the cooker and heat until shimmering. Add chicken, in batches if necessary, and cook, turning once, for 5 minutes or until browned on both sides. Using tongs, transfer chicken to a plate.

5. Add apples and onion to the cooker; cook, stirring often, for 3 to 5 minutes or until onion is translucent. Cancel cooking.

6. Add garlic, brown sugar, onion powder, water, chili sauce, vinegar, tomato paste, mustard, maple syrup and Worcestershire sauce, stirring well. Return chicken and any accumulated juices to the cooker, turning to coat with sauce and finishing with the skin side up; the thighs will need to be in a couple of layers, so stack them like bricks, rather than one right on top of another, so the steam can move around them.

7. Place steam rack on top of chicken and, keeping the casserole dish level, lower it onto the rack. Close and lock the lid. Cook on high pressure for 20 minutes. Let stand, covered, until the float valve drops down. Remove casserole dish and steam rack. Check to make sure an instant-read thermometer inserted in the center of a thigh registers 165°F (74°C) and rice is tender; if more cooking time is needed for both the chicken and rice, return steam rack and dish to the pot and reset to high pressure for 5 minutes (see tip).

8. Transfer chicken to a serving platter and spoon barbecue sauce over top.

9. Stir almonds and parsley into rice. Serve with chicken.

TIPS

Do not substitute another type of rice for the brown rice in this recipe. Other types of rice require different cooking times and will not turn out as intended.

If just the rice is done after the initial cooking time in step 7, cover the dish and set it aside while you continue cooking the chicken. If only the chicken is done, transfer the chicken to the platter, return the rack and casserole dish to the pot and reset to high pressure for 2 minutes.

The chicken will release some liquid into the pot as it cooks, but if your cooker requires more than 3 cups (750 mL) liquid to reach pressure, add more water as needed in step 6 and then follow the next tip to thicken your sauce.

After step 7, if the sauce is not cooked to your desired consistency, transfer the chicken to the platter, then heat the pressure cooker on High/Sauté/Brown and simmer the sauce, stirring often, until thickened to your liking.

Prepare and measure out all of your ingredients ahead of time and have them ready to quickly add to the pressure cooker. This helpful style of food preparation is called *mise en place*, meaning "everything in its place."

Chicken Marsala

In this embodiment of Italian-inspired simplicity, a creamy wine and mushroom sauce adds a delightful depth of flavor to a surprisingly easy dish. Serve it over long-grain white rice or wide egg noodles.

MAKES 4 SERVINGS		
8	boneless skinless chicken thighs (about 1½ lbs/750 g total)	8
	Kosher salt and freshly ground black pepper	
1 tbsp	virgin olive oil	15 mL
1 tbsp	butter	15 mL
1 cup	thinly sliced cremini mushrooms	250 mL
1	clove garlic, minced	1
½ cup	sweet Marsala	125 mL
1 cup	low-sodium chicken stock (page 206) or ready-to-use chicken broth	250 mL
3 tbsp	cornstarch	45 mL
3 tbsp	cold water	45 mL
2 tbsp	chopped fresh parsley	30 mL

TIPS

If you can find only bone-in chicken thighs, you will need about 2¾ lbs (1.375 kg). Remove the skin and debone them by using a paring or boning knife to cut a line through the meat along either side of the bone. Expose the bone, scraping away any small pieces of meat. Separate the end of the bone from the meat. Trim off any leftover bone or gristle still on the thigh.

The chicken will release some liquid into the pot as it cooks, but if your cooker requires more than 2 cups (500 mL) liquid to reach pressure, add more water as needed in step 3. In step 5, you may need to simmer the sauce for 5 to 10 minutes longer to slightly thicken the sauce.

1. Season chicken with salt and pepper. Heat the pressure cooker on High/Sauté/Brown. Add oil and heat until shimmering. Working in batches, add chicken and cook, turning once, for 5 minutes or until browned on both sides. Using tongs, transfer chicken to a plate.

2. Add butter to the cooker and heat until melted. Add mushrooms and cook, stirring often, for 5 minutes or until just starting to brown. Add garlic and cook, stirring, for 1 minute. Add Marsala and boil, scraping up any browned bits from the bottom of the pot, for 5 minutes or until Marsala is almost evaporated. Cancel cooking.

3. Add stock, stirring well. Return chicken and any accumulated juices to the cooker. Close and lock the lid. Cook on high pressure for 6 minutes. Quickly release the pressure. Check to make sure an instant-read thermometer inserted in the center of a thigh registers 165°F (74°C); if more cooking time is needed, reset to high pressure for 1 minute. Using tongs, transfer chicken to a plate and tent with foil to keep warm.

4. In a small bowl, whisk together cornstarch and cold water.

5. Heat the cooker on High/Sauté/Brown. Stir in cornstarch mixture and cook, stirring occasionally, for 7 minutes or until sauce is slightly thickened. Return chicken and any accumulated juices to the cooker and simmer for 5 minutes, turning chicken to coat with sauce.

6. Transfer chicken to individual serving plates and spoon sauce over top. Sprinkle with parsley.

Pineapple Coconut Chicken

I love the combination of tangy barbecue sauce, sweet pineapple and spicy hot pepper flakes that coats these tender chicken thighs. This tantalizing dish goes perfectly with a simple side of rice or steamed vegetables.

MAKES 4 SERVINGS

2 cups	diced pineapple	500 mL
1 cup	barbecue sauce (see tip)	250 mL
1 cup	coconut milk	250 mL
1 tsp	hot pepper flakes	5 mL
8	boneless skinless chicken thighs (about 1½ lbs/750 g total)	8
	Kosher salt	
⅓ cup	unsweetened shredded coconut	75 mL

TIPS

Sweet and Sassy Barbecue Sauce (page 211) has the perfect balance of flavors for this recipe, but you can also use your favorite barbecue sauce.

When quickly releasing pressure, remove the lid carefully, allowing steam to escape away from you.

1. Arrange pineapple in an even layer on the bottom of the pressure cooker. Set aside.

2. In a large bowl, combine barbecue sauce, coconut milk and hot pepper flakes, stirring well.

3. Season chicken with salt. Dip chicken in sauce, turning to coat. Arrange chicken on top of pineapple. Pour in the remaining sauce.

4. Close and lock the lid. Cook on high pressure for 9 minutes. Quickly release the pressure. Check to make sure an instant-read thermometer inserted in the center of a thigh registers 165°F (74°C); if more cooking time is needed, reset to high pressure for 1 minute. Using tongs, transfer chicken to a serving platter and tent with foil to keep warm.

5. Heat the cooker on High/Sauté/Brown. Cook, stirring often, for 5 to 7 minutes or until sauce is thickened to your liking. Drizzle pineapple sauce over chicken. Serve garnished with coconut.

Santa Fe Chicken with Corn and Tomatoes

What could be better than this dish's outstanding flavor? Why, the fact that it is so versatile. You can serve it over tortilla chips, as here, or over rice, in tortillas or as a topping for salads. You can also make it ahead and freeze it for later.

MAKES 8 SERVINGS

2 tbsp	vegetable oil	30 mL
1½ lbs	bone-in skin-on chicken breasts	750 g
1	onion, chopped	1
1 cup	low-sodium chicken stock (page 206) or ready-to-use chicken broth	250 mL
1	can (14 to 19 oz/398 to 540 mL) black beans, drained and rinsed	1
1	can (14 oz/398 mL) diced tomatoes, with juice	1
1	can (4 oz/114 mL) diced green chiles	1
1 cup	frozen corn kernels	250 mL
¼ cup	chopped fresh cilantro	60 mL
1 tsp	ground cumin	5 mL
⅛ tsp	cayenne pepper	0.5 mL
	Kosher salt	
	Tortilla chips	

1. Heat the pressure cooker on High/Sauté/Brown. Add oil and heat until shimmering. Working in batches, add chicken and cook, turning once, for 5 minutes or until browned on both sides. Using tongs, transfer chicken to a plate.

2. Add onion to the cooker and cook, stirring, for 4 to 6 minutes or until lightly browned. Stir in stock, scraping up any browned bits from the bottom of the pot. Cancel cooking.

3. Stir in beans, tomatoes, chiles, corn, cilantro, cumin and cayenne. Arrange chicken, skin side up, on top and add any accumulated juices. Close and lock the lid. Cook on high pressure for 15 minutes. Check to make sure an instant-read thermometer inserted in the center of a breast registers 165°F (74°C); if more cooking time is needed, reset to high pressure for 3 minutes. Let stand, covered, for 10 minutes, then release any remaining pressure.

4. Using tongs, transfer chicken to a cutting board. Using two forks, shred chicken, discarding bones and skin.

5. Season sauce with salt to taste. Return chicken to the cooker, stirring to combine. Serve over tortilla chips.

TIPS

Do not use boneless skinless chicken breasts, as you will not get the intended results.

If you want to use fresh tomatoes, you'll need about 5 plum (Roma) tomatoes or 2 large tomatoes, weighing about 1 lb (500 g).

This recipe contains about 1¾ cups (425 mL) liquid. If your cooker requires more than 2 cups (500 mL) liquid to reach pressure, this recipe is not an ideal choice.

Leftovers can be frozen in an airtight container for up to 3 months.

Greek Chicken with Tabbouleh

Inspired by the bright and fresh flavors of Greek cuisine, chicken breasts get an aromatic rub of lemon and fresh seasonings. A bulgur tabbouleh gets steamed in the same pot for an easy one-pot meal infused with flavor.

MAKES 4 SERVINGS

- 6-inch (15 cm) round metal baking pan
- Tall steam rack

1 cup	coarse bulgur, rinsed	250 mL
3 cups	low-sodium chicken stock (page 206) or ready-to-use chicken broth, divided	750 mL
6 tsp	virgin olive oil, divided	30 mL
1	clove garlic, minced	1
4 tsp	minced fresh oregano, divided	20 mL
1 tsp	grated lemon zest, divided	5 mL
	Kosher salt and freshly ground black pepper	
4	bone-in skin-on chicken breasts (about 1½ lbs/750 g total)	4
	Juice of 1 lemon	
2 tbsp	chopped fresh parsley	30 mL
8 oz	cherry tomatoes, quartered	250 g

TIPS

Do not be tempted to use boneless chicken breasts, as the cooking time is substantially different.

Leftover lemon zest can be measured into individual ice cube trays, covered with water and frozen until ready to use.

1. In the baking pan, combine bulgur, 2 cups (500 mL) stock and 2 tsp (10 mL) oil. Set aside.

2. In a small bowl, combine garlic, 3 tsp (15 mL) oregano, 1 tsp (5 mL) lemon zest, 1 tsp (5 mL) salt and ¼ tsp (1 mL) pepper. Rub chicken with mixture.

3. Heat the pressure cooker on High/Sauté/Brown. Add the remaining oil and heat until shimmering. Working in batches, add chicken, skin side down, and cook for 3 minutes or until skin is browned. Using tongs, transfer chicken to a plate.

4. Add the remaining stock and 1 tbsp (15 mL) lemon juice to the cooker and cook, scraping up any browned bits from the bottom of the pot, for 1 minute. Cancel cooking.

5. Return chicken to the cooker, arranging it skin side up. Place steam rack on top of chicken and, keeping the baking pan level, lower it onto the rack. Close and lock the lid. Cook on high pressure for 12 minutes. Quickly release the pressure. Remove baking pan and steam rack. Check to make sure an instant-read thermometer inserted in the center of a breast registers 165°F (74°C); if more cooking time is needed, reset to high pressure for 2 minutes. Using tongs, transfer chicken to a serving platter and cover with foil.

6. Sprinkle parsley and the remaining oregano and lemon juice over bulgur. Season with salt and pepper. Cover with foil and let stand for 5 minutes. Using a fork, fluff bulgur gently and toss with cherry tomatoes. Serve with chicken, drizzling with sauce from the pot.

Tangy Chicken Lettuce Wraps

I love the way savory, sweet, salty and crunchy are all combined in this recipe. Wrapped up in crisp lettuce leaves, it makes for a sensational dish that is hard to resist.

MAKES 4 SERVINGS

1½ lbs	chicken breast tenders, cut lengthwise into thin strips	750 g
	Kosher salt and freshly ground black pepper	
2	cloves garlic, minced	2
3 tbsp	hoisin sauce	45 mL
3 tbsp	unseasoned rice vinegar	45 mL
2 tbsp	sesame oil	30 mL
8 oz	shiitake mushrooms, stemmed and sliced	250 g
¼ cup	low-sodium chicken stock (page 206) or ready-to-use chicken broth	60 mL
1	bag (14 oz/400 g) shredded coleslaw mix (about 3 cups/ 750 mL)	1
3 tbsp	soy sauce	45 mL
4	green onions, thinly sliced, divided	4
12	Bibb lettuce leaves	12
	Additional hoisin sauce (optional)	

1. Season chicken with salt and pepper. In a medium bowl, combine garlic, hoisin sauce and vinegar. Add chicken, turning to coat, and let stand for 10 minutes.

2. Heat the pressure cooker on High/ Sauté/Brown. Add oil and heat until shimmering. Working in batches, use tongs to transfer chicken to the cooker; reserve marinade. Cook chicken, stirring, for 3 to 5 minutes or until just browned on all sides. Using tongs, transfer chicken to a plate.

3. Add mushrooms to the cooker and cook, stirring, for 4 to 6 minutes or until lightly browned. Stir in stock, scraping up any browned bits from the bottom of the pot. Cancel cooking.

4. Add coleslaw mix and soy sauce, stirring well. Close and lock the lid. Cook on high pressure for 3 minutes. Quickly release the pressure.

5. Heat the cooker on High/Sauté/ Brown. Stir in the reserved marinade. Return chicken and any accumulated juices to the cooker, along with half the green onions, and boil, stirring, for 2 to 3 minutes or until chicken is no longer pink inside and sauce is slightly thickened.

6. Spoon chicken mixture onto lettuce leaves and sprinkle with the remaining green onions. Serve with hoisin sauce, if desired.

VARIATION

For added crunch and a slightly different flavor, substitute a broccoli slaw mix for the traditional coleslaw mix.

TIPS

Cut your chicken breasts into strips of equal size. If they are very thick, you may need to cut them both horizontally and vertically.

Hoisin sauce can be found in the Asian food section of the grocery store. It is a full-flavored sauce that complements a variety of dishes.

Chicken Wings in Tomatillo Sauce

Who said wings should be served only as an appetizer? I can dive into them as a main course or a light meal just about any time. The sweet, sour and fiery sauce adds so much interest, these zesty wings are just plain hard to resist.

MAKES 4 SERVINGS

- Steamer basket
- Blender

12	chicken wings, sections split apart, wing tips removed	12
1 tsp	dried oregano	5 mL
	Kosher salt and freshly ground black pepper	
9	tomatillos, husked, rinsed and coarsely chopped (see tip)	9
3	serrano peppers, coarsely chopped	3
½ cup	lightly packed fresh cilantro leaves, divided	125 mL
6 tbsp	water	90 mL
1 tbsp	vegetable oil	15 mL
6 tbsp	finely chopped onion	90 mL
1	clove garlic, minced	1
2 tbsp	apple cider vinegar	30 mL

TIPS

You can use canned whole tomatillos, drained, if you cannot find fresh.

You can substitute 1 jalapeño pepper for the 3 serrano peppers, if you prefer. If you like a less spicy sauce, you may want to remove some or all of the seeds from the peppers.

If serving this as a main course, allow 6 wing sections per person. If serving this as an appetizer alongside other appetizers, allow for 2 wing sections per person.

1. Season wings with oregano, salt and pepper. Add 1 cup (250 mL) water (or the amount required by your cooker to reach pressure) to the pressure cooker and place the steamer basket in the pot. Arrange wings in the basket with as much of their surface exposed as possible. Close and lock the lid. Cook on high pressure for 15 minutes. Check to make sure the juices run clear when chicken is pierced with a fork; if more cooking time is needed, reset to high pressure for 2 minutes.

2. Meanwhile, in blender, combine tomatillos, serrano peppers, ¼ cup (60 mL) cilantro, 1 tsp (5 mL) salt and water; blend until coarsely puréed. Transfer sauce to a large bowl.

3. When the cooking time is done, quickly release the pressure. Using tongs, transfer wings to tomatillo sauce and toss to coat. Remove steamer basket from pot and discard liquid.

4. Heat the cooker on High/Sauté/Brown. Add oil and heat until shimmering. Add onion and cook, stirring often, for 3 to 5 minutes or until translucent. Add garlic and cook, stirring, for 1 minute or until fragrant. Add vinegar and boil, scraping up any browned bits from the bottom of the pot, for 1 minute or until reduced by half. Add wings and tomatillo sauce; cook, tossing often, for 3 to 5 minutes or until wings are coated with sauce and slightly caramelized.

5. Transfer wings to a serving platter. Chop the remaining cilantro and sprinkle over top.

Leftover Turkey, Mushroom and Fettuccine Casserole

This is the perfect dish for using up all those turkey leftovers from Thanksgiving. It has been a favorite in my family for a long time. The combination of turkey, pasta and mushrooms in a creamy, garlicky sauce just screams comfort food, and — even better — it is so simple to make.

MAKES 6 SERVINGS

8 oz	fettuccine pasta, broken in half	250 g
2 cups	low-sodium chicken stock (page 206) or ready-to-use chicken broth	500 mL
2	cloves garlic, minced	2
2 cups	cubed cooked turkey	500 mL
1/4 tsp	freshly ground black pepper	1 mL
1	can (4 oz/114 mL) mushroom pieces and stems, drained	1
1	jar (15 oz/425 mL) Alfredo sauce	1
1 tbsp	white wine (optional)	15 mL
1/4 cup	freshly grated Parmesan cheese	60 mL

TIPS

This recipe is ideal for 6-quart (6 L) or smaller pressure cookers, or cookers that require only 2 cups (500 mL) or less liquid to reach pressure.

When quickly releasing pressure, remove the lid carefully, allowing steam to escape away from you.

1. In the pressure cooker, combine fettuccine and stock. Close and lock the lid. Cook on high pressure for 2 minutes. Quickly release the pressure. Stir pasta, then drain and return to the cooker.

2. Stir in garlic, turkey, pepper, mushrooms, Alfredo sauce and wine (if using). Heat the cooker on High/Sauté/Brown and cook, stirring gently, for 3 to 4 minutes or until heated through. Serve garnished with Parmesan.

VARIATION

Rotisserie chicken is a great substitute for the turkey in this recipe. A typical rotisserie chicken weighs about 2½ lbs (1.25 kg) and will yield about 3½ cups (875 mL) cubed chicken. The leftover chicken works well on top of salad or in a sandwich.

Florentine Pork Loin Roast

This succulent Italian-inspired dish is exquisitely seasoned. Classic roasts have been a favorite for centuries in Florence, Italy, and it's easy to see why. Not only is a roast easy to prepare, but it also makes a showstopping dinner party presentation — and you can even make it ahead of time.

MAKES 4 SERVINGS

- Mortar and pestle or small food processor
- Kitchen string
- Steam rack
- Rimmed baking sheet, lined with foil, with roasting rack set on top

2½ lb	bone-in pork loin roast	1.25 kg
2	cloves garlic, chopped	2
5	fresh sage leaves, chopped	5
1 tbsp	chopped fresh rosemary leaves	15 mL
1 tsp	ground fennel seeds	5 mL
½ tsp	freshly ground black pepper	2 mL
¼ cup	virgin olive oil, divided	60 mL
	Kosher salt	
¾ cup	dry white wine (such as Sauvignon Blanc or Pinot Grigio)	175 mL
¼ cup	water (see tip)	60 mL

1. Using a sharp knife, cut in between the bones of the pork loin to within 1 inch (2.5 cm) of the bottom of the roast. Set aside.

2. Using the mortar and pestle, mash garlic, sage, rosemary, fennel and pepper into a paste (or process to a paste in a small food processor).

3. Using your hands, rub 2 tbsp (30 mL) oil and the paste all over roast, including in the cuts between the bones. Season with salt. Tie the roast with kitchen string to prevent ribs from falling apart.

4. Place the steam rack in the pressure cooker and add wine and water. Place roast, loin side down, on the rack. Cook on high pressure for 25 minutes.

5. Meanwhile, preheat oven to 475°F (240°C).

6. When the cooking time is done, quickly release the pressure. Check to make sure an instant-read thermometer inserted in the center of the roast registers at least 155°F (68°C) for medium; if more cooking time is needed, reset to high pressure for 5 minutes.

7. Transfer roast to prepared roasting pan, loin side up, and drizzle with the remaining oil. Bake for 5 minutes or until surface is just crisped. Transfer roast to a cutting board, cover with foil and let rest for 15 minutes.

8. Cut roast into individual servings and transfer to a serving platter. Serve immediately.

TIPS

Make sure you purchase a bone-in pork loin roast, which is different from a pork tenderloin.

For a more attractive presentation, ask your butcher to French the bones of your roast. Or, to French them yourself, use a sharp knife to cut the membrane in between the top 2 to 3 inches (5 to 7.5 cm) of bone. Then, using your knife, strip away the meat, fat and membrane from around the bone to expose it.

Add more water in step 4 if required by your cooker to reach pressure. The measurements here are for 6-quart (6 L) or smaller pressure cookers.

Pork Roast with Green Apple and Prosciutto

If you've ever had a Hasselback potato, you know how incredibly delicious it is, with its crisp exterior and tender interior. So I had to wonder: Why stop at potatoes? Here's my take on using the same technique with a pork roast, its numerous slices stuffed with apples and pancetta for a symphony of flavor and applause-worthy presentation.

MAKES 6 SERVINGS

- Kitchen string

3 lb	pork single loin roast (less than 8 inches/20 cm long), untied	1.5 kg
1	tart green apple (such as Granny Smith), cut into 12 thin slices	1
12	thin slices prosciutto	12
2 tbsp	dried herbes de Provence	30 mL
	Kosher salt	
2 tbsp	virgin olive oil	30 mL
1 cup	low-sodium chicken stock (page 206) or ready-to-use chicken broth	250 mL

TIPS

You can also use Cortland, Empire or Honeycrisp apples. The best varieties for this recipe are apples that hold their shape when baking and have a tart flavor.

You can substitute round slices of pancetta for the prosciutto.

1. Cutting only about three-quarters of the way to the bottom, cut roast crosswise into twelve ½-inch (1 cm) slices. Add an apple slice and a prosciutto slice to each cut, folding and arranging them so they fit evenly in the cuts. Tie the roast horizontally with kitchen string so it retains its shape. Season roast with herbes de Provence and salt.

2. Heat the pressure cooker on High/Sauté/Brown. Add oil and heat until shimmering. Add roast and cook, turning carefully, for 8 to 10 minutes or until browned on all sides. Cancel cooking.

3. Position the roast with the cut side up and add stock. Close and lock the lid. Cook on high pressure for 25 minutes. Let stand, covered, until the float valve drops down. Check to make sure an instant-read thermometer inserted in the center of the roast registers at least 160°F (71°C) for medium; if more cooking time is needed, reset to high pressure for 5 minutes.

4. Using tongs, transfer roast to a serving platter and remove string. Drizzle cooking juices over top. Cut through to the bottom of each slice to serve.

Pork Medallions with Red Pepper Sauce

Frustrated by dry, overcooked pork tenderloin? You will be thrilled with the results you'll get from your pressure cooker. This recipe gives you moist, tender, perfectly done pork, served with an exquisite red pepper sauce.

MAKES 4 SERVINGS

- Blender

1¼ lb	pork tenderloin, trimmed and cut in half crosswise	625 g
	Kosher salt and freshly ground black pepper	
2 tbsp	vegetable oil, divided	30 mL
2	red bell peppers, cut into 1-inch (2.5 cm) pieces	2
¼ cup	finely chopped onion	60 mL
1	clove garlic, minced	1
¼ cup	apple cider vinegar	60 mL
1	bay leaf	1
1 tsp	ground cumin	5 mL
1 cup	low-sodium chicken stock (page 206) or ready-to-use chicken broth	250 mL
2 tbsp	butter	30 mL
2 tbsp	freshly squeezed lemon juice	30 mL
2 tbsp	chopped fresh cilantro	30 mL

TIP

When blending the hot sauce in step 4, start pulsing very slowly and hold your hand on the cover. Hot liquids can blow the top off the blender and cause burns and a serious mess.

1. Season pork with salt and pepper. Heat the pressure cooker on High/Sauté/Brown. Add 1 tbsp (15 mL) oil and heat until shimmering. Working with one pork loin at a time, add pork and cook, turning often, for 7 minutes or until browned on all sides. Transfer pork to a plate.

2. Add the remaining oil to the cooker and heat until shimmering. Add red peppers and onion; cook, stirring often, for 3 to 5 minutes or until onion is translucent. Add garlic and cook, stirring, for 1 minute or until fragrant. Add vinegar and cook, scraping up any browned bits from the bottom of the pot, for 1 minute. Cancel cooking.

3. Add bay leaf, cumin and stock, stirring well. Return pork and any accumulated juices to the cooker. Close and lock the lid. Cook on high pressure for 1 minute. Let stand, covered, for 15 minutes, then release any remaining pressure. Check to make sure an instant-read thermometer inserted in the center of the loin registers at least 155°F (68°C) for medium; if more cooking time is needed, reset to high pressure for 5 minutes. Discard bay leaf. Transfer pork to a cutting board, tent with foil and let rest until sauce is finished.

4. Carefully transfer sauce from cooker to blender. Add butter and lemon juice; pulse until almost smooth.

5. Slice pork across the grain into medallions. Serve drizzled with red pepper sauce and garnished with cilantro.

Apple and Maple Glazed Pork Chops

Pressure cooking pork chops renders them moist and tender, a clear winner over the often-dry pan-fried chops. Finishing them with a rich glaze makes them an easy weeknight favorite.

MAKES 4 SERVINGS

4	boneless pork loin chops, about 1 inch (2.5 cm) thick	4
	Kosher salt and freshly ground black pepper	
1 tbsp	vegetable oil	15 mL
½ cup	low-sodium chicken stock (page 206) or ready-to-use chicken broth (see tip)	125 mL
½ cup	apple cider vinegar	125 mL
½ tsp	onion powder	2 mL
½ cup	apple jelly	125 mL
3 tbsp	pure maple syrup	45 mL
2 tbsp	Dijon mustard	30 mL
1 tbsp	soy sauce	15 mL

TIPS

To prevent your chops from curling up at the edges, before browning make a few tiny cuts in the fat and skin around the edges, without cutting into the meat.

Add more stock in step 2 if required by your cooker to reach pressure. In step 3, you may need to increase the simmering time to thicken your glaze.

1. Season pork with salt and pepper. Heat the pressure cooker on High/ Sauté/Brown. Add oil and heat until shimmering. Add pork and cook, turning once, for 5 to 7 minutes or until browned. Using tongs, transfer pork to a plate. Cancel cooking and discard any remaining oil in cooker.

2. Add stock, vinegar and onion powder to the cooker, stirring well. Return pork and any accumulated juices to the cooker. Close and lock the lid. Cook on high pressure for 7 to 8 minutes. Quickly release the pressure. Check to make sure an instant-read thermometer inserted in the thickest part of a pork chop registers at least 160°F (71°C) for medium; if more cooking time is needed, reset to high pressure for 1 minute. Using tongs, transfer chops to a clean plate. Discard cooking liquid.

3. Add apple jelly, maple syrup, mustard and soy sauce to the cooker, stirring well. Heat the cooker on High/Sauté/ Brown. Cook, stirring, for 3 to 5 minutes or until glaze is just bubbling and is a medium caramel color, and a rubber spatula just starts to make trails on the bottom of the pot.

4. Return chops and any accumulated juices to the cooker and turn to coat in glaze.

5. Transfer chops to a serving platter and pour the remaining glaze over top. Serve immediately.

Cuban Braised Pork Chops with Mojo

Jumping with flavor, these Cuban-inspired pork chops are an inviting way to change up everyday pork. The spices and citrus merge to make a vibrant, satisfying dish.

MAKES 4 SERVINGS

1 cup	guava jelly or apricot jam	250 mL
¾ cup	orange juice, divided	175 mL
¼ cup	Dijon mustard	60 mL
¼ cup	freshly squeezed lime juice	60 mL
¼ cup	apple cider vinegar	60 mL
1 tsp	kosher salt	5 mL
1 tbsp	onion powder	15 mL
2 tsp	ground cumin	10 mL
2 tsp	dried oregano	10 mL
4	thick-cut pork chops (about 1 inch/2.5 cm thick)	4
2 tbsp	vegetable oil	30 mL
½	red onion, finely chopped	½
2	cloves garlic, minced	2
	Chopped fresh cilantro	

TIPS

Guava jelly can be found in Latin and Caribbean markets or online. While it is the more traditional glaze for these chops, the apricot jam also works very well.

Two limes will yield about ¼ cup (60 mL) juice.

1. In a small bowl, combine jam, ¼ cup (60 mL) orange juice and mustard. Set aside.

2. In the pressure cooker, combine the remaining orange juice, lime juice and vinegar.

3. In a small bowl, combine salt, onion powder, cumin and oregano. Rub mixture into pork.

4. Transfer pork to the cooker. Close and lock the lid. Cook on high pressure for 8 minutes. Let stand, covered, for 10 minutes, then release any remaining pressure. Using tongs, transfer pork to a plate, cover with foil and let rest for 5 minutes. Discard cooking liquid. Wipe out the cooker's inner pot.

5. Heat the cooker on High/Sauté/Brown. Add oil and heat until shimmering. Add onion and cook, stirring, for 3 to 5 minutes or until translucent. Add garlic and cook, stirring, for 1 minute.

6. Pat pork chops dry. Working in batches, add chops to the cooker and cook, turning once, for 4 to 6 minutes or until browned on both sides and just a hint of pink remains inside. Using tongs, transfer chops to a clean plate.

7. Add jam glaze to the cooker and cook, stirring, for 2 to 3 minutes or until warmed. Add chops, turning to coat.

8. Transfer chops to a serving platter, spoon glaze over top and garnish with cilantro.

Pork Carnitas with Roasted Pineapple Habanero Salsa

Warm tortillas are filled with chunks of crispy, savory pork topped with a citrusy, spicy salsa in this mouthwatering Mexican dish.

MAKES 4 SERVINGS

- Preheat broiler, with rack set 8 inches (20 cm) from the heat
- Baking sheet, lined with foil

Roasted Pineapple Habanero Salsa

2	slices fresh pineapple (½ inch/ 1 cm thick)	2
5 tsp	virgin olive oil	25 mL
1	small red onion, finely chopped	1
1	habanero pepper, minced (with seeds)	1
3 tbsp	chopped fresh cilantro	45 mL
1 tsp	kosher salt	5 mL
2 tbsp	freshly squeezed lime juice	30 mL

Pork Carnitas

1 cup	orange or pineapple juice	250 mL
½ cup	water	125 mL
2	bay leaves	2
2 lbs	pork belly	1 kg
3 tbsp	virgin olive oil, divided	45 mL
	Kosher salt and freshly ground black pepper	
1 tbsp	ground cumin	15 mL
1 tbsp	dried oregano	15 mL
6	cloves garlic, minced	6
2	onions, chopped	2
1	jalapeño pepper, seeded and finely chopped	1
8	taco-size (6-inch/15 cm) flour tortillas	8
2 tbsp	chopped fresh cilantro	30 mL

1. *Salsa:* Place pineapple slices on prepared baking sheet and brush on both sides with oil. Broil, turning once, for 16 minutes or until tender and nicely browned on both sides. Let cool, then finely chop pineapple and discard core.

2. In a medium bowl, combine pineapple, onion, habanero, cilantro, salt and lime juice, stirring well. Set aside.

3. *Carnitas:* In the pressure cooker, combine orange juice, water and bay leaves.

4. Using a very sharp knife, score top of pork belly in a crosshatch pattern. Brush 2 tbsp (30 mL) oil over top. Season generously with salt and pepper. Sprinkle with cumin and oregano.

5. Transfer pork to the cooker. Add garlic, onions and jalapeño on top. Close and lock the lid. Cook on high pressure for 45 minutes. Let stand, covered, for 10 minutes, then release any remaining pressure. Check to make sure the fat is rendered and the meat is fork-tender; if more cooking time is needed, reset to high pressure for 10 minutes.

6. Using tongs, transfer pork to a cutting board, tent with foil and let rest for 10 minutes. Cut into 1½ inch (4 cm) pieces. Strain juice from cooker and discard all but ½ cup (125 mL) juice. Skim fat from juice. Wash and dry the cooker's inner pot.

7. Heat the cooker on High/Sauté/Brown. Add the remaining oil and heat until shimmering. Add pork, in batches if necessary, and cook, turning once, for 5 minutes or until crispy. Using tongs, transfer pork to a serving bowl and drizzle with the reserved juice. Carefully wipe out the cooker's inner pot.

8. Add tortillas, one at a time, to the cooker and cook, turning once, for 2 minutes or until lightly browned on both sides.

9. Transfer tortillas to individual serving plates. Arrange pork in center of tortillas and spoon salsa on top. Serve garnished with cilantro.

TIPS

The salsa can be made up to 1 day ahead, covered and refrigerated. Remove from the refrigerator 30 minutes before serving.

You can substitute boneless pork shoulder blade roast for the pork belly. Cut the roast into 1-inch (2.5 cm) cubes before adding it to the pressure cooker. Reduce the cooking time in step 5 to 30 minutes.

Pork Enchiladas with Chiles and Cheese

Tender shredded pork gets a lively treatment with this intensely flavored mix of chiles, tomatoes, onions and herbs. Cooking under pressure gives the ingredients a deep, rich flavor and cuts the cooking time substantially.

MAKES 4 SERVINGS

- Blender
- 13- by 9-inch (33 by 23 cm) glass baking dish, sprayed with nonstick cooking spray

1 lb	plum (Roma) tomatoes (about 4), roughly chopped	500 g
4	cloves garlic, minced	4
2	dried ancho chile peppers, seeded and roughly sliced (see tip)	2
2	chipotle peppers, finely chopped, with 2 tbsp (30 mL) adobo sauce	2
1	jalapeño pepper, roughly sliced	1
1	onion, sliced	1
1	bay leaf	1
2 tsp	dried oregano	10 mL
1 tsp	ground cumin	5 mL
½ tsp	ground coriander	2 mL
1 cup	low-sodium chicken stock (page 206) or ready-to-use chicken broth	250 mL
1½ lbs	boneless pork shoulder blade roast, cubed	750 g
	Kosher salt and freshly ground black pepper	
1 tbsp	freshly squeezed lime juice	15 mL
4 tbsp	chopped fresh cilantro leaves and fine stems, divided	60 mL
8	burrito-size (10-inch/25 cm) flour tortillas	8
2 cups	shredded Monterey Jack cheese	500 mL
	Sour cream (optional)	

1. In the pressure cooker, combine tomatoes, garlic, ancho chiles, chipotles with adobo sauce, jalapeño, onion, bay leaf, oregano, cumin, coriander and stock.

2. Season pork with salt and pepper. Transfer pork to the cooker. Close and lock the lid. Cook on high pressure for 10 minutes. Quickly release the pressure. Check to make sure the pork is fork-tender; if more cooking time is needed, reset to high pressure for 2 minutes. Discard bay leaf. Using tongs, transfer pork to a bowl and trim off any fat; set aside.

3. Transfer sauce from cooker to blender and add lime juice. Starting on low speed, blend, gradually increasing speed until sauce is smooth. Transfer to a wide bowl and stir in 3 tbsp (45 mL) cilantro.

4. Stir ¼ cup (60 mL) sauce into the pork. Season to taste with salt and pepper.

5. Position rack in the middle of the oven. Preheat oven to 400°F (200°C).

6. Spoon ¾ cup (175 mL) sauce into prepared baking dish, spreading to coat the bottom. Dip a tortilla in sauce in bowl, letting excess sauce drip off, and transfer to a plate. Add one-eighth of the pork mixture down the middle of the tortilla. Sprinkle with 3 tbsp (45 mL) cheese. Roll up tortilla and arrange seam side down in baking dish. Repeat with the remaining tortillas. Spoon all but 3 tbsp (45 mL) sauce over tortillas. Sprinkle the remaining cheese over top. Spoon the remaining sauce over cheese.

7. Cover dish with foil and bake for 15 minutes. Remove foil and bake for 10 minutes or until cheese is melted. Garnish with the remaining cilantro. Serve with sour cream, if desired.

TIPS

To make the dried ancho chiles easier to handle, arrange them on a microwave-safe plate and microwave on High for 12 seconds or until soft and fragrant.

Prepare and measure out all of your ingredients ahead of time and have them ready to quickly add to the pressure cooker. This helpful style of food preparation is called *mise en place*, meaning "everything in its place."

When releasing pressure quickly, keep your hands and face away from the hole on top of the steam release handle so you don't get scalded by the escaping steam.

Caribbean Jerk Pork with Mango and Black Bean Salsa

A pork shoulder yields sensational results when it's rubbed with a spicy jerk seasoning and then cooked under pressure for fall-apart tenderness and impressive flavor. The cooling and earthy salsa completes the dish.

MAKES 6 SERVINGS

Mango and Black Bean Salsa

3	mangos, diced	3
1	large red onion, finely chopped	1
1	can (14 to 19 oz/398 to 540 mL) black beans, drained and rinsed	1
3 cups	diced pineapple (about ¾ fresh pineapple, cored)	750 mL
½ cup	chopped fresh cilantro	125 mL
¼ tsp	kosher salt	1 mL

Jerk Pork

2 tbsp	packed light brown sugar	30 mL
2 tsp	ground allspice	10 mL
1½ tsp	ground cumin	7 mL
1 tsp	kosher salt	5 mL
½ tsp	dried thyme	2 mL
¼ tsp	cayenne pepper	1 mL
¼ tsp	ground cinnamon	1 mL
5 tsp	virgin olive oil, divided	25 mL
4	cloves garlic, smashed	4
2 lb	boneless pork shoulder blade roast	1 kg
1 cup	low-sodium beef bone broth (page 208) or ready-to-use beef broth	250 mL
2 tbsp	freshly squeezed lime juice	30 mL
12	taco-size (6-inch/15 cm) flour tortillas	12

1. *Salsa:* In a medium bowl, stir together mangos, onion, beans, pineapple, cilantro and salt until well combined. Set aside.

2. *Jerk Pork:* In a small bowl, combine brown sugar, allspice, cumin, salt, thyme, cayenne, cinnamon and 2 tsp (10 mL) oil. Rub 1 clove garlic, then spice mixture, all over pork; reserve garlic.

3. Heat the pressure cooker on High/Sauté/Brown. Add the remaining oil and heat until shimmering. Add pork and cook, turning, for 8 minutes or until browned on all sides. Cancel cooking.

4. Add the reserved garlic, the remaining garlic, broth and lime juice. Close and lock the lid. Cook on high pressure for 45 minutes. Let stand, covered, for 10 minutes, then release any remaining pressure. Check to make sure an instant-read thermometer inserted in the thickest part of the roast registers 165°F (74°C) for medium-well; if more cooking time is needed, reset to high pressure for 10 minutes. Transfer pork to a cutting board, tent with foil and let rest for 5 minutes. Discard cooking liquid.

5. Using two forks, shred pork, discarding any fat. Arrange pork in center of tortillas and spoon salsa on top. Serve immediately.

TIP

The salsa can be prepared up to 3 days ahead, covered and stored in the refrigerator. It makes a great topping for fish and chicken. If using it as a dip or for meats that do not have a spicy seasoning, add 1 minced seeded jalapeño.

Root Beer Pulled Pork Sandwiches

These delightful pulled pork sandwiches are tender and packed with slow-braised flavor. They are sure to please even the pickiest of barbecue lovers at your table. Keep the shredded pork warm in the cooker so family members can make their own sandwiches as they come and go.

MAKES 6 SERVINGS

2 tbsp	dried onion flakes	30 mL
1 tbsp	beef bouillon granules	15 mL
1½ tsp	kosher salt	7 mL
½ tsp	freshly ground black pepper	2 mL
¼ tsp	paprika	1 mL
⅛ tsp	onion powder	0.5 mL
⅛ tsp	celery salt	0.5 mL
3 lb	boneless pork shoulder blade roast, cut into 3 equal pieces	1.5 kg
¾ cup	barbecue sauce, divided	175 mL
½ cup	root beer	125 mL
¼ cup	water	60 mL
6	hamburger buns, split	6

TIPS

You can substitute half of a 1-oz (28 g) packet of dried onion soup mix for the dry rub seasonings.

Add more water in step 2 if required by your cooker to reach pressure.

You can double this recipe if using a 6-quart (6 L) or larger pressure cooker.

For a tangy, crunchy sandwich, serve with a spoonful of coleslaw on top of the pork.

1. In a small bowl, combine onion flakes, bouillon, salt, pepper, paprika, onion powder and celery powder. Rub mixture into pork and transfer pork to the pressure cooker.

2. In the same bowl, whisk together ¼ cup (60 mL) barbecue sauce, root beer and water. Pour over pork.

3. Close and lock the lid. Cook on high pressure for 50 minutes. Let stand, covered, for 10 minutes, then release any remaining pressure. Check to make sure an instant-read thermometer inserted in the thickest part of the roast registers 165°F (74°C) for medium-well; if more cooking time is needed, reset to high pressure for 10 minutes. Transfer pork to a bowl, tent with foil and let rest for 5 minutes.

4. Preheat broiler.

5. Using two forks, shred pork, discarding any fat.

6. Pour cooking liquid into a measuring cup and skim off fat. Return ¼ cup (60 mL) sauce to the cooker and discard the remaining liquid. Add shredded pork and the remaining barbecue sauce. Heat the cooker on High/Sauté/Brown. Cook, stirring, for 3 to 5 minutes or until sauce is thickened to your liking.

7. Arrange buns, cut side up, on a baking sheet. Broil for 2 to 3 minutes or until toasted.

8. Serve pork mixture on toasted buns.

Thai Pork Lettuce Wraps

These Thai-inspired wraps hit on so many different notes: sweet, citrus, spicy, savory and loads of crunch. They will make your mouth water and delight your taste buds.

1½ lbs	pork tenderloin, cut into thin strips	750 g
	Kosher salt and freshly ground black pepper	
2	cloves garlic, minced	2
1 tbsp	grated gingerroot	15 mL
2 tbsp	soy sauce	30 mL
2 tbsp	Thai sweet chili sauce	30 mL
1 tbsp	freshly squeezed lime juice	15 mL
1 tbsp	virgin olive oil	15 mL
4	green onions (white and light green parts only), sliced, divided	4
1	carrot, julienned (see tip, page 67)	1
1	red bell pepper, julienned	1
1	can (8 oz/250 mL) water chestnuts, drained and chopped	1
6 tbsp	low-sodium beef bone broth (page 208) or ready-to-use beef broth	90 mL
¼ cup	creamy peanut butter	60 mL
1 tsp	Sriracha	5 mL
8	Bibb lettuce leaves	8
2 tbsp	chopped peanuts	30 mL
	Additional Sriracha (optional)	

1. Season pork with salt and pepper. In a medium bowl, combine garlic, ginger, soy sauce, chili sauce and lime juice. Add pork, turning to coat, and let stand for 30 minutes.

2. Heat the pressure cooker on High/Sauté/Brown. Add oil and heat until shimmering. Working in batches, use tongs to transfer pork to the cooker; reserve marinade. Cook pork, stirring, for 3 to 5 minutes or until browned on all sides. Using tongs, transfer pork to a plate as it is browned. Cancel cooking.

3. Return all pork and any accumulated juices to the cooker. Add half the green onions, carrot, red pepper, water chestnuts, reserved marinade, broth and peanut butter, stirring well. Close and lock the lid. Cook on high pressure for 5 minutes. Quickly release the pressure. Check to make sure just a hint of pink remains in pork; if more cooking time is needed, reset to high pressure for 1 minute. Stir in Sriracha.

4. Spoon pork mixture onto lettuce leaves. Drizzle with more sauce from the pot, if desired. Serve sprinkled with peanuts and the remaining green onions. Serve with additional Sriracha, if desired.

TIPS

When releasing pressure quickly, keep your hands and face away from the hole on top of the steam release handle so you don't get scalded by the escaping steam.

To make this recipe gluten-free, use gluten-free soy sauce or substitute tamari or coconut amino acids.

While I love crisp cooling lettuce leaves as a wrap, you can also use 6-inch (15 cm) flour tortillas.

Traditional Pork and Beans

The key to tantalizing pork and beans has always been a long and slow cooking process — until now. Pressure cooking makes for tender beans, and the sweet, caramelly sauce and smoky bacon immerse the beans in rich flavor.

MAKES 8 SERVINGS		
2 cups	dried navy (white pea) beans, rinsed	500 mL
	Water	
1 lb	slab side bacon, cut into cubes	500 g
1	onion, chopped	1
¼ cup	packed dark brown sugar	60 mL
2 tsp	dry mustard	10 mL
¼ tsp	freshly ground black pepper	1 mL
2 tbsp	pure maple syrup	30 mL
2 tbsp	tomato paste	30 mL

TIPS

You can substitute Great Northern beans for the navy beans, but do not use any other type of bean, as the consistency will not be ideal.

If you cannot find slab bacon, substitute thick-cut bacon and cut it into 1-inch (2.5 cm) pieces.

I love lots of bacon in my beans, but if you prefer, you can reduce the amount of bacon to 8 oz (250 g). Do not reduce it any further, as the bacon adds smoky, salty flavor and a nice texture to the bean dish.

1. Place beans in a large bowl, add 8 cups (2 L) cold water and let soak at room temperature for 8 hours or overnight. Drain and rinse beans. Set aside.

2. Heat the pressure cooker on High/ Sauté/Brown. Add bacon, in batches if necessary, and cook, stirring often, for 5 minutes or until fat is rendered and bacon is slightly crispy. Transfer bacon to a plate lined with paper towels. Discard all but 1 tbsp (15 mL) fat from the cooker.

3. Add onion to the cooker and cook, stirring often, for 3 to 5 minutes or until translucent. Cancel cooking.

4. Add brown sugar, mustard, pepper, 2½ cups (625 mL) water, maple syrup and tomato paste, stirring well. Stir in beans. Close and lock the lid. Cook on high pressure for 35 minutes. Let stand, covered, for 10 minutes, then release any remaining pressure. Check to make sure beans are tender; if more cooking time is needed, reset to high pressure for 5 minutes.

5. Stir in bacon. Heat the cooker on High/ Sauté/Brown. Cook, stirring often and scraping up any browned bits from the bottom of the pot, for 5 to 9 minutes or until mixture is the desired consistency.

Hot and Tangy Barbecue Spareribs

These tender ribs, with their hot and tangy barbecue sauce, are mouthwatering and fall-off-the-bone tender. Make them for guests or for a quick and easy family dinner.

MAKES 6 SERVINGS

Spareribs

1 tbsp	kosher salt	15 mL
1 tbsp	paprika	15 mL
1 tsp	freshly ground black pepper	5 mL
2	slabs pork spareribs (about 6 lbs/3 kg)	2

Hot and Tangy Barbecue Sauce

4	cloves garlic, minced	4
2 tsp	dried onion flakes	10 mL
2 tsp	chili powder	10 mL
2 tsp	ground mustard	10 mL
1/4 tsp	cayenne pepper	1 mL
1 1/2 cups	low-sodium beef bone broth (page 208) or ready-to-use beef broth	375 mL
1/3 cup	ketchup	75 mL
3 tbsp	apple cider vinegar	45 mL
2 tbsp	freshly squeezed lemon juice	30 mL
1 tbsp	light (fancy) molasses	15 mL
1 tbsp	Worcestershire sauce	15 mL
1 tbsp	cornstarch	15 mL
2 tbsp	cold water	30 mL
	Kosher salt and freshly ground black pepper	

1. *Ribs:* In a small bowl, combine salt, paprika and pepper. Rub mixture evenly over ribs. Cut ribs into 4 sections per slab.

2. *Sauce:* In the pressure cooker, combine garlic, onion flakes, chili powder, mustard, cayenne, broth, ketchup, vinegar, lemon juice, molasses and Worcestershire sauce, stirring well.

3. Add ribs to the cooker, tossing to coat in sauce, then stand ribs vertically in the pot. Close and lock the lid. Cook on high pressure for 25 minutes. Let stand, covered, for 10 minutes, then release any remaining pressure. The ribs should be falling off the bone; if more cooking time is needed, reset to high pressure for 5 minutes. Transfer ribs to a serving platter and tent with foil to keep warm.

4. In a small bowl, whisk together cornstarch and cold water.

5. Heat the cooker on High/Sauté/Brown. Stir in cornstarch mixture and cook, stirring, for 4 minutes or until sauce is thickened. Skim off any excess fat from sauce. Season to taste with salt and pepper. Spoon sauce over ribs.

VARIATION

Sweet and Sassy Barbecue Spareribs: Replace the Hot and Tangy Barbecue Sauce with 1 cup (250 mL) Sweet and Sassy Barbecue Sauce (page 211) and 1 1/2 cups (375 mL) low-sodium homemade or ready-to-use beef broth.

Ready-to-Go Bacon and Egg Muffins (page 24)

French Onion Soup (page 37)

Bouillabaisse (page 44)

Rancher's Hearty Beef Chili (page 62)

Lobster Mac (variation, page 64)

Honey Bourbon Chicken Leg Quarters (page 72)
and Glazed Brussels Sprouts with Bacon (page 113)

Pork Roast with Green Apple and Prosciutto (page 84)

Apple and Maple Glazed Pork Chops (page 86)
and Green Beans with Toasted Almonds (page 115)

Penne with Italian Sausage and Peppers

This recipe mimics the technique used by Italian chefs when preparing a pasta dish. They toss lightly cooked pasta into the sauce during the last few minutes of cooking so that the sauce is absorbed into the pasta. Similarly rich flavors are achieved here by pressure cooking the pasta in the sauce.

MAKES 4 SERVINGS

2 tbsp	virgin olive oil, divided	30 mL
1 lb	hot or sweet Italian sausage (bulk or casings removed)	500 g
1	onion, finely chopped	1
1	green bell pepper, roughly chopped	1
1 lb	dried penne pasta	500 g
3 cups	marinara sauce (homemade or store-bought)	750 mL
	Water	
2 tbsp	chopped fresh basil	30 mL
	Kosher salt and freshly ground black pepper	
	Freshly grated Parmesan cheese	

1. Heat the pressure cooker on High/Sauté/Brown. Add 1 tbsp (15 mL) oil and heat until shimmering. Add sausage, onion and green pepper; cook, breaking up sausage and stirring, for 5 to 7 minutes or until sausage is no longer pink. Cancel cooking.

2. Stir in penne and marinara sauce. Add enough water to just cover pasta, then add another 1 cup (250 mL). Close and lock the lid. Cook on low pressure for 4 minutes or for half the time recommended for al dente on the pasta package, whichever is greater. Quickly release the pressure.

3. Stir in basil and the remaining oil. Season to taste with salt and pepper. Let stand for 2 minutes. Serve with Parmesan.

TIPS

If you purchase sausage in links or in tubes, cut the end open and squeeze the sausage out of the casing or packaging.

You can substitute another dried tubular semolina pasta, such as ziti, rigatoni or mostaccioli, for the penne. Do not use a strand-type pasta, such as spaghetti. Do not use any fresh pasta, or pasta that take under 5 minutes to cook.

If using store-bought marinara sauce, use a 24-oz (682 mL) jar or can.

Smoky Beef Brisket and Carrots

The long, slow cooking time for brisket is shortened substantially in the pressure cooker without compromising any flavor. Even the staunchest of connoisseurs will find this barbecue brisket satisfying, tender and packed with flavor.

- 13- by 9-inch (33 by 23 cm) baking dish
- Rimmed baking sheet
- 2 sheets of heavy-duty foil, edges folded up
- Steamer basket

Brisket

1 tbsp	paprika	15 mL
1 tbsp	dry mustard	15 mL
1 tsp	chili powder	5 mL
3 tbsp	Worcestershire sauce	45 mL
	Virgin olive oil	
4 lb	piece beef brisket (see tip), cut into quarters	2 kg
2 tsp	kosher salt	10 mL
1	onion, finely chopped	1
5	cloves garlic, sliced	5
1/4 cup	packed brown sugar	60 mL
1	bottle (12 oz/341 mL) lager beer	1
1 cup	barbecue sauce	250 mL
2 tsp	liquid smoke	10 mL

Carrots

12	carrots, cut diagonally into 1/2-inch (1 cm) slices	12
1 tbsp	extra virgin olive oil	15 mL
1 tbsp	finely chopped fresh thyme	15 mL
	Kosher salt	

1. *Brisket:* In the baking dish, combine paprika, mustard, chili powder, Worcestershire sauce and 2 tbsp (30 mL) oil. Add brisket and turn to coat. Cover dish with plastic wrap and let stand for 30 minutes.

2. Remove brisket from marinade, discarding marinade, and season with salt. Heat the pressure cooker on High/Sauté/Brown. Add 1 tbsp (15 mL) oil and heat until shimmering. Working in batches, add brisket and cook, turning often, for 3 to 5 minutes or until browned on all sides, adding more oil as needed. Transfer brisket to baking sheet.

3. Add onion to the cooker and cook, stirring, for 3 to 5 minutes or until translucent. Add garlic and cook, stirring, for 1 minute or until fragrant. Cancel cooking.

4. Add brown sugar, beer, barbecue sauce and liquid smoke, stirring well. Return brisket and any accumulated juices to the cooker. Close and lock the lid. Cook on high pressure for 75 minutes. Quickly release the pressure.

5. *Carrots:* Meanwhile, arrange carrots on prepared foil sheets, dividing evenly. Drizzle with oil and sprinkle with thyme and salt to taste. Fold foil into tent-style packets and seal edges tightly. Place packets in steamer basket.

6. Place the steamer basket on top of the brisket. Close and lock the lid. Cook on high pressure for 15 minutes. Quickly release the pressure. The brisket should be fork-tender; if more cooking time is needed, reset to high pressure for 5 minutes. Remove carrot packets and set aside.

7. Transfer brisket to a cutting board and let cool slightly, then thinly slice across the grain.

8. Heat the cooker on High/Sauté/ Brown. Return brisket slices and any accumulated juices to the cooker. Simmer, uncovered, for 15 to 20 minutes or until brisket is done to your liking.

9. Carefully open carrot packets and transfer carrots to a serving dish. Serve with brisket.

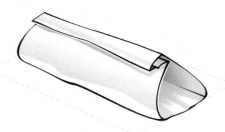

How to fold a tent-style foil packet

TIPS

Your brisket should be "boneless," with deckle off. This cut of brisket is often called "cut 120." It has bones 1 to 4 removed and the hard fat, known as deckle, trimmed off. You can ask your butcher to trim your brisket to these specifications, if it's not already done.

When quickly releasing pressure, remove the lid carefully, allowing steam to escape away from you.

In step 6, if your brisket needs more than 5 minutes additional cooking time, remove the carrot packets before continuing.

All-Time Favorite Pot Roast

My mother was a wonderful cook, and this dish was one of my favorite meals when I was growing up. The pressure cooker version takes much less time, but the roast remains a family favorite. Any leftovers are great for easy and tasty sandwiches for lunch.

MAKES 6 SERVINGS

3 lb	boneless beef chuck roast (less than 8 inches/20 cm in diameter)	1.5 kg
	Kosher salt and freshly ground black pepper	
2 tbsp	virgin olive oil	30 mL
1 tbsp	horseradish powder	15 mL
2	bay leaves	2
1½ cups	low-sodium beef bone broth (page 208) or ready-to-use beef broth	375 mL
8	carrots, cut into 4-inch (10 cm) lengths (see tip)	8
6	red-skinned potatoes, cut in half	6
2	onions, cut into ½-inch (1 cm) wedges	2
2	stalks celery, chopped	2
1 tsp	celery salt	5 mL

1. Season roast with salt and pepper. Heat the pressure cooker on High/Sauté/Brown. Add oil and heat until shimmering. Add roast and cook, turning occasionally, for 8 to 10 minutes or until browned on all sides. Cancel cooking.

2. Sprinkle roast all over with horseradish powder. Add bay leaves and broth. Close and lock the lid. Cook on high pressure for 65 minutes. Quickly release the pressure.

3. Add carrots, potatoes, onions and celery around roast. Sprinkle with celery salt. Cook on high pressure for 5 minutes. Let stand, covered, for 10 minutes, then release any remaining pressure. Check to make sure an instant-read thermometer inserted in the center of the roast registers at least 160°F (71°C) for medium and vegetables are fork-tender; if more cooking time is needed, reset to high pressure for 10 minutes. Discard bay leaves. Transfer roast to a cutting board, cover with foil and let stand for 5 minutes.

4. Slice roast across the grain and transfer to a serving platter. Using a slotted spoon, remove vegetables from the cooker and arrange around roast. Drizzle roast with some of the cooking juices.

TIPS

Choose a roast that is no thicker than 3 inches (7.5 cm); for thicker roasts, the cooking times would be longer.

Make sure your carrot sticks are of roughly equal width, for even cooking. If your carrots are more than ¾ inch (2 cm) in diameter, cut them lengthwise. Or use 4 cups (1 L) baby carrots to make preparation easier.

If you would like to make gravy for your roast, in a small bowl, whisk together 1 tbsp (15 mL) cornstarch and 1 tbsp (15 mL) cold water. After step 3, transfer the vegetables from the cooker to a bowl and keep warm. Heat the cooker on High/Sauté/Brown. Add the cornstarch mixture and cook, whisking, for 5 to 7 minutes or until gravy is thickened to your liking. Serve gravy with roast and vegetables.

Classic Beef Stroganoff

When my daughter comes home for school breaks, she often requests beef stroganoff. I have tried many versions, and this one easily stands out as the best. The chuck roast ensures tender and full-flavored beef chunks, while the pressure cooker seals the deep mushroom and beef partnership and makes for a tender, juicy stroganoff.

MAKES 6 SERVINGS

1½ lbs	boneless beef chuck roast, cut into 1-inch (2.5 cm) cubes	750 g
	Kosher salt and freshly ground black pepper	
1 tbsp	garlic powder	15 mL
2 tbsp	virgin olive oil	30 mL
1 lb	sliced mushrooms	500 g
1	onion, halved and sliced	1
1 cup	dry white wine	250 mL
1 tbsp	Dijon mustard	15 mL
1¼ cups	low-sodium beef bone broth (page 208) or ready-to-use beef broth (see tip)	300 mL
1 tbsp	all-purpose flour	15 mL
¼ cup	water	60 mL
8 oz	sour cream	250 g
12 oz	wide egg noodles	375 g
¼ cup	coarsely chopped fresh parsley	60 mL

TIP

Add more beef broth if required by your cooker to reach pressure. The measurements here are for 6-quart (6 L) or smaller pressure cookers. Many larger cookers require more than 1 cup (250 mL) broth. If you add more than 1 cup (250) more broth, increase the flour to 2 tbsp (30 mL).

1. Generously season beef with salt and pepper. Sprinkle with garlic powder. Heat the pressure cooker on High/Sauté/Brown. Add oil and heat until shimmering. Add beef, in batches if necessary, and cook, stirring often, for 5 minutes or until browned on all sides. Using a slotted spoon, transfer beef to a plate and set aside.

2. Add mushrooms and onion to the cooker and cook, stirring often, for 7 to 9 minutes or until mushrooms have released most of their liquid and onion is lightly browned. Add wine and mustard; boil, scraping up any browned bits from the bottom of the pot, for 3 minutes or until wine is reduced by half. Cancel cooking.

3. Return beef and any accumulated juices to the cooker and add broth, stirring well. Close and lock the lid. Cook on high pressure for 15 minutes. Quickly release the pressure. Check to make sure the beef is fork-tender; if more cooking time is needed, reset to high pressure for 3 minutes.

4. In a small bowl, whisk together flour and water, blending well.

5. Heat the cooker on High/Sauté/Brown. Stir in flour mixture and sour cream; cook, stirring often, for 5 minutes or until sauce is your desired consistency.

6. Meanwhile, cook egg noodles on the stovetop according to package directions.

7. Serve stroganoff over egg noodles, garnished with parsley.

Beef Barbacoa Tacos with Chiles

In this dish, beef is cooked to perfection in a savory blend of chipotle chiles, garlic, onion and spices. You will never again have the urge to stop for takeout Mexican when you can indulge your cravings so quickly and easily at home.

MAKES 8 SERVINGS

4	chipotle peppers, finely chopped, with 2 tbsp (30 mL) adobo sauce	4
4	cloves garlic, minced	4
1	onion, finely chopped, divided	1
3	bay leaves	3
1 tbsp	ground cumin	15 mL
2 tsp	ground oregano	10 mL
1/2 tsp	ground cloves	2 mL
1 cup	low-sodium beef bone broth (page 208) or ready-to-use beef broth	250 mL
1/4 cup	apple cider vinegar	60 mL
2 tbsp	vegetable oil	30 mL
3 lbs	boneless beef chuck roast, cut into 3-inch (7.5 cm) chunks	1.5 kg
	Kosher salt	
16	taco-size (6-inch/15 cm) flour tortillas	16
	Fresh cilantro leaves	
1	lime, cut into 8 wedges	1

1. In a large bowl, combine chipotles with adobo sauce, garlic, half the onion, bay leaves, cumin, oregano, cloves, broth and vinegar. Set aside.

2. Heat the pressure cooker on High/Sauté/Brown. Add oil and heat until shimmering. Working in batches, add beef and cook, stirring often, for 5 to 7 minutes or until browned on all sides. Using a slotted spoon, transfer beef to a plate as it is browned. Cancel cooking.

3. Return all beef and any accumulated juices to the cooker. Pour chipotle mixture over beef. Close and lock the lid. Cook on high pressure for 60 minutes. Quickly release the pressure. Check to make sure the beef is fork-tender; if more cooking time is needed, reset to high pressure for 5 minutes. Discard bay leaves.

4. Transfer beef to a bowl. Using two forks, shred beef into bite-size pieces.

5. Heat the cooker on High/Sauté/Brown. Cook, stirring, for 3 to 5 minutes or until sauce is reduced by half. Return beef to the cooker and stir well to coat with sauce. Season to taste with salt.

6. Divide beef mixture evenly among tortillas. Drizzle with more sauce, if desired. Serve garnished with the remaining onion, cilantro and a lime wedge.

TIP

Beef Barbacoa can be prepared ahead of time and refrigerated in an airtight container for up to 5 days or frozen for up to 3 months. To reheat, defrost beef if frozen. In a saucepan, cook beef, stirring, over medium heat until warmed through. Or reheat in your pressure cooker using the High/Sauté/Brown setting.

Sweet-and-Sour Beef and Broccoli

Now you can make this takeout classic at home in record time and with your own quality ingredients.

MAKES 6 SERVINGS

- 2 sheets of heavy-duty foil, sprayed with nonstick cooking spray

4 cups	broccoli florets (about 1 head)	1 L
1½ lbs	boneless beef top sirloin steak, cut into thin strips	750 kg
	Kosher salt and freshly ground black pepper	
2 tbsp	virgin olive oil	30 mL
1	onion, chopped	1
4	cloves garlic, minced	4
¾ cup	low-sodium beef bone broth (page 208) or ready-to-use beef broth	175 mL
⅓ cup	packed light brown sugar	75 mL
⅔ cup	pineapple juice	150 mL
⅓ cup	unseasoned rice vinegar	75 mL
3 tbsp	ketchup	45 mL
1 tbsp	soy sauce	15 mL
1 tbsp	cornstarch	15 mL
1 tbsp	cold water	15 mL
2 cups	hot cooked white rice	500 mL
	Toasted sesame seeds (optional)	

1. Arrange broccoli on prepared foil sheets, dividing evenly. Fold foil into tent-style packets and seal edges tightly (see illustration, page 99). Set aside.

2. Season beef with salt and pepper. Heat the pressure cooker on High/Sauté/Brown. Add oil and heat until shimmering. Working in batches, add beef and cook, stirring, for 3 to 5 minutes or until browned on all sides. Using a slotted spoon, transfer beef to a plate.

3. Add onion to the cooker and cook, stirring, for 3 to 5 minutes or until translucent. Add garlic and cook, stirring, for 1 minute or until fragrant. Add broth and cook, scraping up any browned bits from the bottom of the pot, for 2 minutes or until combined. Add brown sugar, pineapple juice, vinegar, ketchup and soy sauce; cook, stirring, for 2 minutes or until sugar is dissolved. Cancel cooking.

4. Return beef and any accumulated juices to the cooker, stirring well. Place broccoli packets on top of beef mixture. Close and lock the lid. Cook on high pressure for 13 minutes. Quickly release the pressure. Open a packet and check to make sure the broccoli is tender; if more cooking time is needed, reseal packet and reset to high pressure for 2 minutes. Remove foil packets from pot and set aside.

5. In a small bowl, combine cornstarch and cold water.

6. Heat the cooker on High/Sauté/Brown. Stir in cornstarch mixture and cook, stirring, for 5 minutes or until sauce is thickened to your liking. Stir in broccoli. Serve over rice, garnished with sesame seeds (if using).

TIP

Do not let cooked rice stand at room temperature for any length of time. Rice should be served immediately or refrigerated.

Toasty French Dip Sandwiches with Horseradish Crème

These melt-in-your-mouth sandwiches will delight your family and friends. The top sirloin roast comes out moist, tender and steeped in flavor. Then it is thinly sliced, layered on ciabatta rolls and topped with caramelized onions for a sublime meal.

MAKES 4 SERVINGS		

- Rimmed baking sheet

¼ cup	prepared horseradish	60 mL
8 oz	crème fraîche	250 g
	Kosher salt	
	Butter	
4	onions, chopped	4
1 tsp	granulated sugar	5 mL
¼ tsp	baking soda	1 mL
	Water	
1	packet (1 oz/28 g) dried onion soup mix	1
1 tsp	garlic powder	5 mL
¼ tsp	ground oregano	1 mL
¼ tsp	ground thyme	1 mL
1¾ cups	low-sodium beef bone broth (page 208) or ready-to-use beef broth	425 mL
2 tsp	Worcestershire sauce	10 mL
2 lb	boneless beef top sirloin roast	1 kg
4	soft ciabatta or French rolls, split	4

1. In a small bowl, combine horseradish and crème fraîche. Season with salt. Cover and refrigerate until ready to use.

2. Heat the pressure cooker on High/Sauté/Brown. Add 1 tbsp (15 mL) butter and heat until melted. Add onions, sugar and baking soda; cook, stirring often, for 7 to 9 minutes or until the bottom of the pot is covered in a pale brown coating (this is the fond). Add 2 tbsp (30 mL) water, using a wooden spoon to scrape up any browned bits from the bottom of the pot, and cook, stirring often, for 2 minutes or until fond has built up again. Continue cooking, adding water and scraping up browned bits every 3 minutes, for 25 minutes or until onions are dark brown. Cancel cooking. Transfer onions to a plate, cover and set aside.

3. Add soup mix, garlic powder, oregano, thyme, broth and Worcestershire sauce to the cooker, stirring well. Add roast. Close and lock the lid. Cook on high pressure for 45 minutes. Let stand, covered, for 10 minutes, then release any remaining pressure. Check to make sure an instant-read thermometer inserted in the center of the roast registers at least 160°F (71°C) for medium; if more cooking time is needed, reset to high pressure for 15 minutes. Transfer roast to a cutting board, cover with foil and let rest for 5 minutes.

4. Meanwhile, preheat broiler.

5. Thinly slice roast across the grain. Strain broth and skim off fat; set aside.

6. Butter cut side of rolls and place rolls, buttered side up, on baking sheet. Broil until lightly toasted. Remove top halves of rolls and set aside.

7. Arrange beef slices and caramelized onions on bottom halves of rolls. Broil for 1 to 2 minutes or until onions are warmed through. Drizzle onions with horseradish crème and cover with top halves of rolls. Serve with the reserved broth on the side for dipping.

VARIATION

Top the bottom half of each toasted roll with 1 to 2 slices of provolone cheese before adding the beef.

TIPS

Prepare and measure out all of your ingredients ahead of time and have them ready to quickly add to the pressure cooker. This helpful style of food preparation is called *mise en place*, meaning "everything in its place."

The horseradish crème can be covered and refrigerated for up to 5 days. You may want to make it at least 4 hours before use, to build flavors.

Tex-Mex Meatloaf with Braised Chipotle-Tomatillo Butternut Squash

Green chiles add a little zing of flavor to this twist on a classic meatloaf, and butternut squash gets an inviting infusion of a tart and spicy sauce. What makes this dish even more enjoyable is that it's a complete meal done in one pot.

MAKES 6 SERVINGS

- Blender
- 4 sheets of heavy-duty foil, sprayed with nonstick cooking spray
- Steamer basket

Squash

1½ tbsp	coconut oil	22 mL
4	tomatillos, husked, rinsed and quartered	4
3	cloves garlic, minced	3
2	chipotle peppers in adobo sauce	2
¼ cup	water	60 mL
3 cups	cubed butternut squash (1-inch/2.5 cm cubes)	750 mL
	Kosher salt	
2 tbsp	grated queso añejo or other Mexican cheese	30 mL

Meatloaf

1½ lbs	ground beef	750 g
1	small onion, finely chopped	1
½ cup	freshly grated Parmesan cheese	125 mL
¼ cup	plain dry bread crumbs	60 mL
¼ cup	cornmeal	60 mL
1 tsp	ground cumin	5 mL
1 tsp	kosher salt	5 mL
½ tsp	freshly ground black pepper	2 mL
1	can (4 oz/114 mL) diced green chiles	1
4 tsp	milk	20 mL
1	large egg, beaten	1
1 cup	low-sodium beef bone broth (page 208) or ready-to-use beef broth (see tip)	250 mL

1. *Squash:* Heat the pressure cooker on High/Sauté/Brown. Add oil and heat until shimmering. Add tomatillos and cook, stirring often, for 9 to 11 minutes or until browned and softened. Add garlic and cook, stirring, for 1 minute or until fragrant. Cancel cooking.

2. Carefully transfer tomatillo mixture to blender. Add chipotles and water; blend until slightly puréed.

3. Arrange squash on prepared foil sheets, dividing evenly. Season with salt. Fold up edges of foil and drizzle tomatillo sauce over squash. Fold foil into tent-style packets and seal edges tightly (see illustration, page 99). Set aside.

4. *Meatloaf:* In a large bowl, using your hands, combine beef, onion, Parmesan, bread crumbs, cornmeal, cumin, salt, pepper, chiles and milk. Gently mix in egg until just combined. Form meat mixture into a long loaf.

5. Transfer loaf to the steamer basket, forming it into a ring around the center and pinching the ends together. Add broth to the cooker. Place the basket in the cooker. Carefully arrange squash packets on top of the meatloaf. Close and lock the lid. Cook on high pressure for 10 minutes. Let stand, covered, for 10 minutes, then release any remaining pressure. Remove the foil packets. Check to make sure an instant-read thermometer inserted in the center of the meatloaf registers at least 165°F (74°C); if more cooking time is needed, reset to high pressure for 2 minutes. Discard cooking liquid.

6. Open foil packets and transfer squash to a large serving bowl. Garnish with queso.

7. Cut meatloaf into wedges and serve with squash.

TIPS

Choose tomatillos that have a tight-fitting husk and are firm to the touch. If the husk is slightly loose, check the interior fruit to make sure it is unwrinkled and bright green.

After removing the husk from the tomatillo, make sure to scrub off all the sticky residue on the fruit.

Add more broth in step 5 if required by your cooker to reach pressure.

Baked Cheesy Beef Rotini Casserole

The epitome of comfort food, this dish is bursting with ground beef, mushrooms and twisted pasta, and layered with loads of mozzarella, for a scrumptious, dreamy meal in a pot.

MAKES 6 TO 8 SERVINGS

- 11- by 7-inch (28 by 18 cm) glass baking dish, sprayed with nonstick cooking spray

2 tbsp	butter	30 mL
8 oz	sliced mushrooms	250 g
1	onion, chopped	1
2	cloves garlic, minced	2
1½ lbs	ground beef	750 g
3 tbsp	red wine	45 mL
1 lb	dried rotini or cavatappi pasta	500 g
1	can (15 oz/425 mL) tomato purée	1
1 tsp	kosher salt	5 mL
	Water	
2 cups	shredded mozzarella cheese	500 mL

TIPS

This recipe is suitable for 6- to 8-quart (6 to 8 L) pressure cookers. You can halve it for smaller cookers.

If you prefer, you can substitute ground pork or bulk turkey sausage for the beef.

When quickly releasing pressure, remove the lid carefully, allowing steam to escape away from you.

1. Heat the pressure cooker on High/Sauté/Brown. Add butter and heat until melted. Add mushrooms and onion; cook, stirring, for 3 to 5 minutes or until mushrooms have released most of their liquid and onion is translucent. Add garlic and cook, stirring, for 1 minute or until fragrant.

2. Add beef and cook, breaking it up with a spoon, for 7 minutes or until no longer pink. Add wine and cook, scraping up any browned bits from the bottom of the pot, for 2 minutes or until wine has evaporated. Cancel cooking.

3. Add pasta, tomato purée and salt, stirring well. Add enough water to just cover pasta. Close and lock the lid. Cook on low pressure for 5 minutes. Quickly release the pressure. Stir and let stand for 2 minutes.

4. Meanwhile, preheat broiler.

5. Spoon half the pasta mixture into prepared baking dish. Evenly sprinkle with half the cheese. Spoon the remaining pasta mixture on top and sprinkle with the remaining cheese.

6. Broil for 3 to 5 minutes or until cheese is melted and golden brown. Let stand for 5 minutes before serving.

Side Dishes

Beets with Orange Tarragon Vinaigrette and Walnuts

Beets have always been a favorite of mine, and with their excellent health benefits, beets are back in favor again. Topping steamed beets with an inviting orange tarragon vinaigrette and crunchy walnuts gives them a whole new boost of taste.

MAKES 6 SERVINGS

- Blender

6	medium beets (about 2 lbs/1 kg)	6
2½ cups	water	625 mL
¾ cup	virgin olive oil, divided	175 mL
2 tbsp	minced fresh tarragon, divided	30 mL
1	shallot, peeled	1
1	clove garlic, peeled	1
½ tsp	kosher salt	2 mL
¼ tsp	freshly ground black pepper	1 mL
¼ cup	white wine vinegar	60 mL
1 tbsp	Dijon mustard	15 mL
2 tsp	grated orange zest	10 mL
1 tsp	liquid honey	5 mL
¼ cup	chopped walnuts	60 mL
	Crumbled chèvre (optional)	

TIPS

You can use a commercial tarragon vinegar, if you prefer, and skip step 3. You will still need ½ cup (125 mL) virgin olive oil (or you can use extra virgin, if you prefer) and 1 tbsp (15 mL) minced fresh tarragon.

Do not substitute dried tarragon for the fresh, as the taste will be bitter.

You can get about 6 to 8 tsp (30 to 40 mL) zest from 1 orange. Make sure you do not cut into the white, pithy part of the orange, which is bitter.

1. Cut greens from beets, leaving 1 inch (2.5 cm) stem on. (Greens can be discarded or saved for later.) Do not cut root end. Scrub beets well.

2. Add beets and water to the pressure cooker. Close and lock the lid. Cook on high pressure for 18 minutes.

3. Meanwhile, in a small saucepan, combine ¼ cup (60 mL) oil and 1 tbsp (15 mL) tarragon. Cook over medium heat, stirring often, for 2 minutes or until small bubbles start to appear. Remove from heat and let stand for 5 minutes.

4. In blender, combine shallot, garlic, the remaining tarragon, salt, pepper, vinegar, mustard, orange zest and honey; process for 15 seconds or until finely chopped. With the blender running, through the feed tube, slowly add tarragon oil and the remaining oil, then blend for 15 seconds or until emulsified.

5. When the beet cooking time is done, quickly release the pressure. Check to make sure the beets are firm but fork-tender; if more cooking time is needed, reset to high pressure for 2 minutes.

6. Transfer beets to a bowl of ice water and let cool. Peel beets and discard skins. Cut each beet into 6 wedges and transfer to a serving bowl.

7. Drizzle beets with vinaigrette and toss gently to coat. Sprinkle with walnuts. Serve garnished with chèvre, if desired.

Sweet and Spicy Broccoli and Cauliflower Salad

This dish is perfect on a warm summer day as a light and refreshing lunch. I also love it served as a side for broiled fish. It will certainly steal the show.

MAKES 6 TO 8 SERVINGS

- Small covered jar or oil-and-vinegar bottle
- Tall steam rack
- Steamer basket

4	canned anchovy fillets, drained and finely chopped	4
1	serrano or jalapeño pepper, finely chopped (see tip)	1
1 tbsp	drained capers	15 mL
	Grated zest and juice of 1 orange	
¼ cup	extra virgin olive oil	60 mL
	Kosher salt and freshly ground black pepper	
3 cups	cauliflower florets	750 mL
3 cups	Romanesco cauliflower florets	750 mL
2 cups	broccoli florets	500 mL
2	seedless oranges, peeled and supremed (see tip)	2

1. In the jar, combine anchovies, serrano pepper, capers, orange zest and orange juice; cover and shake well. Add oil, cover and shake to emulsify. Season to taste with salt and pepper. Set aside.

2. Add 1 cup (250 mL) water (or the amount required by your cooker to reach pressure) to the pressure cooker and place the steam rack in the pot. Arrange cauliflower, Romanesco cauliflower and broccoli in the steamer basket and place the basket on the rack. Close and lock the lid. Cook on low pressure for 5 minutes. Quickly release the pressure. Check to make sure the florets are firm but tender; if more cooking time is needed, close the lid and let stand for 2 minutes.

3. Transfer the florets to a serving dish and let cool. Arrange orange slices in and around the florets. Serve drizzled with anchovy dressing.

TIPS

If you prefer a spicier dressing, include the seeds of the serrano or jalapeño pepper. Discard the seeds if you favor a milder dressing.

If you are unable to find Romanesco cauliflower, you can use twice as much regular cauliflower.

To supreme an orange, first use a small sharp knife (a serrated tomato knife works well) to cut off the peel and white pith. Holding the orange in your hand over a bowl to catch the juices, carefully slice in between the membranes and the flesh, keeping the knife as close as possible to the membrane, to remove the individual segments, leaving the membranes behind.

Broccoli and Cauliflower au Gratin

This casserole dish is reminiscent of many traditional holiday side dishes I have eaten over the years. The creamy cheese sauce flows through the vegetables and steaming the vegetables keeps them tender-crisp. A broil to finish the dish turns the topping that nice golden brown.

- Steamer basket
- 6-cup (1.5 L) casserole dish, buttered

2 tbsp	butter	30 mL
½	medium onion, finely chopped	½
1 cup	salt-free chicken stock (page 207) or ready-to-use chicken broth	250 mL
½ tsp	kosher salt	2 mL
⅛ tsp	freshly ground black pepper	0.5 mL
3 cups	broccoli florets	750 mL
3 cups	cauliflower florets	750 mL
4 oz	brick-style cream cheese, softened	125 g
1½ cups	shredded Monterey Jack cheese, divided	375 mL
¼ cup	sour cream	60 mL
½ tsp	paprika	2 mL
⅓ cup	dry bread crumbs	75 mL
1 tbsp	butter, melted	15 mL

1. Heat the pressure cooker on High/Sauté/Brown. Add 2 tbsp (30 mL) butter and heat until melted. Add onion and cook, stirring occasionally, for 3 to 5 minutes or until translucent. Stir in stock, salt and pepper. Cancel cooking.

2. Arrange broccoli and cauliflower in the steamer basket and add basket to the cooker.

3. Close and lock the lid. Cook on high pressure for 3 minutes. Quickly release the pressure. Remove basket and transfer florets to prepared casserole dish.

4. Preheat broiler.

5. Heat the pressure cooker on High/Sauté/Brown. Stir in cream cheese, 1 cup (250 mL) Monterey Jack, sour cream and paprika until melted and well combined. Pour over florets. Gently move florets with a spoon to allow mixture to seep throughout. Sprinkle with the remaining Monterey Jack.

6. In a small bowl, combine bread crumbs and melted butter. Sprinkle over casserole.

7. Broil for 5 minutes or until cheese is melted and crumbs are golden brown. Serve.

TIPS

This recipe has 1 cup (250 mL) liquid. You may need to add more stock or water if required by your cooker to reach pressure. Place a steam rack under the steamer basket so the florets are not resting in the water.

Leftover broccoli and cauliflower stems can be shredded and used in salads or chopped and used to make homemade vegetable stock.

Glazed Brussels Sprouts with Bacon

As some would say, everything is better with bacon! Well, that is certainly true for Brussels sprouts. This just may turn into your new favorite way to make these darling little balls of green.

MAKES 4 SERVINGS

	Nonstick cooking spray	
4	slices thick-cut bacon, finely chopped	4
1	large shallot, thinly sliced	1
3	cloves garlic, minced	3
1 lb	Brussels sprouts, trimmed and cut in half	500 g
½ tsp	kosher salt	2 mL
¼ tsp	freshly ground black pepper	1 mL
1 cup	low-sodium chicken stock (page 206) or ready-to-use chicken broth	250 mL
1 tbsp	balsamic vinegar reduction (see tip)	15 mL
½ cup	chopped pecans, toasted (see tip)	125 mL

1. Spray the pressure cooker pot with cooking spray. Heat the pressure cooker on High/Sauté/Brown. Add bacon and cook, stirring, for 4 to 5 minutes or until medium-crisp. Using a slotted spoon, transfer bacon to a plate lined with paper towels.

2. Add shallot to the cooker and cook, stirring, for 3 to 4 minutes or until softened. Add garlic and cook, stirring, for 1 minute or until fragrant. Cancel cooking.

3. Add Brussels sprouts, salt, pepper, stock and vinegar reduction, stirring well. Close and lock the lid. Cook on high pressure for 2 minutes. Quickly release the pressure. Check to make sure a fork inserted in the stem end of a sprout pierces it easily and the sauce has the consistency of a glaze; if more cooking time is needed, close the lid and let stand for 2 minutes.

4. Transfer sprout mixture to a serving bowl and sprinkle with pecans and bacon.

TIPS

Choose Brussels sprouts that are uniform in size, for even cooking.

You can purchase balsamic vinegar reduction or make your own. In a small saucepan, bring 1 cup (250 mL) balsamic vinegar and ¼ cup (60 mL) liquid honey or pure maple syrup to a boil over high heat. Reduce heat and simmer for 10 minutes or until reduced to about ⅓ cup (75 mL). Let cool. Leftover balsamic vinegar reduction can be drizzled over a caprese salad, cut fruits or roasted vegetables.

You can toast the pecans in your pressure cooker before beginning step 1. Heat the pressure cooker on High/Sauté/Brown, add the pecans and cook, stirring, for 2 to 3 minutes or until fragrant. Transfer the pecans to a plate to cool. (They can also be toasted in a skillet over medium-high heat for 2 to 3 minutes.)

Ginger and Hoisin Glazed Carrots

These carrots are a colorful and deliciously sweet complement to any main course. You can easily double this recipe to serve at a holiday gathering.

MAKES 6 SERVINGS

3 tbsp	butter, divided	45 mL
1	clove garlic, minced	1
2 tbsp	sliced gingerroot	30 mL
2 lbs	carrots, cut diagonally into ½-inch (1 cm) thick slices	1 kg
¾ cup	water	175 mL
½ cup	orange juice	125 mL
3 tbsp	hoisin sauce	45 mL

TIPS

A 2- by 1-inch (5- by 2.5-cm) piece of ginger will yield about 2 tbsp (30 mL) slices.

This recipe has 1¼ cups (300 mL) liquid. You may need to add more water if required by your cooker to reach pressure.

You can substitute pure maple syrup for the hoisin sauce, if you prefer.

1. Heat the pressure cooker on High/Sauté/Brown. Add 1 tbsp (15 mL) butter and heat until melted. Add garlic and ginger; cook, stirring, for 1 to 2 minutes or until fragrant. Add carrots, water and orange juice. Cancel cooking.

2. Close and lock the lid. Cook on high pressure for 4 minutes. Quickly release the pressure. Check to make sure the carrots are just fork-tender; if more cooking time is needed, close the lid and let stand for 2 minutes. Drain carrots and discard ginger. Return carrots to the cooker.

3. Heat the cooker on High/Sauté/Brown. Add hoisin sauce and the remaining butter; cook, stirring often, for 5 minutes or until carrots are glazed. Serve warm.

Green Beans with Toasted Almonds

This recipe makes a quick and easy company-worthy side dish, but really, it is perfect any time, company or not. The toasted almonds lend a nutty crunch to the beans, and the butter, garlic and lemon add a delightful flavor boost.

MAKES 6 SERVINGS

- Steam rack
- Steamer basket

1½ lbs	thin French green beans, trimmed	750 g
2 tbsp	butter	30 mL
2 tbsp	virgin olive oil	30 mL
½ cup	slivered almonds	125 mL
1	clove garlic, minced	1
	Juice of 1 lemon	
	Kosher salt and freshly ground black pepper	

TIPS

At the market, pick out each bean individually to make sure you have the best quality and even size and shape.

You can use regular green beans, but increase the steaming time in step 1 to 6 minutes.

1. Add 1 cup (250 mL) water (or the amount required by your cooker to reach pressure) to the pressure cooker and place the steam rack in the pot. Add beans to the steamer basket and place the basket on the rack. Close and lock the lid. Cook on high pressure for 3 minutes. Quickly release the pressure. Check to make sure the beans are just tender-crisp; if more cooking time is needed, reset to high pressure for 1 minute.

2. Remove the steamer basket and plunge beans into cold water to quickly cool them. Drain and spread on paper towels to dry. Remove the steam rack, drain the water from the pot and wipe the pot dry.

3. Heat the cooker on High/Sauté/Brown. Add butter and oil; heat until butter is melted. Add almonds and cook, stirring, for 3 to 5 minutes or until golden brown all over. Using a slotted spoon, transfer almonds to a plate.

4. Add garlic to the cooker and cook, stirring, for 1 minute or until fragrant. Add beans and cook, stirring occasionally, for 6 to 8 minutes or until tender-crisp and lightly browned. Stir in lemon juice and season to taste with salt and pepper. Serve sprinkled with almonds.

Easy Boston Baked Beans

My version of this traditional recipe takes advantage of cooking under pressure to do away with the long stovetop cooking times, yet still delivers outstanding results. If you enjoy a rich and hearty bean dish, you will love the depth of flavor that cooking under pressure gives this classic.

MAKES 6 SERVINGS

2 cups	dried navy (white pea) beans, rinsed	500 mL
	Water	
6	slices thick-cut bacon, finely chopped	6
1	onion, finely chopped	1
1 tsp	dry mustard	5 mL
½ tsp	ground cloves	2 mL
1 tbsp	virgin olive oil	15 mL
½ cup	packed brown sugar	125 mL
¼ cup	dark (cooking) molasses	60 mL
3 tbsp	tomato paste	45 mL
2 tbsp	bourbon (optional)	30 mL
2 tbsp	prepared yellow mustard	30 mL

TIPS

When pressure-cooking beans of any type, make sure to fill the pot no more than halfway full; otherwise, the exhaust valve may become clogged as the beans froth up under pressure.

You can double or triple this recipe if you have a large enough pressure cooker.

1. Place beans in a large bowl, cover with 8 cups (2 L) cold water and let stand at room temperature for 8 hours or overnight. Drain and rinse beans.

2. Heat the cooker on High/Sauté/Brown. Add bacon and onion; cook, stirring, for 4 to 5 minutes or until bacon is medium-crisp. Cancel cooking.

3. Transfer beans to the cooker and add dry mustard, cloves, 3 cups (750 mL) water and oil, stirring well. Close and lock the lid. Cook on high pressure for 20 minutes. Let stand, covered, for 10 minutes, then release any remaining pressure. Check to make sure the beans are just tender (they will soften more in step 4); if more cooking time is needed, reset to high pressure for 4 minutes.

4. Heat the cooker on High/Sauté/Brown. Add brown sugar, molasses, tomato paste, bourbon (if using) and yellow mustard; cook, stirring often, for 5 to 7 minutes or until thickened to your liking.

Chickpea and Lentil Salad

This salad is a protein powerhouse. Complemented with nutrient-rich Swiss chard and a sweet and tangy dressing, it makes a delectable side dish — or even a fantastic light meal.

MAKES 2 TO 4 SERVINGS

- Steam rack
- Steamer basket

¼ cup	virgin olive oil, divided	60 mL
2	onions, halved and sliced	2
3	cloves garlic, minced	3
1 cup	dried green (Puy) lentils, rinsed	250 mL
2 cups	water	500 mL
6	Swiss chard leaves, tough stems removed	6
1 tbsp	pomegranate molasses	15 mL
1 tbsp	freshly squeezed lemon juice	15 mL
1 tsp	kosher salt	5 mL
1	can (14 to 15 oz/398 to 425 mL) chickpeas, drained and rinsed (see tip)	1
	Kosher salt and freshly ground black pepper	
3	green onions, sliced	3

TIPS

If served as a main dish, this recipe makes 2 servings.

If you have extra virgin olive oil on hand as well as virgin, use extra virgin in step 5.

Instead of using canned chickpeas, you can use soaked dried chickpeas; cook according to the directions in the chart on page 215 before adding them to the salad.

1. Heat the pressure cooker on High/Sauté/Brown. Add 2 tbsp (30 mL) oil and heat until shimmering. Add onions and cook, stirring often, for 3 to 5 minutes or until translucent. Add garlic and cook for 12 to 15 minutes or until onions are slightly caramelized. Cancel cooking.

2. Add lentils and water, stirring well. Close and lock the lid. Cook on high pressure for 10 minutes. Let stand, covered, until the float valve drops down. Check to make sure the lentils are tender; if more cooking time is needed, close the lid and let stand, stirring occasionally, for 2 to 3 minutes.

3. Drain and rinse lentils, reserving liquid. Transfer lentils to a large bowl and let cool.

4. Return 1 cup (250 mL) of the reserved liquid (or the amount required by your cooker to reach pressure) to the cooker and place the steam rack in the pot. Add Swiss chard to the steamer basket and place basket on the rack. Close and lock the lid. Cook on high pressure for 2 minutes. Quickly release the pressure. Check to make the Swiss chard is done to your liking; if more cooking time is needed, close the lid and let stand for 2 minutes. Remove steamer basket and let Swiss chard cool.

5. In a small bowl, combine molasses, lemon juice and salt. Gradually whisk in the remaining oil.

6. Add Swiss chard and chickpeas to the lentils. Drizzle with dressing and toss gently to combine. Season to taste with salt and pepper. Serve garnished with green onions.

Tangy Three-Bean Salad

For large family gatherings, one of my aunts would bring the most fabulous combination of colorful cooked beans and fresh green beans from her garden, marinated in a sweet and tangy dressing. The store-bought canned versions never even came close. The pressure cooker makes it easy to create this delicious three-bean salad modeled after hers.

MAKES 6 SERVINGS

- Tall steam rack
- Steamer basket
- Sheet of heavy-duty foil

1 cup	dried chickpeas, rinsed	250 mL
1 cup	borlotti (cranberry) beans, rinsed	250 mL
	Water	
1	small red onion, finely chopped	1
⅓ cup	apple cider vinegar	75 mL
1 tbsp	granulated sugar	15 mL
1	clove garlic, smashed	1
1	bay leaf	1
1 tsp	vegetable oil	5 mL
1½ cups	frozen green beans	375 mL
2	stalks celery, chopped	2
½ cup	finely chopped fresh parsley	125 mL
¼ cup	virgin olive oil	60 mL
	Kosher salt and freshly ground black pepper	

1. Place chickpeas and borlotti beans in separate large bowls and cover each with 4 cups (1 L) cold water. Let soak at room temperature for 8 hours or overnight. Drain and rinse beans, keeping them separate.

2. In a small bowl, combine onion, vinegar and sugar. Set aside.

3. In the pressure cooker, combine chickpeas, garlic, bay leaf, 4 cups (1 L) water and vegetable oil. Place steam rack in the pot. Add borlotti beans to the steamer basket and place the basket on the rack.

4. Arrange frozen green beans in center of foil sheet. Fold foil into a flat packet around the beans and seal edges tightly (see illustration, page 67). Rest the ends of the packet on the edges of the steamer basket, suspending the packet above the borlotti beans.

5. Close and lock the lid. Cook on high pressure for 13 minutes. Let stand, covered, for 10 minutes, then release any remaining pressure. Remove the green bean packet and open it carefully, and remove the steamer basket. Check to make sure the chickpeas, borlotti beans and green beans and are done to your liking; if more cooking time is needed for any of the beans, return them to the cooker and reset to high pressure for 2 minutes.

6. Drain chickpeas and borlotti beans, discarding bay leaf and cooking liquid, and rinse under cold water until cool. Transfer to a serving bowl.

7. Carefully open foil packet and plunge green beans into a bowl of ice water to cool. Cut beans into 1-inch (2.5 cm) slices, if necessary.

8. Add green beans to the serving bowl and stir in marinated onion, celery, parsley and olive oil until combined. Season to taste with salt and pepper. Serve immediately or cover and refrigerate for up to 1 day before serving.

TIPS

Do not substitute any other legume for the chickpeas or borlotti beans, as the cooking times and stacking order are specifically designed for these beans. Other legumes will not give similar results.

The green beans need to be frozen before use in this recipe so they will not be overcooked. You can use garden fresh beans, but freeze them first.

Chickpea, Mozzarella and Tomato Salad

This salad is inspired by the traditional caprese salad, but with the added protein and earthy flavor of chickpeas. A simple tahini and maple dressing complements it nicely. Just make sure you plan ahead, since the chickpeas turn out best if soaked overnight.

MAKES 4 SERVINGS

2 cups	dried chickpeas, rinsed	500 mL
8 cups	cold water	2 L
4 cups	low-sodium vegetable stock (page 204) or ready-to-use vegetable broth	1 L
¼ cup	tahini	60 mL
2 tbsp	freshly squeezed lemon juice	30 mL
1 tbsp	pure maple syrup	15 mL
	Hot water	
	Kosher salt and freshly ground black pepper	
20	ciliegine (mini fresh mozzarella) balls (each about ⅓ oz/9 g)	20
20	cherry tomatoes	20
4 cups	lightly packed spinach leaves, tough stems removed	1 L

TIP

You can prepare this salad through step 5 up to 3 days ahead; cover tightly and refrigerate. Let stand for 30 minutes at room temperature before continuing with step 6.

1. Place chickpeas in a large bowl, add cold water and let soak at room temperature for 8 hours or overnight. Drain and rinse chickpeas.

2. Add chickpeas and stock to the pressure cooker. Close and lock the lid. Cook on high pressure for 16 minutes. Let stand, covered, until the float valve drops down. Check to make sure the chickpeas are tender; if more cooking time is needed, reset to high pressure for 3 minutes.

3. Drain chickpeas, discard cooking liquid and rinse under cold water until cool.

4. In a small bowl, whisk together tahini, lemon juice and maple syrup. Whisk in hot water, 1 tbsp (15 mL) at a time, until dressing is your desired consistency. Season to taste with salt and pepper.

5. In a large bowl, combine chickpeas, ciliegine and tomatoes. Drizzle with dressing and toss gently to combine.

6. Arrange spinach on individual serving plates and top with chickpea mixture.

Homestyle Potato Salad

Potato salad is one of those classic sides that goes well with many main dishes. On a hot summer day, it is especially nice to make this quick and easy recipe in the pressure cooker, so you aren't steaming up your kitchen.

MAKES 6 SERVINGS

- Steam rack

3	large eggs	3
6	small red-skinned potatoes (about 12 oz/375 g)	6
1	stalk celery, chopped	1
¼ cup	chopped red onion	60 mL
	Kosher salt and freshly ground black pepper	
1 tbsp	chopped fresh dill	15 mL
½ cup	mayonnaise	125 mL
2 tsp	prepared yellow mustard	10 mL
1 tsp	apple cider vinegar	5 mL
2 tbsp	fresh parsley leaves	30 mL

TIPS

Eggs cooked in the pressure cooker do not need to be aged to make peeling them easier.

If you prefer, you can substitute plain yogurt for the mayonnaise; decrease the apple cider vinegar to ½ tsp (2 mL).

1. Add 1 cup (250 mL) water (or the amount required by your cooker to reach pressure) to the pressure cooker and place the steam rack in the pot. Place the eggs on the rack. Close and lock the lid. Cook on low pressure for 6 minutes. Let stand, covered, until the float valve drops down.

2. Transfer eggs to a bowl of cold water to chill, refreshing water as necessary to keep cold. Drain water from cooker. When cool enough to handle, peel and chop eggs and set aside.

3. In the cooker, combine potatoes and 1 cup (250 mL) cold water (or the amount required by your cooker to reach pressure). Close and lock the lid. Cook on high pressure for 4 minutes. Let stand, covered, for 3 minutes, then release any remaining pressure. The potatoes should be fork-tender; if more cooking time is needed, reset to high pressure for 1 minute.

4. Transfer potatoes to a cutting board. When cool enough to handle, cut potatoes into ½-inch (1 cm) cubes.

5. In a large bowl, combine potatoes, celery and onion. Season to taste with salt and pepper, tossing gently. Add eggs and dill.

6. In a small bowl, combine mayonnaise, mustard and vinegar, mixing well. Gently fold into potato salad. Cover and refrigerate for at least 1 hour, until chilled, or up to 1 day. Just before serving, garnish with parsley.

Creamy Garlic and Chive Mashed Potatoes

These mashed potatoes are blended with loads of butter, cream and sautéed garlic. The fresh chives add an extra nuance to the taste and texture. I love that I don't have to peel the potatoes ahead of time, since the skins pretty much fall right off after pressure cooking.

MAKES 4 SERVINGS

- Steam rack

4	russet potatoes (about 1¼ lbs/625 g total)	4
5 tbsp	butter, softened, divided	75 mL
3	cloves garlic, minced	3
¼ cup	low-sodium chicken stock (page 206) or ready-to-use chicken broth	60 mL
½ cup	heavy or whipping (35%) cream (approx.)	125 mL
1 tbsp	chopped fresh chives	15 mL
	Kosher salt and freshly ground black pepper	

TIPS

To cut the pressure cooking time in half, peel and quarter the potatoes before adding them to the cooker. Place them in a steamer basket instead of on a rack. Cook on high pressure for 8 minutes.

If you prefer, you can leave the potato skins on in step 2.

Mash potatoes just until they are your desired consistency and everything is combined. Do not over-mash potatoes, or they will not be as fluffy.

1. Add 1 cup (250 mL) water (or the amount required by your cooker to reach pressure) to the pressure cooker and place the steam rack in the pot. Using a fork, poke holes in the potatoes in a few places. Place potatoes on the rack. Close and lock the lid. Cook on high pressure for 16 minutes. Quickly release the pressure. Check to make sure the potatoes are fork-tender; if more cooking time is needed, reset to high pressure for 3 minutes.

2. Transfer potatoes to a cutting board. Drain water from the cooker. When potatoes are cool enough to handle, use your hands to rub off the skins. Discard skins. Cut potatoes into sixths.

3. Heat the pressure cooker on High/Sauté/Brown. Add 2 tbsp (30 mL) butter and heat until melted. Add garlic and cook, stirring, for 1 minute or until fragrant. Add stock and cook, scraping up any browned bits from the bottom of the pot, for 2 minutes. Add potatoes and the remaining butter and start mashing potatoes. When butter is absorbed, cancel cooking.

4. Slowly add cream, mashing, until potatoes are your desired consistency. (Use only as much cream as is needed to reach that consistency.) Stir in chives and season to taste with salt and pepper. Transfer to a serving bowl. Serve warm.

Pecan-Crusted Sweet Potato Casserole

Sweet potato casseroles are a tradition for many holiday parties. When your oven is packed with all your other fixings, you can make this dish in your multicooker. You can choose to pressure-cook or slow-cook it (see variation), depending upon the timing that suits you best.

- Steamer basket
- Stand or hand mixer
- 4-cup (1 L) round casserole dish, sprayed with nonstick cooking spray
- Steam rack

2 lbs	sweet potatoes, peeled and cut into ½-inch (1 cm) chunks	1 kg
¼ cup	packed light brown sugar	60 mL
1 tsp	ground cinnamon	5 mL
½ tsp	ground nutmeg	2 mL
¼ tsp	kosher salt	1 mL
2 tbsp	butter, cut into pieces	30 mL
1 tsp	vanilla extract	5 mL
1	large egg	1
2 tbsp	heavy or whipping (35%) cream	30 mL

Pecan Topping

⅓ cup	chopped pecans	75 mL
⅓ cup	packed light brown sugar	75 mL
1 tbsp	all-purpose flour	15 mL
1 tbsp	butter, melted	15 mL

1. Add 1 cup (250 mL) water (or the amount required by your cooker to reach pressure) to the pressure cooker and place the steamer basket in the pot. Place sweet potatoes in the basket. Close and lock the lid. Cook on high pressure for 8 minutes. Quickly release the pressure. Check to make sure the potatoes are fork-tender; if more cooking time is needed, reset to high pressure for 2 minutes.

2. Transfer sweet potatoes to a large bowl. Using the mixer, mix in brown sugar, cinnamon, nutmeg, salt, butter and vanilla until smooth. Mix in egg and cream until combined. Spoon into prepared casserole dish.

3. *Topping:* In a small bowl, combine pecans, brown sugar, flour and butter. Sprinkle over casserole.

4. Replenish the water in the cooker as needed and place the steam rack in the pot. Place casserole dish on the rack. Close and lock the lid. Cook on high pressure for 15 minutes. Quickly release the pressure. Serve warm.

VARIATION

Slow Cooker Sweet Potato Casserole: You will not need the steamer basket, mixer or steam rack. Omit the egg and cream. In the pressure cooker, combine sweet potatoes, brown sugar, cinnamon, nutmeg and salt. Close and lock the lid, making sure the steam vent is open. Press Slow Cook and adjust the temperature to the lowest setting. Cook for 7 to 7½ hours or until sweet potatoes are fork-tender. Gently stir in butter and vanilla. Transfer potatoes to a serving dish and sprinkle with pecan topping.

Stuffed Acorn Squash

I have always loved the slightly sweet taste and fibrous texture of acorn squash. What I particularly love about this recipe is that the squash functions as a bowl for delightfully seasoned quinoa and brown rice.

MAKES 4 SERVINGS		

• Steam rack

1 tbsp	butter	15 mL
1	onion, finely chopped	1
2	cloves garlic, minced	2
1/2 cup	quinoa, rinsed	125 mL
1 cup	short- or long-grain brown rice, rinsed	250 mL
1 tsp	finely chopped fresh rosemary	5 mL
1 tsp	finely chopped fresh thyme	5 mL
3¾ cups	low-sodium chicken stock (page 206) or ready-to-use chicken broth	925 mL
2	medium acorn squash, cut in half lengthwise and seeded	2
¾ cup	freshly grated Parmesan cheese, divided	175 mL
	Kosher salt and freshly ground black pepper	

TIP

If only the rice needs more cooking time at the end of step 2, simply set the squash aside and keep it warm while you continue cooking the rice mixture. If only the squash needs more cooking time, transfer the rice mixture to a large bowl, add 1 cup (250 mL) water (or the amount required by your cooker to reach pressure) to the pressure cooker and return the rack and squash to the pot to continue cooking. In the meantime, you can complete step 4.

1. Heat the pressure cooker on High/Sauté/Brown. Add butter and heat until melted. Add onion and cook, stirring, for 3 to 5 minutes or until translucent. Add garlic and cook, stirring, for 1 minute. Add quinoa and cook, stirring, for 2 minutes or until lightly toasted. Cancel cooking.

2. Add rice, rosemary, thyme and stock, stirring well. Place steam rack over rice mixture. Arrange squash halves, cut side up, on the rack. Close and lock the lid. Cook on high pressure for 6 minutes. Quickly release the pressure. Remove squash and rack. Check to make sure the squash and rice are tender; if both need more cooking time, return rack and squash to pot and reset to high pressure for 2 minutes (see tip).

3. Remove squash and rack from the pot. Drain any liquid from the center of the squash and set aside.

4. Stir ½ cup (125 mL) Parmesan into the rice mixture. Season to taste with salt and pepper. Let stand for 5 minutes or until slightly thickened.

5. Spoon rice mixture into the center of each squash, dividing evenly. Sprinkle with the remaining Parmesan. Serve immediately.

Butternut Squash and Spiced Millet Pilaf

Cumin and cardamom add just the right touch of spice to this millet pilaf, while the butternut squash adds a touch of sweetness. This dish works well with Indian fare, but you may find you also enjoy it as a side for Mediterranean or Moroccan dishes.

MAKES 4 SERVINGS

1 tbsp	ghee (see tip)	15 mL
1 tbsp	cumin seeds	15 mL
½ tsp	ground cardamom	2 mL
1½ cups	cubed butternut squash	375 mL
1	onion, halved and thinly sliced	1
2 cups	millet, rinsed	500 mL
1	bay leaf	1
1 tsp	kosher salt	5 mL
3 cups	water	750 mL

TIPS

Ghee is a type of clarified butter found in Indian cuisine. It is commonly believed to have many health benefits. Ghee can be found in the Indian cooking section of most well-stocked grocery stores. You can substitute butter or virgin olive oil for the ghee.

This recipe can be doubled, but make sure to fill the pot no more than halfway; otherwise, the exhaust valve may become clogged, resulting in excess pressure.

1. Heat the pressure cooker on High/Sauté/Brown. Add ghee and heat until melted. Add cumin seeds and cardamom; cook, stirring, for 1 minute or until seeds begin to sputter. Add squash and onion; cook, stirring, for 3 to 5 minutes or until just softened. Add millet, stirring to coat with ghee. Cancel cooking.

2. Add bay leaf, salt and water, stirring well. Close and lock the lid. Cook on high pressure for 1 minute. Let stand, covered, for 10 minutes, then release any remaining pressure. Check to make sure millet is al dente; if more cooking time is needed, reset to high pressure for 3 minutes. Discard bay leaf. Fluff millet with a fork and serve warm.

Spicy Basmati Rice with Lentils, Green Onions and Almonds

Take your typical rice dish up to new levels with this combination of basmati rice, lentils, green onions and a spicy dash of curry. Finish it off with slivered almonds for a unique and flavorful side dish.

MAKES 4 SERVINGS		
¼ cup	slivered almonds	60 mL
1½ cups	basmati rice, rinsed	375 mL
2 cups	salt-free chicken stock (page 207) or ready-to-use chicken broth	500 mL
2 tsp	curry powder, divided	10 mL
6 tbsp	dried red lentils, rinsed	90 mL
¼ cup	minced onion	60 mL
2	cloves garlic, minced	2
	Kosher salt	
4	green onions, sliced	4

TIPS

Do not substitute green lentils for the red lentils, as the cooking time is substantially different.

If you prefer a less spicy rice, add ½ tsp (2 mL) curry powder in step 2, then stir in additional curry powder to taste in step 3.

Do not add more curry powder than is specified in step 2 unless you have previous experience with this recipe and know you would prefer more spice. Pressure cooking amplifies the spiciness of chile peppers.

1. Heat the pressure cooker on High/Sauté/Brown. Add almonds and cook, stirring, for 2 to 3 minutes or until lightly toasted and fragrant. Transfer to a plate and let cool. Cancel cooking.

2. Add rice, stock and 1 tsp (5 mL) curry powder to the cooker, stirring well. Arrange lentils, onion and garlic on top, making sure they are covered by stock; do not stir. Close and lock the lid. Cook on high pressure for 3 minutes. Let stand, covered, for 10 minutes, then release any remaining pressure. Check to make sure the lentils are tender; if more cooking time is needed, reset to high pressure for 1 minute, then quickly release the pressure. Stir in almonds and season to taste with salt.

3. Transfer to a serving bowl. Sprinkle with the remaining curry powder and garnish with green onions. Serve immediately.

Spanish Rice

Here, a traditional rice pilaf is infused with Southwestern seasonings to make it a perfect accompaniment to your favorite Mexican or Tex-Mex dish. Serve along with beans to accompany your favorite main course, or use as a filling for burritos and tacos.

MAKES 6 SERVINGS

2 cups	long-grain brown rice, rinsed	500 mL
2½ cups	low-sodium chicken stock (page 206) or ready-to-use chicken broth	625 mL
2 cups	canned diced tomatoes, with juice	500 mL
1	onion, finely chopped	1
3 tbsp	chili powder	45 mL
1 tsp	ground cumin	5 mL
1 tsp	garlic powder	5 mL
1 tsp	kosher salt	5 mL

TIP

Long-grain white rice also works in this recipe, but I prefer the texture and added nutrients of brown rice. For white rice, use an additional ½ cup (125 mL) stock and cook on high pressure for 4 minutes.

1. In the pressure cooker, combine rice, stock and tomatoes. Add onion, chili powder, cumin, garlic powder and salt, stirring to dissolve.

2. Close and lock the lid. Cook on low pressure for 20 minutes. Let stand, covered, for 10 minutes, then release any remaining pressure. Check to make sure the rice is done to your liking; if more cooking time is needed, close the lid and let stand for 2 minutes. Fluff rice with a fork.

Pea and Saffron Risotto

If you love risotto but don't like to make it at home because it can be challenging to get good results, you are going to love the simplicity and consistently fabulous results from your pressure cooker. This recipe is an ideal accompaniment to many dishes.

MAKES 4 SERVINGS		
1 tbsp	virgin olive oil	15 mL
1	large shallot, minced (about ⅓ cup/75 mL)	1
1	clove garlic, minced	1
1½ cups	Arborio rice	375 mL
½ cup	dry white wine	125 mL
1½ tsp	balsamic vinegar	7 mL
3½ cups	low-sodium chicken stock (page 206) or ready-to-use chicken broth (approx.)	875 mL
2 cups	frozen peas	500 mL
Pinch	saffron threads	Pinch
1 tbsp	freshly squeezed lemon juice	15 mL
1 tbsp	butter (optional)	15 mL
⅓ cup	grated Parmigiano-Reggiano cheese	75 mL
	Kosher salt and freshly ground black pepper	

TIP

Using authentic, full-flavored Parmigiano-Reggiano creates a complex, yet subtle tango of flavors. If you can't find it, you can use regular Parmesan.

1. Heat the pressure cooker on High/Sauté/Brown. Add oil and heat until shimmering. Add shallot and cook, stirring, for 2 to 3 minutes or until softened. Add garlic and cook, stirring, for 30 seconds or until fragrant. Add rice, stirring to coat with oil. Add wine and vinegar; cook, stirring constantly, for 30 seconds or until wine is absorbed. Cancel cooking.

2. Add stock, stirring well. Close and lock the lid. Cook on high pressure for 4 minutes. Quickly release the pressure.

3. Stir in peas, saffron, lemon juice and butter (if using). Heat the cooker on High/Sauté/Brown. Cook, stirring, for 3 to 4 minutes or until peas are warmed through and rice is done to your liking. If the rice gets too thick before the peas are done, stir in more stock, 1 tbsp (15 mL) at a time, until your desired consistency is reached and the peas are cooked through. Cancel cooking.

4. Stir in cheese until well combined. Season to taste with salt and pepper.

Root Beer Pulled Pork Sandwiches (page 93)

Hot and Tangy Barbecue Spareribs (page 96)

Toasty French Dip Sandwiches with Horseradish Crème (page 104)

Stuffed Bell Peppers (page 152)

Potatoes Stuffed with Lentil Chili (page 162)

Bulgur and Chickpea Salad with Lemon Dill Dressing (page 167)

Strawberry Mini Cheesecakes (page 190)

Chocolate, Peanut Butter and Marshmallow Brownies (page 192)

Portobello Mushroom Risotto

Risotto is one of my go-to side dishes for family and friends, for dinners ranging from casual to special-occasion. Pressure-cooking risotto is so much easier than simmering it on the stovetop and delivers consistently fabulous results. The mushrooms add a rich, earthy flavor to the creamy rice.

MAKES 6 SERVINGS

2 cups	finely chopped portobello mushroom caps (see tip)	500 mL
3 to 4 cups	salt-free chicken stock (page 207) or ready-to-use chicken broth	750 mL to 1 L
2 tbsp	virgin olive oil	30 mL
1	large onion, finely chopped	1
1	clove garlic, minced	1
2 cups	Arborio rice	500 mL
½ cup	dry red wine	125 mL
¼ cup	grated Parmigiano-Reggiano cheese	60 mL
2 tbsp	chopped fresh thyme	30 mL
1 tbsp	butter	15 mL
	Kosher salt and freshly ground black pepper	

TIPS

Before chopping the mushroom caps, remove the dark gills by using a spoon to gently scrape the gills out until you see the firm, white cap.

Using authentic, full-flavored Parmigiano-Reggiano creates a complex, yet subtle tango of flavors. If you can't find it, you can use regular Parmesan.

1. Place mushrooms in a 4-cup (1 L) measuring cup and add enough stock to measure 4 cups (1 L). Set aside.

2. Heat the pressure cooker on High/Sauté/Brown. Add oil and heat until shimmering. Add onion and cook, stirring, for 3 to 5 minutes or until translucent. Add garlic and cook, stirring, for 1 minute or until fragrant. Add rice, stirring to coat with oil. Add wine and cook, stirring constantly, for 30 seconds or until wine is evaporated. Cancel cooking.

3. Add mushroom mixture to the pot, stirring well. Close and lock the lid. Cook on high pressure for 4 minutes. Quickly release the pressure.

4. Stir in cheese, thyme and butter. Heat the cooker on High/Sauté/Brown. Cook, stirring, for 1 to 3 minutes or until rice is done to your liking. If the rice gets too thick, stir in more stock, 1 tbsp (15 mL) at a time, until your desired consistency is reached. Season to taste with salt and pepper.

Spoonbread with Maple Butter

Cornbread and cheese lovers rejoice! In this Southern-style side dish, cornmeal and Cheddar cheese unite for a delectably creamy delight you can dig right in to. If you've never had spoonbread before, you will be pleasantly surprised by this soufflé-like side dish. And spoonbread lovers will be charmed by the quick and easy recipe. This spoonbread is a fabulous side dish for barbecue ribs and pork roasts. Try it alongside Smoky Beef Brisket and Carrots (page 98) or Hot and Tangy Barbecue Spareribs (page 96).

MAKES 6 SERVINGS

- Steam rack
- 6-inch (15 cm) round springform pan (see tip), sprayed with nonstick cooking spray

Spoonbread

4	green onions, sliced	4
1 cup	all-purpose baking mix (such as Bisquick)	250 mL
⅔ cup	cornmeal	150 mL
2 tsp	granulated sugar	10 mL
1½ tsp	kosher salt	7 mL
1	large egg	1
2 cups	low-sodium chicken stock (page 206) or ready-to-use chicken broth	500 mL
1 cup	milk	250 mL
1 cup	shredded sharp (old) Cheddar cheese	250 mL
2 tbsp	butter, melted	30 mL

Maple Butter

½ cup	butter, softened	125 mL
2 tbsp	pure maple syrup	30 mL
⅛ tsp	ground cinnamon	0.5 mL

> **TIP**
>
> A 6-inch (15 cm) round metal baking pan can be used in place of the springform pan.

1. *Spoonbread:* Add 1 cup (250 mL) water (or the amount required by your cooker to reach pressure) to the pressure cooker and place the steam rack in the pot.

2. In a large bowl, combine green onions, baking mix, cornmeal, sugar, salt, egg, stock, milk, cheese and butter, mixing well. Pour into prepared springform pan. Place pan on the rack.

3. Close and lock the lid. Cook on high pressure for 18 minutes. Let stand, covered, for 10 minutes, then release any remaining pressure. Check to make sure the spoonbread is soft but not runny when tested with a spoon; if more cooking time is needed, reset to high pressure for 3 minutes.

4. Remove springform pan and rack from the cooker. Let pan stand on the rack for 5 minutes before serving.

5. *Maple Butter:* Meanwhile, in a small bowl, whip together butter, syrup and cinnamon. Serve with spoonbread.

VARIATION

Add ¾ cup (175 mL) creamed corn in step 2 and reduce the milk by ¼ cup (60 mL) for a richer corn texture and flavor.

Paleo Dishes

Butternut Squash Soup

This soup is the ideal comfort food for cool, crisp days. It is creamy, slightly sweet and has a deep, rich flavor from the seasonings. Need to warm up quickly? Then this is the soup for you.

- Immersion blender (see tip)

½ cup	raw green pumpkin seeds (pepitas)	125 mL
2 tbsp	lard or ghee (see tip, page 133)	30 mL
1	onion, chopped	1
4 lbs	butternut squash (about 1 medium), cut into cubes, divided	2 kg
1 tbsp	grated gingerroot	15 mL
¼ tsp	ground nutmeg	1 mL
1	sprig fresh sage	1
4 cups	low-sodium chicken stock (page 206) or ready-to-use chicken broth	1 L
	Kosher salt and freshly ground black pepper	

1. Heat the pressure cooker on High/Sauté/Brown. Add pumpkin seeds and cook, stirring, for 1 to 2 minutes or until lightly toasted and fragrant. Transfer seeds to a plate and set aside.

2. Add lard to the cooker and heat until melted. Add onion and cook, stirring often, for 3 to 5 minutes or until translucent. Add 2 cups (500 mL) squash, ginger, nutmeg and sage; cook, stirring occasionally, for 5 to 7 minutes or until squash is browned. Cancel cooking.

3. Add the remaining squash and stock, stirring well. Close and lock the lid. Cook on high pressure for 15 minutes. Quickly release the pressure. Check to make sure the squash is fork-tender; if more cooking time is needed, reset to high pressure for 3 minutes. Discard sage.

4. Using the immersion blender, blend soup until puréed (or to your desired consistency). Serve garnished with toasted pumpkin seeds.

TIPS

When purchasing ready-to-use chicken broth, check to make sure it is certified gluten-free or has been packaged in a facility where there is no gluten cross-contamination.

Instead of sautéing the squash cubes in step 2, you can roast them in a 350°F (180°C) oven for 20 to 30 minutes, turning occasionally, until browned.

In step 4, instead of using an immersion blender, you can transfer the soup, in batches, to a blender. After blending, return soup to the cooker to reheat as needed. Be very careful when transferring soup, as it is very hot. Do not fill your blender more than half full, to prevent hot soup from spewing out the top.

Italian Chicken and Vegetable Soup

This soup, often called Italian wedding soup, is the perfect marriage of delicate chicken meatballs and a savory combination of vegetables and greens.

MAKES 4 SERVINGS

1 lb	ground chicken	500 g
¼ cup	tapioca flour	60 mL
1 tsp	garlic powder	5 mL
1 tsp	kosher salt	5 mL
1	large egg	1
2 tbsp	coconut amino acids	30 mL
2 tbsp	ghee (see tip) or lard	30 mL
2	carrots, diced	2
1	onion, finely chopped	1
5 cups	low-sodium chicken stock (page 206) or ready-to-use chicken broth (see tip, page 132)	1.25 L
2 tsp	dried parsley	10 mL
1 tsp	garlic powder	5 mL
1 cup	packed spinach leaves, chopped	250 mL
	Nutritional yeast (optional)	

1. In a large bowl, combine chicken, tapioca flour, garlic powder, salt, egg and amino acids, mixing well. Using your hands or a small scoop, form mixture into 1½-inch (4 cm) balls.

2. Heat the pressure cooker on High/Sauté/Brown. Add ghee and heat until shimmering. Add carrots and onion; cook, stirring, for 3 to 5 minutes or until onion is translucent. Move vegetables to the edges of the pot. Working in batches, add meatballs to the center of the pot and cook, turning carefully, for 3 minutes or until lightly browned all over. Using tongs, transfer meatballs to a plate.

3. Add stock, parsley and garlic powder to the cooker and cook, scraping up any browned bits from the bottom of the pot. Cancel cooking.

4. Return meatballs and any accumulated juices to the cooker. Close and lock the lid. Cook on high pressure for 10 minutes. Quickly release the pressure. Check to make sure the meatballs are no longer pink inside; if more cooking time is needed, reset to high pressure for 3 minutes.

5. Add spinach, stirring until wilted. Spoon into individual serving bowls. Serve garnished with nutritional yeast, if desired.

TIPS

Ghee is a type of clarified butter with a nutty flavor. It contains virtually no lactose or milk proteins, so it doesn't cause the inflammation, sensitivities and intolerances that dairy products can. It is considered a healthy oil and has a high smoke point, so it is generally accepted in the paleo diet.

If you prefer your meatballs browner and crispier on the outside, you can bake them on a rimmed baking sheet lined with parchment paper in a 350°F (180°C) oven for 10 to 15 minutes, until browned as desired, instead of frying them in step 2.

Chicken and Sausage Gumbo

This spicy soup certainly packs a hearty punch: it is loaded with vegetables, chicken and andouille sausage for a delectable, full-bodied meal.

3 tbsp	virgin coconut oil (see tip), divided	45 mL
1 lb	boneless skinless chicken thighs, cut into cubes	500 g
1 lb	andouille sausage, thinly sliced diagonally	500 g
2	green bell peppers, finely chopped	2
2	carrots, chopped	2
2	stalks celery, chopped	2
1	white onion, halved and sliced	1
4	cloves garlic, minced	4
6	tomatoes, chopped	6
1	bay leaf	1
1/4 cup	finely chopped fresh parsley	60 mL
1 tsp	dried thyme	5 mL
1 tsp	paprika	5 mL
1/8 tsp	cayenne pepper	0.5 mL
2 cups	low-sodium chicken stock (page 206) or ready-to-use chicken broth	500 mL
	Kosher salt and freshly ground black pepper	
	Hot pepper flakes (optional)	

1. Heat the pressure cooker on High/ Sauté/Brown. Add 1 tbsp (15 mL) coconut oil and heat until melted. Working in batches, add chicken and sausage; cook, stirring, for 5 to 7 minutes or until browned all over, adding more coconut oil as needed between batches. Using a slotted spoon, transfer chicken and sausage to a platter.

2. Add any remaining coconut oil to the cooker and heat until melted. Add green peppers, carrots, celery and onion; cook, stirring often, for 3 to 5 minutes or until onion is translucent. Add garlic and cook, stirring, for 1 minute or until fragrant. Cancel cooking.

3. Return chicken, sausage and any accumulated juices to the cooker. Add tomatoes, bay leaf, parsley, thyme, paprika, cayenne and stock, stirring well. Close and lock the lid. Cook on high pressure for 7 minutes. Quickly release the pressure. Check to make sure the juices run clear when chicken is pierced; if more cooking time is needed, reset to high pressure for 2 minutes. Discard bay leaf. Season to taste with salt and black pepper. Serve garnished with hot pepper flakes, if desired.

TIPS

Coconut oil is considered a healthy oil and as such is generally accepted in the paleo diet.

Check to be sure that the sausage you buy is certified gluten-free or has been packaged in a facility where there is no gluten cross-contamination.

You can use two 28-oz (796 mL) cans of tomatoes instead of the fresh tomatoes.

When purchasing ready-to-use chicken broth, check to make sure it is certified gluten-free or has been packaged in a facility where there is no gluten cross-contamination.

Zuppa Toscana

Now you can make this classic Italian soup in the comfort of your own home, quickly and easily. Serve with a salad and get ready to please the whole family.

1 tbsp	virgin olive oil (see tip, page 136)	15 mL
1 lb	Italian pork or chicken sausage (bulk or casings removed)	500 g
2	large russet potatoes (see tip), cut into 1-inch (2.5 cm) cubes	2
2	cloves garlic, minced	2
1	large onion, chopped	1
4 cups	water	1 L
2 cups	low-sodium chicken stock (page 206) or ready-to-use chicken broth	500 mL
2 cups	chopped trimmed Swiss chard	500 mL
1 cup	coconut milk	250 mL
	Hot pepper flakes	
4	slices bacon, cooked crisp and crumbled	4

1. Heat the pressure cooker on High/Sauté/Brown. Add oil and heat until shimmering. Add sausage and cook, breaking it up with a spoon, for 5 to 7 minutes or until no longer pink. Cancel cooking.

2. Add potatoes, garlic, onion, water and stock, stirring well. Close and lock the lid. Cook on high pressure for 12 minutes. Quickly release the pressure. Check to make sure the potatoes are fork-tender; if more cooking time is needed, reset to high pressure for 2 minutes.

3. Stir in Swiss chard. Close the lid and let stand for 5 minutes. Gently stir in coconut milk. Season to taste with hot pepper flakes.

4. Ladle soup into serving bowls and serve garnished with bacon.

TIPS

Check to be sure that the sausage you buy is certified gluten-free or has been packaged in a facility where there is no gluten cross-contamination.

You can use gluten-free sausage in casings and remove the casings before cooking. Check the packaging to make sure there are no added ingredients that are not paleo-friendly.

Potatoes are often excluded from paleo-approved food lists because of their high carbohydrate and starch content. If you experience blood sugar spikes or have an autoimmune disorder, you may want to skip this recipe.

When purchasing ready-to-use chicken broth, check to make sure it is certified gluten-free or has been packaged in a facility where there is no gluten cross-contamination.

If you like your soup a little creamier, you can mash the potatoes before adding the Swiss chard.

If you like your soup spicier, you can add a pinch of hot pepper flakes with the stock in step 2. This soup will get spicier as it cooks under pressure, so add hot pepper flakes in small amounts to begin with.

Beef Bourguignon

This classic French comfort food dish remains a time-tested favorite, and now you can skip the typically long, slow simmering time without relinquishing any of the rich and hearty flavor.

MAKES 4 SERVINGS

2 tbsp	virgin olive oil (approx.)	30 mL
1 lb	beef flank steak, cut into 2-inch (5 cm) cubes	500 g
8 oz	bacon, cut into ¾-inch (2 cm) pieces	250 g
8 oz	pearl onions (1½ inches/4 cm in diameter)	250 g
5	carrots, chopped	5
2	cloves garlic, minced	2
8 oz	sliced mushrooms	250 g
2 tbsp	fresh parsley leaves, chopped	30 mL
1 tbsp	fresh thyme leaves	15 mL
1 tsp	kosher salt	5 mL
1 cup	dry red wine (such as Pinot Noir)	250 mL
½ cup	low-sodium beef bone broth (page 208) or ready-to-use beef broth	125 mL
1 tbsp	pure maple syrup	15 mL

1. Heat the pressure cooker on High/Sauté/Brown. Add 1 tbsp (15 mL) oil and heat until shimmering. Working in batches, add beef and cook, turning often, for 5 to 7 minutes or until browned all over, adding more oil as needed between batches. Using a slotted spoon, transfer beef to a plate.

2. Add bacon, onions and carrots to the cooker and cook, stirring often, for 5 minutes or until bacon fat is rendered and onion is translucent. Add garlic and cook, stirring, for 1 minute or until fragrant. Cancel cooking.

3. Return beef and any accumulated juices to the cooker. Add mushrooms, parsley, thyme, salt, wine, broth and maple syrup, stirring well. Close and lock the lid. Cook on high pressure for 25 minutes. Quickly release the pressure. Check to make sure the beef is fork-tender; if more cooking time is needed, reset to high pressure for 5 minutes. Stir and spoon into individual serving bowls.

TIPS

Virgin olive oil is considered a healthy oil and is not inflammatory, so it is generally accepted in the paleo diet.

When purchasing ready-to-use beef broth, check to make sure it is certified gluten-free or has been packaged in a facility where there is no gluten cross-contamination.

Spicy Mexican Beef Stew

If you love all things spicy, this stew will become your new comfort food favorite. Hearty chunks of beef are seasoned with chili powder, chipotle peppers and salsa for an elevation of flavor.

MAKES 6 SERVINGS

2½ lbs	boneless beef chuck roast, cut into cubes	1.25 kg
1 tbsp	chili powder	15 mL
	Kosher salt	
2 tbsp	lard or ghee (see tip, page 133)	30 mL
1	onion, thinly sliced	1
6	cloves garlic, minced	6
1 tbsp	tomato paste	15 mL
1	chipotle pepper, minced, with 1 tbsp (15 mL) adobo sauce	1
½ cup	low-sodium beef bone broth (page 208) or ready-to-use beef broth	125 mL
½ cup	tomato salsa	125 mL
	Freshly ground black pepper	
½ cup	minced fresh cilantro	125 mL
2	radishes, thinly sliced	2

1. In a large bowl, combine beef, chili powder and 2 tsp (10 mL) salt.

2. Heat the pressure cooker on High/Sauté/Brown. Add 1 tbsp (15 mL) lard and heat until melted. Working in batches, add beef and cook, stirring occasionally, for 5 minutes or until browned on all sides, adding more lard as needed between batches. Using a slotted spoon, transfer beef to a plate.

3. Add any remaining lard to the cooker and heat until melted. Add onion and cook, stirring often, for 3 to 5 minutes or until translucent. Add garlic and cook, stirring, for 1 minute or until fragrant. Stir in tomato paste. Cancel cooking.

4. Return beef and any accumulated juices to the cooker. Add chipotle with adobo sauce, broth and salsa, stirring well. Close and lock the lid. Cook on high pressure for 30 minutes. Let stand, covered, until the float valve drops down. Check to make sure the beef is fork-tender; if more cooking time is needed, reset to high pressure for 5 minutes. Season to taste with salt and pepper. Serve garnished with cilantro and radishes.

TIPS

When purchasing ready-to-use beef broth, check to make sure it is certified gluten-free or has been packaged in a facility where there is no gluten cross-contamination.

This recipe has about 1¼ cups (300 mL) liquid. If your cooker requires more than this amount to reach pressure, you may want to skip this recipe. Alternatively, you can add more broth as needed and then, before serving, combine 1 tbsp (15 mL) arrowroot flour and 1 tbsp (15 mL) cold water, stir the mixture into the stew and cook on High/Sauté/Brown until thickened to your desired consistency. If you have difficulty digesting starch, do not thicken the stew.

This stew can be refrigerated for up to 3 days or frozen for up to 3 months. Reheat and garnish with cilantro and radishes just before serving.

Hearty Meat Ragù and Spaghetti Squash

This simple one-pot ragù is so satisfying. The sauce cooks in the bottom of the pot while the squash rests on top — a quick and easy preparation, and even easier cleanup.

1 tbsp	lard or ghee (see tip, page 133)	15 mL
1 lb	lean ground beef	500 g
3	cloves garlic, minced	3
1	onion, chopped	1
1	carrot, chopped	1
1	stalk celery, chopped	1
1	can (28 oz/796 mL) crushed tomatoes	1
1	bay leaf	1
	Kosher salt and freshly ground black pepper	
4 lbs	spaghetti squash (1 large or 2 medium)	2 kg
	Paleo Parmesan (see tips; optional)	

TIPS

Here's how to make ⅓ cup (75 mL) Paleo Parmesan, a replacement for Parmesan cheese: In a food processor, combine ⅓ cup (75 mL) raw almonds, 1 tbsp (15 mL) nutritional yeast and a pinch of kosher salt; process until fluffy and no chunks remain. Leftover Paleo Parmesan can be stored in an airtight container in the refrigerator for up to 1 week. Fluff with a fork before using, if necessary.

Instead of the Paleo Parmesan, you can sprinkle the ragù with nutritional yeast, if desired.

1. Heat the pressure cooker on High/Sauté/Brown. Add butter and heat until melted. Add beef, garlic, onion, carrot and celery; cook, stirring and breaking up beef, for 5 to 7 minutes or until beef is no longer pink and vegetables are softened. Stir in tomatoes and bay leaf. Cancel cooking.

2. Using a knife, pierce squash all over. Place squash on top of sauce. Close and lock the lid. Cook on high pressure for 12 minutes. Quickly release the pressure. Check to make sure the skin of the squash gives easily when pressed with a spoon; if more cooking time is needed, reset to high pressure for 3 minutes. Discard bay leaf.

3. Transfer squash to a cutting board and let stand until cool enough to handle. Cut squash in half and remove and discard seeds. Scoop out strands of squash with a fork and transfer to serving bowls.

4. Season sauce to taste with salt and pepper. Spoon sauce over squash strands. Serve sprinkled with Paleo Parmesan, if desired.

Thai Beef Curry

In this recipe, bell peppers, mushrooms and broccoli are wrapped in foil and then cooked on top of the spirited curried beef, for a delicious one-pot meal that preserves the individual flavors and textures.

MAKES 4 SERVINGS

- 2 sheets of heavy-duty foil

1	red bell pepper, sliced	1
8 oz	sliced mushrooms	250 g
2 cups	broccoli florets	500 mL
2 tbsp	virgin coconut oil (see tip, page 134), divided	30 mL
1½ lbs	beef brisket, cut into 1½-inch (4 cm) cubes	750 g
	Kosher salt	
1	onion, finely chopped	1
3	cloves garlic, minced	3
2 tsp	grated gingerroot	10 mL
2 tbsp	Thai red curry paste	30 mL
1 tbsp	coconut amino acids	15 mL
1 tsp	fish sauce	5 mL
1 cup	low-sodium beef bone broth (page 208) or ready-to-use beef broth (see tip, page 137)	250 mL
1	can (14 oz/400 mL) coconut milk	1
2	green onions, sliced diagonally	2

1. Arrange red pepper, mushrooms and broccoli on prepared foil sheets, dividing evenly. Drizzle with 1 tbsp (15 mL) oil. Fold foil into tent-style packets and seal edges tightly (see illustration, page 99). Set aside.

2. Season beef with salt. Heat the pressure cooker on High/Sauté/Brown. Add the remaining oil and heat until shimmering. Working in batches, add beef and cook, stirring, for 3 to 5 minutes or until browned on all sides. Using a slotted spoon, transfer beef to a plate.

3. Add onion to the cooker and cook, stirring often, for 3 to 5 minutes or until translucent. Add garlic and ginger; cook, stirring, for 1 minute or until fragrant. Stir in curry paste, amino acids and fish sauce. Add broth and cook, stirring and scraping up any browned bits from the bottom of the pot, for 2 minutes. Cancel cooking.

4. Return beef and any accumulated juices to the cooker, stirring well. Close and lock the lid. Cook on high pressure for 20 minutes. Quickly release the pressure.

5. Place vegetable packets on top of beef mixture. Close and lock the lid. Cook on high pressure for 15 minutes. Quickly release the pressure. Open a packet and check to make sure the broccoli is tender; if more cooking time is needed, reseal packet and reset to high pressure for 3 minutes. Carefully remove packets and check to make sure the beef is fork-tender; if more cooking time is needed, set packets aside and reset the cooker to high pressure for 3 minutes.

6. Heat the cooker on High/Sauté/Brown. Add coconut milk and cook, stirring, for 5 minutes or until sauce thickens to your liking. Stir in vegetables from foil packets. Serve garnished with green onions.

TIP

This recipe has about 1¼ cups (300 mL) liquid. If your cooker requires more than this amount to reach pressure, you may want to skip this recipe.

Lemon Garlic Chicken

Lemon juice and garlic pair up to give chicken thighs and legs a lively, mouthwatering taste. If you get bored of eating the same old chicken, this recipe is an exciting alternative.

1 tbsp	lard or ghee (see tip, page 133)	15 mL
1	onion, finely chopped	1
1/4 cup	dry white wine	60 mL
4	cloves garlic, minced	4
1 tsp	dried parsley	5 mL
1 tsp	kosher salt	5 mL
1/2 tsp	paprika	2 mL
1/2 cup	low-sodium chicken stock (page 206) or ready-to-use chicken broth	125 mL
3 tbsp	freshly squeezed lemon juice	45 mL
4	bone-in chicken legs (about 1 lb/500 g total)	4
4	bone-in skin-on chicken thighs (about 1 1/2 lbs/750 g total)	4
1 tbsp	arrowroot flour (see tip, page 143)	15 mL

1. Heat the pressure cooker on High/Sauté/Brown. Add lard and heat until melted. Add onion and cook, stirring often, for 3 to 5 minutes or until translucent. Add wine, scraping up any browned bits from the bottom of the pot. Cancel cooking.

2. Add garlic, parsley, salt, paprika, stock and lemon juice, stirring well. Arrange chicken legs and thighs on top, skin side up. Close and lock the lid. Cook on high pressure for 15 minutes. Quickly release the pressure. Check to make sure an instant-read thermometer inserted in the center of a thigh registers 165°F (74°C); if more cooking time is needed, reset to high pressure for 3 minutes. Using tongs, transfer chicken to a serving platter and keep warm.

3. Heat the cooker on High/Sauté/Brown. Spoon out 1/4 cup (60 mL) liquid into a small bowl. Stir in arrowroot. Return mixture to the cooker and cook, stirring, until sauce is thickened to your liking. Spoon sauce over chicken and serve immediately.

TIPS

When purchasing ready-to-use chicken broth, check to make sure it is certified gluten-free or has been packaged in a facility where there is no gluten cross-contamination.

One large lemon will yield about 3 tbsp (45 mL) juice.

The chicken will release some liquid into the pot as it cooks, but if your cooker requires more than 1 1/2 cups (375 mL) liquid to reach pressure, add water or more stock as needed in step 2.

For an appealing garnish, thinly slice a lemon and arrange the slices around the chicken.

Chicken Parmigiana

If you want the fussy eaters in your house to be smiling at dinner, you owe it to yourself to try this Italian comfort food. Since it's so quick and easy, you have nothing to lose and likely a new family favorite as your win.

MAKES 4 SERVINGS

Chicken

1½ cups	almond flour	375 mL
2 tsp	onion powder	10 mL
2 tsp	garlic powder	10 mL
2 tsp	dried oregano	10 mL
2	large eggs	2
8	boneless skinless chicken thighs (about 1½ lbs/750 g total)	8
3 tbsp	ghee (see tip, page 133)	45 mL
1	sprig fresh basil	1
	Nutritional yeast (optional)	

Sauce

2 tbsp	virgin olive oil (see tip)	30 mL
7	cloves garlic, slivered	7
1	can (28 oz/796 mL) crushed tomatoes	1
1 cup	water (see tip)	250 mL
1 tsp	kosher salt	5 mL
¼ tsp	dried oregano	1 mL
Pinch	hot pepper flakes	Pinch

TIPS

Virgin olive oil is considered a healthy oil and is not inflammatory, so it is generally accepted in the paleo diet.

For the sauce, add the water to the empty can and swirl it around to get all the last good pieces of crushed tomatoes out. Then pour into the cooker.

1. *Chicken:* In a medium bowl, combine flour, onion powder, garlic powder and oregano. In a separate bowl, whisk eggs. Dredge chicken first in flour mixture, then in egg and then in flour again, shaking off any excess flour. Discard any excess flour mixture and egg.

2. Heat the pressure cooker on High/Sauté/Brown. Add ghee and heat until shimmering. Working in batches, add dredged chicken and cook, turning once, for 4 to 6 minutes or until browned on both sides. Using tongs, transfer chicken to a plate.

3. *Sauce:* Add oil to the cooker and heat, scraping up any browned bits from the bottom of the pot, until shimmering. Add garlic and cook, stirring, for 1 minute or until fragrant. Stir in tomatoes, water, salt, oregano and hot pepper flakes. Cancel cooking.

4. Arrange chicken in sauce. Place basil sprig on top. Close and lock the lid. Cook on high pressure for 5 minutes. Quickly release the pressure. Check to make sure an instant-read thermometer inserted in the center of a thigh registers 165°F (74°C); if more cooking time is needed, reset to high pressure for 1 minute. Discard basil.

5. Transfer chicken to individual serving plates, spoon sauce on top and serve garnished with nutritional yeast, if desired.

Hungarian Chicken Paprikash

This dish is Old World comfort food at its best. Make it on cold winter evenings when you want a hearty, satisfying chicken dish that is bursting with umami.

Paleo Sour Cream

1	can (14 oz/400 mL) coconut milk, refrigerated for 8 hours or more	1
1 tbsp	freshly squeezed lemon juice (or to taste)	15 mL
⅛ tsp	kosher salt (or to taste)	0.5 mL

Chicken Paprikash

2	cloves garlic, minced	2
2 tbsp	coconut flour	30 mL
1 tbsp	fresh thyme leaves	15 mL
1 tbsp	Hungarian paprika	15 mL
1 cup	low-sodium chicken stock or ready-to-use chicken broth	250 mL
1 tbsp	tomato paste	15 mL
2 tsp	Sriracha	10 mL
4	bone-in skin-on chicken breasts (about 3 lbs/1.5 kg total)	4
1	onion, chopped	1

1. *Paleo Sour Cream:* Open the can of coconut milk and spoon the congealed cream from the top of the can into a small bowl. (Save the coconut milk for use in another recipe; see tip.) Stir in lemon juice and salt until smooth. Taste and adjust lemon juice and salt as desired. Let stand at room temperature.

2. *Chicken Paprikash:* In the pressure cooker, combine garlic, coconut flour, thyme, paprika, stock, tomato paste and Sriracha. Arrange chicken on top. Sprinkle with onion. Close and lock the lid. Cook on high pressure for 12 minutes. Let stand, covered, for 10 minutes, then release any remaining pressure. Check to make sure an instant-read thermometer inserted in the center of a breast registers 165°F (74°C); if more cooking time is needed, reset to high pressure for 2 minutes. Using tongs, transfer chicken to a serving platter and keep warm.

3. Stir paleo sour cream into juices in pot until combined. Spoon sauce over chicken.

TIPS

Hungary produces some of the finest paprika in the world. It is classified into grades based on the quality of the peppers and the thoroughness of the grinding process.

When purchasing ready-to-use chicken broth, check to make sure it is certified gluten-free or has been packaged in a facility where there is no gluten cross-contamination.

After removing the cream from the can of coconut milk, pour the coconut milk into an airtight container and refrigerate for up to 5 days.

The chicken will release some liquid into the pot as it cooks, but if your cooker requires more than 1½ cups (375 mL) liquid to reach pressure, add water or more stock as needed in step 2. In step 3, discard all but 1½ cups (375 mL) liquid before stirring in the sour cream.

Buffalo Chicken and Sweet Potatoes

These fiery chicken breasts are tender, juicy and oozing with flavor. Paired with sweet potatoes, they make a delightful one-pot meal.

MAKES 4 SERVINGS

3 tbsp	ghee (see tip, page 133)	45 mL
1	onion, finely chopped	1
1 lb	sweet potatoes, peeled and diced	500 g
1 tsp	onion powder	5 mL
1 tsp	garlic powder	5 mL
¼ cup	water	60 mL
3 tbsp	Buffalo wing sauce	45 mL
4	boneless skinless chicken breasts (each about 6 oz/175 g)	4
	Kosher salt and freshly ground black pepper	
1 tbsp	arrowroot flour (see tip)	15 mL

TIPS

Arrowroot is a starch that has some acceptance in the paleo community if used in small amounts by individuals who can tolerate it. I have used it here to help the sauce coat the chicken and to thicken the sauce. While it adds to the finished recipe, you can omit it.

This recipe is recommended for 6-quart (6 L) or smaller pressure cookers.

While it may seem like there is not enough liquid in this recipe for the cooker to reach pressure, the chicken will release enough water to make up the difference. If your cooker does not come up to pressure, add more water. You may need more arrowroot flour to thicken the sauce.

1. Heat the pressure cooker on High/Sauté/Brown. Add ghee and heat until melted. Add onion and cook, stirring often, for 3 to 5 minutes or until translucent. Cancel cooking.

2. Add sweet potatoes, onion powder, garlic powder, water and wing sauce, stirring well. Add chicken, turning to coat in sauce; season with salt and pepper. Close and lock the lid. Cook on high pressure for 15 minutes. Quickly release the pressure. Check to make sure an instant-read thermometer inserted in the center of a breast registers 165°F (74°C); if more cooking time is needed, reset to high pressure for 3 minutes. Transfer chicken and sweet potatoes to a serving platter and keep warm.

3. Heat the cooker on High/Sauté/Brown. Spoon out ¼ cup (60 mL) liquid into a small bowl. Stir in arrowroot. Return mixture to the cooker and cook, stirring, for 2 minutes or until sauce is thickened to your liking. Drizzle chicken with sauce. Serve warm.

Mediterranean Chicken Breast Rollups

Stuffed with roasted red peppers and kalamata olives, and bursting with Mediterranean seasonings, these delicate chicken rollups are sure to delight both family and guests. Serve with a side of couscous and a zesty salad for a full Mediterranean meal.

MAKES 4 SERVINGS

- Wooden toothpicks

1 tbsp	dried basil	15 mL
1 tbsp	dried oregano	15 mL
1 tbsp	dried parsley	15 mL
1 tsp	dried thyme	5 mL
1 tsp	dried rosemary	5 mL
1 tsp	garlic powder	5 mL
1 tsp	onion powder	5 mL
4	boneless skinless chicken breasts (about 2 lbs/1 kg total), pounded to ½ inch (1 cm) thick	4
	Kosher salt and freshly ground black pepper	
½ cup	sliced drained roasted red bell peppers	125 mL
¼ cup	chopped drained kalamata olives	60 mL
1 tbsp	virgin olive oil (see tip)	15 mL
1 cup	low-sodium chicken stock (page 206) or ready-to-use chicken broth (see tip, page 142)	250 mL
½ cup	Cashew Feta (see tip; optional)	125 mL

1. In a small bowl, combine basil, oregano, parsley, thyme, rosemary, garlic powder and onion powder. Season chicken on both sides with seasoning mix, salt and pepper.

2. In the same bowl, combine roasted peppers and olives. Arrange mixture in the center of each breast, dividing evenly. Roll breasts up and secure each rollup with a toothpick.

3. Heat the pressure cooker on High/Sauté/Brown. Add oil and heat until shimmering. Add rollups and cook, turning occasionally, for 4 minutes or until lightly browned on all sides. Cancel cooking.

4. Add stock, without stirring. Close and lock the lid. Cook on high pressure for 7 minutes. Quickly release the pressure. Check to make sure the chicken is no longer pink inside; if more cooking time is needed, reset to high pressure for 1 minute.

5. Transfer chicken rollups to a serving platter; discard stock. Serve chicken sprinkled with cashew feta, if desired.

TIPS

Virgin olive oil is considered a healthy oil and is not inflammatory, so it is generally accepted in the paleo diet.

Add more stock if required by your cooker to reach pressure.

Cashew Feta: In a small food processor, combine ½ cup (125 mL) raw cashews, 1 tbsp (15 mL) extra virgin olive oil and 1½ tsp (7 mL) dried oregano; process to a consistency similar to that of crumbled feta cheese.

Island Kalua Pork

This simple pork dish is reminiscent of the popular roasted pork served at a Hawaiian luau. The smoked bacon adds a roasted flavor, and pressure cooking makes this dish fall-apart tender.

MAKES 8 SERVINGS		
3 lb	boneless pork shoulder blade roast, trimmed	1.5 kg
3	cloves garlic, peeled	3
1 tbsp	kosher salt	15 mL
3	slices bacon	3
	Water	
1	green or red cabbage, cored and cut into 6 wedges	1

TIPS

Serve this dish all by itself or over rice.

You can omit the cabbage and skip step 4. Shred the pork and chop the bacon as directed, then serve the pork and bacon in corn tortillas or wrapped in lettuce leaves, with your choice of toppings.

The shredded pork and chopped bacon can be refrigerated in an airtight container for up to 5 days or frozen for up to 3 months. Reheat in a medium saucepan over medium heat, stirring occasionally, until warmed through.

1. Cut pork into 3 even pieces. Cut a slit in each of the pieces and insert a garlic clove in each slit. Season pork with salt.

2. Heat the pressure cooker on High/Sauté/Brown. Add bacon and cook, turning once, for 5 minutes or until slightly crispy. Cancel cooking.

3. Place pork on top of bacon. Add 1 cup (250 mL) water (or the amount required by your cooker to reach pressure). Close and lock the lid. Cook on high pressure for 65 minutes. Let stand, covered, until the float valve drops down. Check to make sure an instant-read thermometer inserted in the thickest part of a pork piece registers 165°F (74°C) for medium-well; if more cooking time is needed, reset to high pressure for 10 minutes. Transfer pork and bacon to a cutting board.

4. Add cabbage to the liquid in the cooker. Close and lock the lid. Cook on high pressure for 5 minutes. Quickly release the pressure. Check to make sure the cabbage is tender and wilted; if more cooking time is needed, reset to high pressure for 1 minute.

5. Meanwhile, using two forks, shred pork, discarding any fat. Chop bacon. Transfer pork to individual serving bowls and top with cabbage and bacon. Serve immediately.

Chipotle Pineapple Pork

This pulled pork is sweet, sassy, entirely heavenly and so versatile that I make a large batch ahead of time so I can have it ready for various meal options during the week — and can still freeze some for later.

MAKES 10 SERVINGS

2½ lb	boneless pork shoulder blade roast, trimmed	1.25 kg
	Kosher salt and freshly ground black pepper	
1 tbsp	virgin olive oil (see tip, page 144)	15 mL
6	cloves garlic, slivered	6
1 tsp	ground cumin	5 mL
1 tsp	ground coriander	5 mL
1 tsp	ground turmeric	5 mL
1 tsp	garlic powder	5 mL
½ tsp	dried oregano	2 mL
¾ cup	low-sodium chicken stock (page 206) or ready-to-use chicken broth (see tip, page 142)	175 mL
1	can (8 oz/227 mL) crushed pineapple in juice	1
2	chipotle peppers, minced, in 1 tbsp (15 mL) adobo sauce	2
2	bay leaves	2
	Chipotle chile powder (optional)	

1. Season pork with salt and pepper. Heat the pressure cooker on High/Sauté/Brown. Add oil and heat until shimmering. Add pork and cook, turning often, for 7 to 9 minutes or until browned on all sides. Cancel cooking.

2. Transfer pork to a cutting board and let stand until cool enough to handle. Cut 1-inch (2.5 cm) slits all over the roast and insert garlic slivers in the slits.

3. In a small bowl, combine cumin, coriander, turmeric, garlic powder and oregano. Rub mixture all over pork.

4. Add stock, pineapple, chipotles and bay leaves to the cooker, stirring well. Place pork on top. Close and lock the lid. Cook on high pressure for 55 minutes. Let stand, covered, for 10 minutes, then release any remaining pressure. Check to make sure an instant-read thermometer inserted in the thickest part of a pork piece registers 165°F (74°C) for medium-well; if more cooking time is needed, reset to high pressure for 10 minutes. Discard bay leaves.

5. Transfer pork to a cutting board. Using two forks, shred pork, discarding any fat. Return pork to the cooker, stirring well. Season to taste with chipotle powder (if using).

TIPS

If you want to use chipotle chile powder, you can find it in the spice section of well-stocked grocery stores. This spice adds a smoky, light, peppery taste that is wonderful in many dishes. I also use it as a backup in case I run out of the chipotle peppers in adobo sauce.

Serve pork in lettuce wraps, make tacos with corn tortillas or add pork on top of salads.

Pulled pork can be refrigerated for up to 3 days or frozen for up to 3 months. Reheat in a medium saucepan over medium heat, stirring occasionally, until warmed through.

Spicy Coffee and Cocoa-Rubbed Beef Roast

Savory, spicy and with a bit of sweetness, this melt-in-your-mouth beef roast is a memorable dish with remarkable depth of flavor.

MAKES 4 SERVINGS

- Blender

1 tbsp	finely ground coffee	15 mL
1 tbsp	paprika	15 mL
1 tbsp	unsweetened cocoa powder	15 mL
1 tsp	hot pepper flakes	5 mL
1 tsp	chili powder	5 mL
½ tsp	ground ginger	2 mL
	Kosher salt and freshly ground black pepper	
2½ lb	boneless beef chuck roast (less than 8 inches/20 cm in diameter)	1.25 kg
6	dried figs, peeled	6
2	onions, cut into wedges, divided	2
2 cups	low-sodium beef bone broth (page 208) or ready-to-use beef broth	500 mL
3 tbsp	balsamic vinegar (see tip)	45 mL

1. In a large bowl, combine coffee, paprika, cocoa, hot pepper flakes, chili powder, ginger, 2 tsp (10 mL) salt and ½ tsp (2 mL) black pepper, mixing well. Rub mixture all over beef. Cover with plastic wrap and let stand for 30 minutes.

2. In blender, combine figs, half the onions, broth and vinegar; purée until smooth.

3. Place beef in the pressure cooker and arrange the remaining onions on top. Pour in purée. Close and lock the lid. Cook on high pressure for 55 minutes. Let stand, covered, until the float valve drops down. Check to make sure the beef is fork-tender; if more cooking time is needed, reset to high pressure for 10 minutes. Transfer roast to a cutting board, cover with foil and let stand for 5 minutes.

4. Slice roast across the grain and transfer to a serving platter. Season broth to taste with salt and pepper. Drizzle some sauce over beef and spoon the remainder into a gravy boat for serving.

TIPS

When purchasing ready-to-use beef broth, check to make sure it is certified gluten-free or has been packaged in a facility where there is no gluten cross-contamination.

Vinegar contains a very small amount of acetic acid, which can contribute to the net acid load in your diet; however, if you consume roughly one-third of your diet as vegetables and fruits, a little acid every once in a while should not be problematic.

If desired, you can shred the beef and serve it over rice or on corn tortillas. In step 3, cook on high pressure for 65 minutes. Check to make sure the beef is easily shredded with a fork.

Maple Mustard Brisket

Even the staunchest of barbecue brisket connoisseurs will find this version satisfying, tender and packed with flavor.

- 13- by 9-inch (33 by 23 cm) baking dish
- Rimmed baking sheet

1 tbsp	paprika	15 mL
1 tbsp	dry mustard	15 mL
1 tsp	chili powder	5 mL
3 tbsp	Worcestershire sauce	45 mL
	Lard or ghee (see tip, page 133)	
4 lb	piece beef brisket (see tip), cut into quarters	2 kg
2 tsp	kosher salt	10 mL
1	onion, finely chopped	1
5	cloves garlic, sliced	5
1 cup	low-sodium beef bone broth (page 208) or ready-to-use beef broth (see tip, page 149)	250 mL
1 cup	barbecue sauce	250 mL
¼ cup	pure maple syrup	60 mL

1. In baking dish, combine paprika, mustard, chili powder, Worcestershire sauce and 2 tbsp (30 mL) lard. Add brisket and turn to coat. Cover dish with plastic wrap and let stand for 30 minutes.

2. Remove brisket from marinade, discarding marinade, and season with salt. Heat the pressure cooker on High/Sauté/Brown. Add 1 tbsp (15 mL) lard and heat until melted. Working in batches, add brisket and cook, turning often, for 3 to 5 minutes or until browned on all sides, adding more lard as needed between batches. Transfer brisket to baking sheet.

3. Add onion to the cooker and cook, stirring, for 3 to 5 minutes or until translucent. Add garlic and cook, stirring, for 1 minute or until fragrant. Cancel cooking.

4. Add broth, barbecue sauce and maple syrup, stirring well. Return brisket and any accumulated juices to the cooker. Close and lock the lid. Cook on high pressure for 90 minutes. Quickly release the pressure. Check to make sure the beef is fork-tender; if more cooking time is needed, reset to high pressure for 15 minutes. Transfer brisket to a cutting board and let cool slightly, then thinly slice across the grain.

5. Heat the cooker on High/Sauté/Brown. Return brisket slices and any accumulated juices to the cooker. Simmer, uncovered, for 15 to 20 minutes or until brisket is done to your liking. Serve immediately.

TIPS

Your brisket should be "boneless," with deckle off. This cut of brisket is often called "cut 120." It has bones 1 to 4 removed and the hard fat, known as deckle, trimmed off.

This recipe is best suited for 6-quart (6 L) or larger pressure cookers.

This recipe has about 2½ cups (625 mL) liquid. If your cooker requires more liquid to reach pressure, add as much water in step 4 as is required.

Mongolian Beef

This takeout favorite is easy to make at home in your pressure cooker, with fresh, quality ingredients — and you don't have to leave the house or wait for delivery.

MAKES 6 SERVINGS

2 lbs	beef flank steak, cut into ½-inch (1 cm) strips	1 kg
	Kosher salt and freshly ground black pepper	
2 tbsp	virgin coconut oil (see tip)	30 mL
4	cloves garlic, minced	4
4	dates, chopped	4
2 tsp	minced gingerroot	10 mL
¾ cup	low-sodium beef bone broth (page 208) or ready-to-use beef broth	175 mL
⅓ cup	pure maple syrup	75 mL
⅓ cup	coconut amino acids	75 mL
1 tbsp	arrowroot flour (see tip)	15 mL
3 tbsp	water	45 mL
3	green onions, cut into 1-inch (2.5 cm) pieces	3

1. Season beef with salt and pepper. Heat the pressure cooker on High/Sauté/Brown. Add oil and heat until shimmering. Working in batches, add beef and cook, turning occasionally, for 3 to 5 minutes or until browned on all sides. Using a slotted spoon, transfer beef to a plate.

2. Add garlic to the cooker and cook, stirring, for 1 minute or until fragrant. Cancel cooking.

3. Return beef and any accumulated juices to the cooker. Add dates, ginger, broth, maple syrup and amino acids, stirring well. Close and lock the lid. Cook on high pressure for 12 minutes. Check to make sure the beef is fork-tender; if more cooking time is needed, reset to high pressure for 3 minutes. Quickly release the pressure.

4. In a small bowl, whisk together arrowroot and water.

5. Heat the cooker on High/Sauté/Brown. Add arrowroot mixture and cook, stirring, until sauce is thickened to your liking. Transfer to a serving bowl and garnish with green onions.

TIPS

Coconut oil is considered a healthy oil and as such is generally accepted in the paleo diet.

When purchasing ready-to-use beef broth, check to make sure it is certified gluten-free or has been packaged in a facility where there is no gluten cross-contamination.

Arrowroot is a starch that has some acceptance in the paleo community if used in small amounts by individuals who can tolerate it. While it adds to the finished recipe, you can omit it.

If your cooker requires more than 2⅔ cups (650 mL) liquid to reach pressure, add as much water in step 3 as is required.

Mouthwatering Beef Short Ribs with Onions

These full-flavored beef short ribs have extra depth of flavor thanks to porcini mushrooms. You can eat these the day you cook them, but for a richer taste and reduced fat, make them a day ahead.

5 lbs	bone-in beef short ribs, cut into 3-rib sections	2.5 kg
	Kosher salt and freshly ground black pepper	
3 tbsp	lard or ghee (see tip, page 133), divided	45 mL
3	carrots, chopped	3
2	stalks celery, chopped	2
1	large onion, chopped	1
½ oz	dried porcini mushrooms, coarsely chopped	15 g
6	cloves garlic, minced	6
1 cup	marinara sauce	250 mL
½ cup	low-sodium beef bone broth (page 208) or ready-to-use beef broth	125 mL
2 tbsp	balsamic vinegar (see tip, page 147)	30 mL
¼ cup	chopped fresh parsley	60 mL

TIPS

When purchasing ready-to-use beef broth, check to make sure it is certified gluten-free or has been packaged in a facility where there is no gluten cross-contamination.

You can serve the ribs, garnished with parsley, immediately after step 3 if desired.

This recipe is recommended for 8-quart (8 L) or larger pressure cookers. It can be cut in half for smaller cookers.

1. Season ribs with salt and pepper. Heat the pressure cooker on High/Sauté/Brown. Add 1 tbsp (15 mL) lard and heat until melted. Working in batches, add ribs and cook, turning, for 5 to 7 minutes or until browned, adding more lard as needed between batches. Using tongs, transfer ribs to a platter.

2. Add any remaining lard to the cooker and heat until melted. Add carrots, celery and onion; cook, stirring, for 3 to 5 minutes or until onion is translucent. Add mushrooms and garlic; cook, stirring, for 1 minute. Stir in marinara sauce, broth and vinegar. Cancel cooking.

3. Return ribs and any accumulated juices to the cooker. Close and lock the lid. Cook on high pressure for 35 minutes. Let stand, covered, for 10 minutes, then release any remaining pressure. Check to make sure the ribs are pull-apart tender; if more cooking time is needed, reset to high pressure for 5 minutes.

4. Once the pot is cool enough to handle, remove the inner pot from the cooker housing. Cover pot tightly and refrigerate for 12 to 24 hours.

5. Scrape off any congealed fat from the top of the ribs and discard. Return pot to cooker housing. Heat the cooker on High/Sauté/Brown. Cook, uncovered, for 15 to 20 minutes or until ribs are heated through. Serve garnished with parsley.

Meatballs in Tangy Chile Sauce

These darling little meatballs are grain-free and float in a sweet and sassy chile sauce. They are wonderful on spaghetti, in a sub sandwich or as a savory appetizer.

- Blender

1 lb	lean ground beef	500 g
1/4 cup	tapioca flour	60 mL
1 tsp	garlic powder	5 mL
1 tsp	kosher salt	5 mL
1/2 tsp	freshly ground black pepper	2 mL
1	large egg	1
3	cloves garlic	3
2	jalapeño peppers, stemmed and seeded	2
1/2 cup	coconut or apple cider vinegar	125 mL
6 tbsp	water	90 mL
1/3 cup	liquid honey	75 mL
1 1/2 tbsp	fish sauce	22 mL
4 tsp	arrowroot flour (see tip, page 149)	20 mL
3 tbsp	cold water	45 mL

1. In a large bowl, combine beef, flour, garlic powder, salt, pepper and egg, mixing well. Using your hands or a small scoop, form mixture into 1 1/2-inch (4 cm) balls. Set aside.

2. In blender, combine garlic, jalapeños, vinegar, 6 tbsp (90 mL) water, honey and fish sauce; blend until almost smooth.

3. Heat the pressure cooker on High/Sauté/Brown. Scrape in sauce and cook, stirring, for 5 minutes or until reduced by half.

4. In a small bowl, whisk together arrowroot and cold water. Add to the cooker and cook, stirring, for 1 minute or until sauce is thickened. Cancel cooking.

5. Add meatballs, turning to coat in sauce. Close and lock the lid. Cook on low pressure for 30 minutes. Quickly release the pressure. Check to make sure the meatballs are no longer pink inside; if more cooking time is needed, reset to high pressure for 5 minutes.

VARIATION

Slow Cooker Meatballs: Preheat oven to 350°F (180°C). After forming the meatballs in step 1, place them on a foil-lined rimmed baking sheet. Bake for 25 minutes or until browned. Meanwhile, prepare the sauce as directed in steps 2 to 4. In step 5, after adding the meatballs, close and lock the lid, making sure the steam vent is open. Press Slow Cook and adjust the temperature to the lowest setting. Cook for 2 to 4 hours or until meatballs are no longer pink inside.

TIPS

If your cooker requires more than 1 1/4 cups (300 mL) liquid to reach pressure, you can double the recipe and add more water as needed. If your sauce does not have a glaze consistency by the end of step 5, transfer the meatballs to a plate and cover with foil to keep warm. Cook the sauce on High/Sauté/Brown to your desired thickness. Return meatballs to the cooker, stirring to coat, before serving.

Leftover meatballs can be stored in an airtight container in the refrigerator for up to 5 days or frozen for up to 3 months.

Stuffed Bell Peppers

Colorful bell peppers are the bowls of choice for this savory combination of ground beef, tomatoes, olives and spicy jalapeño, making them the ultimate complete one-pot meal.

• Steam rack

1 tbsp	virgin olive oil (see tip)	15 mL
1	onion, finely chopped	1
1	clove garlic, minced	1
12 oz	ground beef	375 g
2 tsp	ground cumin	10 mL
2 tsp	dried parsley	10 mL
1 tsp	paprika	5 mL
½ tsp	kosher salt	2 mL
3	plum (Roma) tomatoes, diced	3
1	jalapeño pepper, seeded and minced	1
¼ cup	sliced drained black olives, divided	60 mL
2	bell peppers (any color), halved lengthwise, ribs and seeds removed	2

TIPS

Virgin olive oil is considered a healthy oil and is not inflammatory, so it is generally accepted in the paleo diet.

By using silicone tongs to remove the peppers from the pressure cooker, you'll avoid poking through the skin of the peppers.

1. Heat the pressure cooker on High/Sauté/Brown. Add oil and heat until shimmering. Add onion and cook, stirring, for 3 to 5 minutes or until translucent. Add garlic and cook, stirring, for 1 minute or until fragrant. Add beef, cumin, parsley, paprika and salt; cook, stirring and breaking up beef, for 7 minutes or until beef is no longer pink. Stir in tomatoes, jalapeño and 2 tbsp (30 mL) olives. Cancel cooking.

2. Spoon beef mixture into bell pepper halves, dividing evenly. Sprinkle with the remaining olives. Wash and dry the cooker's inner pot.

3. Add 1 cup (250 mL) water (or the amount required by your cooker to reach pressure) to the pressure cooker and place the steam rack in the pot. Arrange the filled peppers on the rack. Close and lock the lid. Cook on high pressure for 7 minutes. Quickly release the pressure. Check to make sure the pepper is softened to your liking; if more cooking time is needed, reset to high pressure for 1 minute.

4. Using silicone tongs, transfer peppers to individual serving plates. Serve immediately.

Savory Veal Shanks with Carrots

Often called osso buco, this classic Milanese dish consists of braised veal shanks in a rich tomato and wine broth. The result is one of Italy's most notable and luscious dishes.

MAKES 4 SERVINGS

4	veal shanks (each about 12 oz/375 g)	4
	Kosher salt and freshly ground black pepper	
2 tbsp	ghee (see tip, page 133), divided	30 mL
2	carrots, roughly chopped	2
2	stalks celery, chopped	2
1	onion, chopped	1
3	cloves garlic, minced	3
1 lb	plum (Roma) tomatoes (about 6 or 7), coarsely chopped	500 g
6 tbsp	minced fresh parsley, divided	90 mL
1 cup	low-sodium beef bone broth (page 208) or ready-to-use beef broth	250 mL
1 tbsp	tomato paste	15 mL
1 tbsp	balsamic vinegar (see tip, page 147)	15 mL

1. Season veal with salt and pepper. Heat the pressure cooker on High/Sauté/Brown. Add 1 tbsp (15 mL) ghee and heat until melted. Working in batches, add veal and cook, turning once, for 5 to 7 minutes or until browned on both sides. Transfer shanks to a plate.

2. Add the remaining ghee to the cooker and heat until melted. Add carrots, celery and onion; cook, stirring often, for 3 to 5 minutes or until onion is translucent. Add garlic and cook, stirring, for 1 minute or until fragrant. Stir in tomatoes, 4 tbsp (60 mL) parsley, broth, tomato paste and vinegar. Cancel cooking.

3. Return veal and any accumulated juices to the cooker. Close and lock the lid. Cook on high pressure for 50 minutes. Let stand, covered, until the float valve drops down. Check to make sure the veal is fork-tender; if more cooking time is needed, reset to high pressure for 10 minutes. Using tongs, transfer shanks to individual serving plates.

4. Season sauce to taste with salt and pepper. Spoon sauce over shanks. Serve garnished with the remaining parsley.

TIPS

You can substitute a 14-oz (398 mL) can of diced tomatoes, with juice, for the plum tomatoes.

When purchasing ready-to-use beef broth, check to make sure it is certified gluten-free or has been packaged in a facility where there is no gluten cross-contamination.

This recipe has about 1½ cups (375 mL) liquid. If your cooker requires more liquid to reach pressure, add water or more broth as needed. After step 3, you may need to cook the sauce on High/Sauté/Brown to reduce the sauce to your desired consistency.

Indian Curry Lamb Chops

This recipe calls for lamb sirloin chops instead of rib or loin chops, making for a more economical dish without sacrificing on taste. The pressure cooker helps tenderize this cut, and the seasonings bring the dish to life. You'll get the best results if you marinate the lamb chops, so plan ahead for this dish.

MAKES 2 SERVINGS		

- Blender

2	lamb sirloin chops	2
	Kosher salt	
2 tsp	curry powder, divided	10 mL
4	plum (Roma) tomatoes, halved	4
1	onion, cut into wedges	1
1 tbsp	virgin coconut oil (see tip)	15 mL
5	cloves garlic, minced	5
1¼ cups	chopped fresh cilantro, divided	300 mL
½ cup	dry red wine	125 mL
	Juice of 1 lemon	
4	green onions, sliced	4

TIPS

Make sure to use lamb sirloin chops and not loin chops, as the results will not be the same.

Cooking under pressure greatly intensifies the flavor of some spices, such as curry powder. It is best to add smaller amounts before cooking and then season with more to taste as you're finishing the sauce.

Coconut oil is considered a healthy oil and as such is generally accepted in the paleo diet.

You can substitute water for the wine, if you prefer.

1. Season lamb with salt and 1 tsp (5 mL) curry powder. Cover tightly with plastic wrap and refrigerate for at least 4 hours or up to 24 hours.

2. In blender, combine tomatoes and onion; purée until smooth. Set aside.

3. Heat the pressure cooker on High/Sauté/Brown. Add coconut oil and heat until melted. Working in batches, add lamb and cook, turning once, for 3 to 5 minutes or until browned on both sides. Using tongs, transfer lamb to a plate.

4. Add garlic to the cooker and cook, stirring, for 1 minute or until fragrant. Stir in tomato purée, 1 cup (250 mL) cilantro, wine and lemon juice; bring to a boil. Cancel cooking.

5. Return lamb and any accumulated juices to the cooker, turning lamb to coat with sauce. Close and lock the lid. Cook on high pressure for 8 minutes. Let stand, covered, for 10 minutes, then release any remaining pressure. Check to make sure the lamb is fork-tender; if more cooking time is needed, reset to high pressure for 2 minutes, then quickly release the pressure. Using tongs, transfer lamb to individual serving plates.

6. Stir green onions and the remaining cilantro into sauce. Season to taste with salt and the remaining curry powder. Drizzle sauce over lamb.

Vegetarian and Vegan Dishes

Roasted Garlic Hummus

Making hummus in the pressure cooker is so quick and easy, and this version so delectable, you may never go back to buying prepared hummus or using canned chickpeas. This garlicky concoction is ideal for dipping vegetables or pita bread, and is a wonderful alternative sandwich spread.

MAKES 8 SERVINGS		

• Food processor

2 cups	dried chickpeas	500 mL
	Water	
½ cup	extra virgin olive oil, divided	125 mL
3	cloves garlic, roasted (see tip)	3
1½ tbsp	ground cumin, divided	22 mL
½ tsp	kosher salt	2 mL
	Freshly ground black pepper	
½ cup	tahini	125 mL
2 tbsp	freshly squeezed lemon juice	30 mL

TIPS

To roast garlic, cut off the top of a head of garlic, exposing the tops of the cloves but leaving the outer skin intact. Place garlic on a sheet of heavy-duty foil and drizzle olive oil over the cloves. Seal foil around garlic. Bake in a 350°F (180°C) oven for 50 minutes or until cloves are soft when pierced with a knife. Squeeze out cloves. Store extra cloves in an airtight container in the refrigerator for up to 5 days. They are a great addition to other dips and sauces.

This recipe is meant for pressure cookers that are 6 quarts (6 L) or larger. If you are using a smaller cooker, cut the recipe in half. Do not fill your cooker more than halfway full.

The hummus can be covered and refrigerated for up to 3 days.

1. Place chickpeas in a large bowl, add 8 cups (2 L) cold water and let soak at room temperature for 8 hours or overnight. Drain and rinse chickpeas.

2. In the pressure cooker, combine chickpeas, 4 cups (1 L) water and 1½ tbsp (22 mL) oil. Close and lock the lid. Cook on high pressure for 38 minutes. Let stand, covered, for 10 minutes, then release any remaining pressure. Check to make sure the chickpeas give almost no resistance when pressed between your fingers; if more cooking time is needed, reset to high pressure for 5 minutes. Drain chickpeas.

3. In food processor, combine chickpeas, garlic, 1 tbsp (15 mL) cumin, salt, pepper to taste, tahini, ¼ cup (60 mL) oil and lemon juice. Process until smooth and creamy, adding water if necessary to reach the desired consistency.

4. Transfer hummus to a serving bowl. Using the back of a spoon, make a depression in the hummus and drizzle with the remaining oil. Garnish with the remaining cumin.

Vegetarian Meatball and Tortellini Soup

This unique and satisfying soup is the perfect combination on a cool winter day, with its union of veggie meatballs, cheese tortellini, spinach and seasonings.

MAKES 6 SERVINGS		
2 tbsp	virgin olive oil	30 mL
1	onion, thinly sliced	1
3	cloves garlic, minced	3
2	stalks celery, sliced	2
2 cups	chopped trimmed spinach or kale leaves	500 mL
1 tsp	granulated sugar	5 mL
1 tsp	dried basil	5 mL
1 lb	frozen meatless veggie meatballs	500 g
8 oz	dried cheese tortellini	250 g
6 cups	low-sodium vegetable stock (page 204) or ready-to-use vegetable broth	1.5 L
1½ tbsp	freshly squeezed lemon juice	22 mL
	Kosher salt and freshly ground black pepper	
	Freshly grated Parmesan cheese (optional)	

1. Heat the pressure cooker on High/Sauté/Brown. Add oil and heat until shimmering. Add onion and cook, stirring often, for 3 to 5 minutes or until translucent. Cancel cooking.

2. Add garlic, celery, spinach, sugar, basil, meatballs, tortellini, stock and lemon juice, stirring well. Close and lock the lid. Cook on high pressure for 5 minutes. Quickly release the pressure. Check to make sure the tortellini are fork-tender; if more cooking time is needed, reset to high pressure for 1 minute. Season to taste with salt and pepper. Serve garnished with Parmesan, if desired.

> **TIP**
>
> When releasing pressure quickly, keep your hands and face away from the hole on top of the steam release handle so you don't get scalded by the escaping steam.

Thai Coconut Tofu Soup

Mushrooms, peppers and tofu combine in a fiery sauce that is then blended with coconut milk and lime for a complementary flavor profile.

MAKES 6 SERVINGS

2 tbsp	vegetable oil	30 mL
1	small onion, cut into thin (¼-inch/0.5 cm) strips	1
1	red or green bell pepper, cut into strips	1
8 oz	cremini mushrooms, thinly sliced	250 g
6	wild lime leaves, lightly crushed (optional)	6
1 tbsp	minced gingerroot	15 mL
1 tbsp	packed brown sugar	15 mL
2 tbsp	Thai red curry paste	30 mL
2 tbsp	coconut amino acids	30 mL
14 oz	extra-firm tofu, cut into cubes	425 g
3 cups	low-sodium vegetable stock (page 204) or ready-to-use vegetable broth	750 mL
¾ cup	unsweetened coconut milk	175 mL
2 tbsp	freshly squeezed lime juice	30 mL
	Fresh cilantro leaves	

1. Heat the pressure cooker on High/Sauté/Brown. Add oil and heat until shimmering. Add onion and red pepper; cook, stirring often, for 5 minutes or until softened. Add mushrooms and cook, stirring often, for 5 minutes or until softened. Cancel cooking.

2. Add lime leaves (if using), ginger, brown sugar, red curry paste and amino acids, stirring well. Add tofu and stock. Close and lock the lid. Cook on high pressure for 5 minutes. Quickly release the pressure.

3. Stir in coconut milk and lime juice. Serve garnished with cilantro.

> **TIP**
>
> Look for wild lime leaves at well-stocked Asian grocery stores. They are very common in Thai cooking, but because they are difficult to find and there is no good substitute for them, they are optional in the recipe.

Pinto Bean and Seitan Chili

Pinto beans, seitan, fresh tomatoes and sweet and smoky spices bring life to this hearty chili.

1¼ cups	dried pinto beans, rinsed	300 mL
5 cups	cold water	1.25 L
2 tbsp	vegetable oil	30 mL
1	onion, finely chopped	1
1 tbsp	chili powder	15 mL
8 oz	seitan, diced	250 g
3	large tomatoes, chopped	3
3	cloves garlic, minced	3
1	green bell pepper, chopped	1
2 tsp	granulated sugar	10 mL
1 tsp	paprika	5 mL
½ tsp	chipotle chile powder	2 mL
1	can (28 oz/796 mL) tomato sauce	1
5 cups	low-sodium vegetable stock (page 204) or ready-to-use vegetable broth	1.25 L
	Kosher salt and freshly ground black pepper	
6 tbsp	sour cream (regular or nondairy)	90 mL

TIP

When pressure-cooking beans of any type, make sure to fill the pot no more than halfway full. Do not attempt to double or triple the recipe, or the exhaust valve may become clogged as the beans froth up under pressure. Adding oil with the beans helps to reduce the amount of froth.

1. Place pinto beans in a large bowl, add cold water and let soak at room temperature for 30 minutes. Drain and rinse beans. Set aside.

2. Heat the pressure cooker on High/Sauté/Brown. Add oil and heat until shimmering. Add onion and cook, stirring often, for 3 to 5 minutes or until translucent. Add chili powder and cook, stirring, for 1 minute. Cancel cooking.

3. Add beans, seitan, tomatoes, garlic, green pepper, sugar, paprika, chipotle powder, tomato sauce and stock, stirring well. Close and lock the lid. Cook on high pressure for 25 minutes. Let stand, covered, for 10 minutes, then release any remaining pressure. Check to make sure the beans are tender; if more cooking time is needed, reset to high pressure for 5 minutes. Season to taste with salt and pepper.

4. Spoon into individual serving bowls and top with a dollop of sour cream.

Butternut Squash, Okra and Brown Rice Gumbo

This Cajun-influenced dish is rocking with black soybeans, butternut squash, okra and an array of spicy and vibrant seasonings. The recipe uses a pot-in-pot technique that lets you cook the rice right along with the gumbo.

MAKES 8 SERVINGS

- 2 sheets of heavy-duty foil, sprayed with nonstick cooking spray, edges of foil folded up
- 4-quart (4 L) round casserole dish
- Tall steam rack

1 cup	black soybeans, rinsed	250 mL
	Water	
1½ cups	cubed butternut squash	375 mL
2	okra, sliced	2
6 tbsp	virgin olive oil, divided	90 mL
½ tsp	hot pepper flakes	2 mL
1½ cups	long-grain brown rice	375 mL
2 tsp	kosher salt	10 mL
1	onion, chopped	1
1	green bell pepper, chopped	1
4	cloves garlic, minced	4
1 tbsp	Cajun seasoning	15 mL
1 tbsp	dried oregano	15 mL
2 tsp	dried thyme	10 mL
2 tsp	smoked paprika	10 mL
2 tsp	paprika	10 mL
1 tsp	kosher salt	5 mL
8 cups	low-sodium vegetable stock (page 204) or ready-to-use vegetable broth, divided	2 L
1 tbsp	cornstarch	15 mL
	Hot pepper sauce (optional)	

1. Place soybeans in a large bowl, add 4 cups (1 L) cold water and let soak at room temperature for 8 hours or overnight. Drain and rinse soybeans. Set aside.

2. Arrange squash on 1 prepared foil sheet and okra on the other. Drizzle each with 1 tbsp (15 mL) oil. Sprinkle squash with hot pepper flakes. Fold foil into tent-style packets and seal edges tightly (see illustration, page 99). Set aside.

3. In casserole dish, combine rice, salt, 2¼ cups (550 mL) water and 1 tsp (5 mL) oil. Set aside.

4. Heat the pressure cooker on High/ Sauté/Brown. Add 2 tbsp (30 mL) oil and heat until shimmering. Add onion and green pepper; cook, stirring often, for 3 to 5 minutes or until onion is translucent. Add garlic and cook, stirring, for 1 minute or until fragrant. Cancel cooking.

5. Stir in Cajun seasoning, oregano, thyme, smoked paprika, paprika and salt. Add soybeans, 2 cups (500 mL) stock and the remaining oil, stirring well. Place the steam rack on top of the bean mixture. Keeping the casserole dish level, lower it onto the rack. Rest the foil packets on top of the dish, with the edges of the packets on the rim of the dish.

6. Close and lock the lid. Cook on high pressure for 20 minutes. Let stand, covered, for 10 minutes, then release any remaining pressure. Carefully remove the packets, open them and check to make sure the squash and okra are fork-tender. Remove the casserole dish and rack, and check to make sure the rice and the beans are tender. If all of the components need more cooking time, return the rack and dish to the cooker, reseal the packets and rest them on top of the dish, and reset to high pressure for 4 minutes, then quickly release the pressure (see tip).

7. Remove the foil packets and set aside. Remove the casserole dish and fluff the rice with a fork. Remove the rack. Add the remaining stock to the beans.

8. In a small bowl, combine cornstarch and 1 tbsp (15 mL) cold water.

9. Heat the cooker on High/Sauté/Brown. Stir in cornstarch mixture and cook, stirring, for 5 minutes or until sauce is thickened to your liking. Open the foil packets and add squash and okra to the cooker. Cook, stirring, for 3 minutes or until flavors are melded.

10. Mound a scoopful of rice in the center of each individual serving bowl and spoon gumbo around the rice. Serve with hot pepper sauce, if desired.

VARIATION

You can add 1 lb (500 g) vegetarian andouille sausage, cut into ¾-inch (2 cm) pieces. Sauté the sausage in step 4 with the onions and peppers.

TIP

If only the beans need more cooking time in step 6, reseal the packets and cover the casserole dish to keep the contents warm while you continue cooking the beans. If the beans and one or two of the other meal components need more cooking time, return the rack, dish and/or packets to the cooker as required for the added cooking time and keep the other components warm. If the beans are done but one or more of the other meal components are not, transfer the bean mixture to a large bowl, add 1 cup (250 mL) water (or the amount required by your cooker to reach pressure) to the pressure cooker and return the rack and the necessary items to the pot to continue cooking; continue with step 7, emptying the water from the cooker and returning the bean mixture to it before adding the remaining stock.

Potatoes Stuffed with Lentil Chili

This vegetarian lentil chili is hearty comfort food on its own, but when it's served on top of a baked potato, you get a filling meal that is perfect for a cool fall or winter day.

- Steam rack
- Baking sheet, lined with foil

6	medium baking potatoes, pierced	6
1 tbsp	virgin olive oil	15 mL
2	carrots, chopped	2
1	stalk celery, chopped	1
1	onion, chopped	1
3	cloves garlic, minced	3
1 tbsp	chili powder	15 mL
1 tsp	ground cumin	5 mL
1 tsp	dried oregano	5 mL
½ tsp	dry mustard	2 mL
2 cups	dried green (Puy) lentils, rinsed	500 mL
1	can (14 oz/398 mL) crushed tomatoes	1
3 cups	low-sodium vegetable stock (page 204) or ready-to-use vegetable broth	750 mL
	Kosher salt	

TIPS

Brown lentils can be substituted for the green lentils. Add 2 minutes to the cooking time in step 4. I do not recommend using split red or yellow lentils, as they tend to become mushy when cooked.

For variety, make fewer baked potatoes for stuffing and serve leftover lentil chili as a stand-alone dish.

1. Add 1 cup (250 mL) water (or the amount required by your cooker to reach pressure) to the pressure cooker and place the steam rack in the pot. Arrange potatoes on rack. Close and lock the lid. Cook on high pressure for 10 minutes. Quickly release the pressure. Check to make sure the potatoes are fork-tender; if more cooking time is needed, reset to high pressure for 2 minutes. Transfer potatoes to prepared baking sheet and set aside. Wipe the cooker's inner pot dry.

2. Preheat oven to 425°F (220°C).

3. Heat the cooker on High/Sauté/Brown. Add oil and heat until shimmering. Add carrots, celery and onion; cook, stirring, for 3 to 5 minutes or until onion is translucent. Add garlic, chili powder, cumin, oregano and mustard; cook, stirring, for 1 minute or until fragrant. Cancel cooking.

4. Add lentils, tomatoes and stock, stirring well. Close and lock the lid. Cook on high pressure for 12 minutes. Let stand, covered, until the float valve drops down. Check to make sure the lentils are tender but firm; if more cooking time is needed, reset to high pressure for 3 minutes. Season to taste with salt.

5. Meanwhile, bake potatoes for 10 minutes. Keep warm.

6. Transfer potatoes to individual serving plates and split tops open. Spoon lentil chili over the potatoes. Serve immediately.

Freekeh Tabbouleh

Freekeh is a powerhouse grain that gives this Middle Eastern dish a slightly nutty flavor. The marriage of freekeh, tomatoes, cucumbers and herbs is an experience you will not want to miss.

MAKES 6 SERVINGS

1½ cups	freekeh, rinsed	375 mL
	Kosher salt	
3¾ cups	water	925 mL
3	tomatoes, diced	3
2	medium English cucumbers, cut into small cubes	2
1 cup	minced fresh parsley	250 mL
¼ cup	chopped fresh mint	60 mL
¼ cup	minced green onions	60 mL
½ tsp	paprika	2 mL
¼ cup	virgin olive oil	60 mL
	Juice of 1 lemon	
	Freshly ground black pepper	

TIP

English cucumbers are also called seedless cucumbers. If you cannot find them, regular cucumbers will also work well. You can either remove the seeds or use them with the seeds, as you prefer.

1. In the pressure cooker, combine freekeh, 1 tsp (5 mL) salt and water, stirring well. Close and lock the lid. Cook on high pressure for 6 minutes. Let stand, covered, for 10 minutes, then release any remaining pressure. Check to make sure the freekeh is done to your liking; if more cooking time is needed, cover and let stand for 2 minutes. Transfer freekeh to a large plate and let cool for 30 minutes.

2. In a large bowl, gently combine tomatoes, cucumbers, parsley, mint, green onions, paprika, oil and lemon juice. Gently stir in freekeh. Season to taste with salt and pepper.

Power Bowls with Farro and Ratatouille

This Mediterranean-inspired combination of hearty farro, classic ratatouille and a refreshing vinaigrette is a nourishing, filling one-bowl meal or hearty side dish. The farro adds a nice crunchy, nutty texture, while the ratatouille is loaded with fresh, tender vegetables. You can even prepare the ratatouille and farro ahead and have them ready to assemble for individual servings.

MAKES 6 SERVINGS

- 4-cup (1 L) casserole dish
- Steam rack

Farro

1½ cups	farro, rinsed	375 mL
2 tsp	chopped fresh mint	10 mL
2 tsp	kosher salt	10 mL
1 cup	unsweetened apple cider	250 mL
	Water	

Ratatouille

6 tbsp	virgin olive oil, divided	90 mL
1	eggplant (about 1 lb/500 g), unpeeled, cut into 1-inch (2.5 cm) pieces	1
3	zucchini, unpeeled, cut into 1-inch (2.5 cm) pieces	3
3	onions, cut into 1-inch (2.5 cm) squares	3
3	green bell peppers, cut into 1-inch (2.5 cm) squares	3
5	cloves garlic, minced	5
4	fully ripe tomatoes, seeded and cut into 1-inch (2.5 cm) squares	4
2 tsp	kosher salt	10 mL
½ tsp	freshly ground black pepper	2 mL
½ cup	water	125 mL

Vinaigrette

2	cloves garlic, minced	2
½ tsp	freshly ground black pepper	2 mL
7 tbsp	extra virgin olive oil	105 mL
2 tbsp	apple cider vinegar	30 mL
2 cups	trimmed arugula leaves (optional)	500 mL
½ cup	crumbled feta or shaved Parmesan cheese	125 mL
	Fresh basil leaves	

1. *Farro:* In the casserole dish, combine farro, mint, salt, apple cider and ½ cup (125 mL) water.

2. Add 1 cup (250 mL) water (or the amount required by your cooker to reach pressure) to the pressure cooker and place the steam rack in the pot. Keeping the casserole dish level, lower it onto the rack. Close and lock the lid. Cook on high pressure for 10 minutes. Let stand, covered, for 10 minutes, then release any remaining pressure. Check to make sure the farro is tender; if more cooking time is required, reset to high pressure for 1 minute. Remove the dish from the pot. Fluff farro with a fork and let cool. Discard water and wipe the cooker's inner pot dry.

3. *Ratatouille:* Heat the cooker on High/Sauté/Brown. Add ¼ cup (60 mL) oil and heat until shimmering. Add eggplant and cook, stirring often, for 7 minutes or until softened. Using a slotted spoon, transfer eggplant to a bowl.

4. Add zucchini to the cooker and cook, stirring often, for 7 minutes or until browned. Using a slotted spoon, add zucchini to the eggplant.

5. Add the remaining oil to the cooker and heat until shimmering. Add onions and green peppers; cook, stirring often, for 5 to 7 minutes or until onions are translucent. Add garlic and cook, stirring, for 1 minute or until fragrant. Cancel cooking.

6. Return eggplant and zucchini to the cooker. Add tomatoes, salt, pepper and water, stirring well. Close and lock the lid. Cook on high pressure for 4 minutes. Quickly release the pressure.

7. Heat the cooker on High/Sauté/Brown. Cook ratatouille, stirring occasionally, for 5 to 10 minutes or until liquid is reduced to your liking. Cancel cooking. Let ratatouille cool.

8. *Vinaigrette:* In a small bowl, whisk together garlic, pepper, oil and vinegar.

9. Arrange arugula (if using) in individual serving bowls. Divide farro and ratatouille evenly among bowls. Drizzle with vinaigrette. Sprinkle with feta. Serve garnished with basil.

TIPS

The farro can be cooked up to 3 days ahead. Cool, cover and refrigerate until ready to assemble.

Make sure the vegetables for the ratatouille are cut into pieces that are at least 1 inch (2.5 cm) square or cubed. They may turn out mushy if cut any smaller.

The ratatouille develops a deeper flavor if refrigerated for up to 24 hours, and will keep for up to 3 days. Assemble with the other ingredients just before serving.

The arugula adds a nice peppery flavor base to this dish. But you can feel free to omit it or substitute another green of your choice.

For more protein, top each bowl with a poached egg.

Quinoa, Carrot and Parsnip Medley

Quinoa and vegetables combine for a balanced main dish or a hearty side dish. The South Asian infusion of spices adds to the appeal of this savory dish.

MAKES 4 TO 6 SERVINGS

2 tbsp	virgin olive oil	30 mL
1	carrot, chopped	1
1	parsnip, chopped	1
3	cloves garlic, minced	3
1½ cups	quinoa, rinsed	375 mL
2 tsp	grated gingerroot	10 mL
1 tbsp	ground cumin	15 mL
2 tsp	paprika	10 mL
1 tsp	ground coriander	5 mL
1 tsp	ground turmeric	5 mL
⅛ tsp	cayenne pepper	0.5 mL
2¼ cups	low-sodium vegetable stock (page 204) or ready-to-use vegetable broth	550 mL
¼ cup	chopped cashews	60 mL

1. Heat the pressure cooker on High/Sauté/Brown. Add oil and heat until shimmering. Add carrot and parsnip; cook, stirring, for 3 minutes or until slightly softened. Add garlic and cook, stirring, for 1 minute or until fragrant. Cancel cooking.

2. Add quinoa, ginger, cumin, paprika, coriander, turmeric, cayenne and stock, stirring well. Close and lock the lid. Cook on high pressure for 1 minute. Let stand, covered, for 10 minutes, then release any remaining pressure. Fluff quinoa, cover and let stand for 5 minutes. Stir in cashews.

> **TIP**
> Place a steam rack and steamer basket on top of the quinoa mixture and toss in your favorite greens to be steamed on top.

Bulgur and Chickpea Salad with Lemon Dill Dressing

This Middle Eastern–influenced salad is packed with grains, chickpeas, cucumbers and red peppers and finished with a lemony dill dressing. The bulgur adds a chewy, nutty taste to the creamy chickpeas. The vegetables and herbs bring it all together.

MAKES 4 SERVINGS

Salad

2 cups	dried chickpeas, rinsed	500 mL
	Water	
1 cup	medium-grind bulgur	250 mL
2 tsp	kosher salt, divided	10 mL
1¼ cups	boiling water	300 mL
1	shallot, minced	1
1	bay leaf	1
1 tbsp	virgin olive oil	15 mL
1	red bell pepper, finely chopped	1
1	English cucumber, diced	1
⅓ cup	finely chopped red onion	75 mL

Lemon Dill Dressing

1	clove garlic, minced	1
½ cup	finely chopped fresh dill	125 mL
1 tsp	ground cumin	5 mL
1 tsp	granulated sugar	5 mL
¼ cup	freshly squeezed lemon juice	60 mL
¼ cup	virgin olive oil	60 mL

1. *Salad:* Place chickpeas in a large bowl, add 8 cups (2 L) cold water and let soak at room temperature for 8 hours or overnight. Drain and rinse chickpeas. Set aside.

2. In another large bowl, combine bulgur, ½ tsp (2 mL) salt and boiling water. Cover tightly with plastic wrap and let stand for 30 minutes or until water is completely absorbed. Let cool.

3. In the pressure cooker, combine chickpeas, shallot, bay leaf, 4 cups (1 L) water and oil. Close and lock the lid. Cook on high pressure for 18 minutes. Let stand, covered, until the float valve drops down. Check to make sure the chickpeas are tender; if more cooking time is needed, reset to high pressure for 2 minutes. Discard bay leaf. Drain and rinse chickpeas. Transfer chickpeas to a large bowl and let cool.

4. *Dressing:* In a small bowl, whisk together garlic, dill, cumin, sugar, the remaining salt, lemon juice and oil.

5. Add bulgur, red pepper, cucumber and onion to the cooled chickpeas. Pour dressing over salad and toss to coat.

TIPS

If you have extra virgin olive oil on hand as well as virgin, use extra virgin in step 4.

When pressure-cooking beans of any type, make sure to fill the pot no more than halfway full. Do not attempt to double or triple the recipe, or the exhaust valve may become clogged as the beans froth up under pressure. Adding oil with the beans helps to reduce the amount of froth.

Chickpea, Tomato, Cucumber and Black Olive Salad

Transport yourself to the Mediterranean with this lively and nutritious cornucopia of chickpeas, tomatoes, cucumbers and olives marinated in a zesty Mediterranean dressing.

MAKES 4 SERVINGS		
2 cups	dried chickpeas, rinsed	500 mL
	Water	
1	shallot, minced	1
1	bay leaf	1
6 tbsp	virgin olive oil, divided	90 mL
1	clove garlic, minced	1
1 tbsp	chopped fresh rosemary	15 mL
1 tsp	hot pepper flakes	5 mL
1 tsp	kosher salt	5 mL
¼ cup	freshly squeezed lemon juice	60 mL
8	cherry tomatoes, quartered	8
2	cucumbers, peeled and coarsely chopped	2
½ cup	drained black olives	125 mL

TIPS

When pressure-cooking beans of any type, make sure to fill the pot no more than halfway full. Do not attempt to double or triple the recipe, or the exhaust valve may become clogged as the beans froth up under pressure. Adding oil with the beans helps to reduce the amount of froth.

Add ¼ cup (60 mL) pearl-size bocconcini (fresh mozzarella balls) to the salad in step 4. If you are unable to find pearl-size, select the next largest size and cut into bite-size pieces.

1. Place chickpeas in a large bowl, add 8 cups (2 L) cold water and let soak at room temperature for 8 hours or overnight. Drain and rinse chickpeas.

2. In the pressure cooker, combine chickpeas, shallot, bay leaf, 4 cups (1 L) water and 1 tbsp (15 mL) oil. Close and lock the lid. Cook on high pressure for 18 minutes. Let stand, covered, until the float valve drops down. Check to make sure the chickpeas are tender; if more cooking time is needed, reset to high pressure for 2 minutes. Discard bay leaf. Drain and rinse chickpeas. Transfer chickpeas to a large bowl and let cool.

3. In a small bowl, whisk together garlic, rosemary, hot pepper flakes, salt, lemon juice and the remaining oil.

4. Add tomatoes, cucumbers and olives to the cooled chickpeas. Pour dressing over salad and toss to coat. Refrigerate for at least 30 minutes, until chilled, or for up to 8 hours.

Black Bean and Corn Salad

This colorful and refreshing combination of beans, corn, bell peppers, tomatoes and avocados makes a refreshing meal or side dish. The tangy and zesty dressing takes this salad to new mouthwatering heights.

2 cups	dried black beans, rinsed	500 mL
	Water	
1	bay leaf	1
2 tbsp	chopped fresh parsley	30 mL
6 tbsp	virgin olive oil, divided	90 mL
1	shallot, minced	1
1	clove garlic, minced	1
2 tbsp	granulated sugar	30 mL
2 tsp	kosher salt	10 mL
½ tsp	ground cumin	2 mL
⅛ tsp	cayenne pepper	0.5 mL
3 tbsp	freshly squeezed lime juice	45 mL
2	plum (Roma) tomatoes, chopped	2
1	yellow bell pepper, chopped	1
1 cup	corn kernels	250 mL
2	avocados (preferably Haas)	2

TIPS

When pressure-cooking beans of any type, make sure to fill the pot no more than halfway full. Do not attempt to double or triple the recipe, or the exhaust valve may become clogged as the beans froth up under pressure. Adding oil with the beans helps to reduce the amount of froth.

This salad can also be used as a savory filling for quesadillas.

1. Place beans in a large bowl, add 8 cups (2 L) cold water and let soak at room temperature for 8 hours or overnight. Drain and rinse beans.

2. In the pressure cooker, combine beans, bay leaf, parsley, 4 cups (1 L) water and 1 tbsp (15 mL) oil. Close and lock the lid. Cook on high pressure for 5 minutes. Let stand, covered, until the float valve drops down. Discard bay leaf. Drain and rinse beans. Transfer beans to a large bowl and let cool.

3. In a small bowl, whisk together shallot, garlic, sugar, salt, cumin, cayenne, lime juice and the remaining oil.

4. Add tomatoes, yellow pepper and corn to the cooled beans. Pour dressing over salad and toss to coat. Refrigerate for at least 30 minutes, until chilled, or for up to 8 hours.

5. Just before serving, chop avocados, add to the salad and toss gently to combine.

Cauliflower, Fennel and Navy Bean Salad

This salad is very light and bright with its combination of cauliflower florets, shaved fennel and navy beans. The caper and thyme vinaigrette pulls it all together.

MAKES 4 TO 6 SERVINGS

¾ cup	dried navy (white pea) beans, rinsed	175 mL
3 cups	cold water	750 mL
1½ cups	salt-free vegetable stock (page 205) or ready-to-use vegetable broth	375 mL
5 tbsp	virgin olive oil, divided	75 mL
1	small head cauliflower (about 1¾ lbs/875 g)	1
1	fennel bulb	1
1	small red onion	1
1	clove garlic, minced	1
1	shallot, minced	1
	Leaves from 2 sprigs fresh thyme	
2 tbsp	chopped drained capers	30 mL
2 tbsp	red wine vinegar	30 mL
	Kosher salt and freshly ground black pepper	
½ cup	crumbled Cashew Feta (see tip) or feta cheese (optional)	125 mL

1. Place beans in a large bowl, add cold water and let soak at room temperature for 8 hours or overnight. Drain and rinse beans.

2. In the pressure cooker, combine beans, stock and 1 tbsp (15 mL) oil. Close and lock the lid. Cook on high pressure for 7 minutes. Let stand, covered, until the float valve drops down. Check to make sure the beans are tender; if more cooking time is needed, reset to high pressure for 1 minute. Drain and rinse beans. Transfer beans to a large bowl and let cool.

3. Meanwhile, cut cauliflower into 1-inch (2.5 cm) florets, shave fennel into long, thin strips (see tip) and finely chop onion. Add cauliflower, fennel and onion to the beans.

4. In a medium bowl, combine garlic, shallot, thyme, capers, vinegar and the remaining oil. Season to taste with salt and pepper.

5. Drizzle vinaigrette over salad and toss to coat. Garnish with cashew feta, if desired.

TIPS

Cashew Feta: In a small food processor, combine ½ cup (125 mL) raw cashews, 1 tbsp (15 mL) extra virgin olive oil and 1½ tsp (7 mL) dried oregano; process to a consistency similar to crumbled feta cheese.

Use a potato peeler or a box grater to shave the fennel into 2- to 3-inch (5 to 7.5 cm) long pieces.

This salad will serve 6 as a side dish or 4 as a main dish.

The salad can be covered and refrigerated for up to 3 days.

Sweet Rice and Adzuki Beans

This traditional Japanese dish, served on special occasions, is thought to bring good luck. Whether you need some luck or just want to serve a memorable side dish, you'll want to dive right in!

MAKES 4 SERVINGS

1/3 cup	dried adzuki beans, rinsed	75 mL
	Water	
1 cup	sweet brown rice, rinsed	250 mL
1/2 tsp	kosher salt	2 mL
1 tbsp	black sesame seeds, toasted (see tip)	15 mL
	Rice vinegar (optional)	

TIPS

To toast sesame seeds, add them to a small skillet and cook over medium-high heat, stirring, for 1 minute or until fragrant.

Quickly rinse bowls with warm water before adding the rice mixture, to reduce sticking.

1. Place beans in a large bowl, add 1¼ cups (300 mL) cold water and let soak at room temperature for 8 hours or overnight. Drain and rinse beans. Set aside.

2. In the pressure cooker, combine rice and 3½ cups (875 mL) water. Let soak for 30 minutes.

3. Add beans and salt, stirring well. Close and lock the lid. Cook on high pressure for 25 minutes. Let stand, covered, until the float valve drops down. Check to make sure the rice and beans are tender; if more cooking time is needed, reset to high pressure for 4 minutes. Let stand, uncovered, for 5 minutes.

4. Spoon rice mixture into individual serving bowls and garnish with sesame seeds. Serve with a drop of vinegar, if desired.

Tuscan Pasta and Beans

Here, lovely cannellini beans pair up with tiny tubular pasta in a zesty tomato sauce — perfect for those times when you want to curl up with pure comfort food and watch a movie.

MAKES 4 SERVINGS

- Immersion blender (see tip)

1½ cups	dried cannellini (white kidney) beans, rinsed	375 mL
	Water	
1 tbsp	butter	15 mL
	Virgin olive oil	
1	onion, chopped	1
3	cloves garlic, minced	3
1	sprig fresh rosemary	1
1 tsp	dried oregano	5 mL
Pinch	hot pepper flakes	Pinch
2	plum (Roma) tomatoes, chopped	2
2 tsp	kosher salt	10 mL
½ tsp	freshly ground black pepper	2 mL
2 tbsp	tomato paste	30 mL
8 oz	ditalini or other small tubular pasta	250 g

1. Place beans in a large bowl, add 6 cups (1.5 L) cold water and let soak at room temperature for 8 hours or overnight. Drain and rinse beans. Set aside.

2. Heat the pressure cooker on High/Sauté/Brown. Add butter and 1 tbsp (15 mL) oil; heat until melted and shimmering. Add onion and cook, stirring often, for 3 to 5 minutes or until translucent. Add garlic and cook, stirring, for 1 minute or until fragrant. Cancel cooking.

3. Add beans, rosemary, oregano, hot pepper flakes and 4 cups (1 L) water, stirring well. Close and lock the lid. Cook on high pressure for 9 minutes.

Let stand, covered, until the float valve drops down. Check to make sure the beans are tender; if more cooking time is needed, reset to high pressure for 2 minutes. Discard rosemary sprig.

4. Add tomatoes, salt, black pepper and tomato paste. Using the immersion blender, purée bean mixture until creamy.

5. Stir in pasta. Add enough water to just cover pasta plus ½ cup (125 mL) more. Close and lock the lid. Cook on high pressure for half the time indicated on the pasta package. Quickly release the pressure. Stir well.

6. Spoon into individual serving bowls and serve with a swirl of olive oil.

TIPS

Instead of the immersion blender, you can use a stand blender in step 4. Working in batches, transfer the bean mixture to the blender. Begin by pulsing the ingredients, then slowly increase the speed. (Quickly blending hot ingredients can cause the cover to pop off and the ingredients to spew out the top.) Return the bean mixture to the cooker and continue with step 5.

If you have extra virgin olive oil on hand as well as virgin, use extra virgin in step 6.

This recipe is designed for 6- to 8-quart (6 to 8 L) pressure cookers. You can cut it in half for smaller cookers.

Lentil Sloppy Joes

If you're looking for a crowd-pleasing meatless main dish, then this is the perfect choice. Green lentils provide a powerhouse base for onions, peppers, tomato sauce and some spice. Serve it on buns, add your favorite toppings and enjoy!

MAKES 6 SERVINGS

1 tbsp	vegetable oil	15 mL
2	stalks celery, finely chopped	2
1	onion, finely chopped	1
1	green bell pepper, finely chopped	1
1	clove garlic, minced	1
2 tsp	chili powder	10 mL
1 tsp	ground cumin	5 mL
1 cup	dried green (Puy) lentils, rinsed	250 mL
1 tsp	granulated sugar	5 mL
3¼ cups	Traditional Tomato Sauce (page 209)	800 mL
3 cups	water	750 mL
2 tbsp	tomato paste	30 mL
1 tbsp	Worcestershire sauce	15 mL
½ tsp	Sriracha (optional)	2 mL
	Kosher salt	
6	hamburger buns, split and toasted	6

Optional Toppings
Coleslaw

Sliced onions

Pickles

Shredded cheese

1. Heat the pressure cooker on High/Sauté/Brown. Add oil and heat until shimmering. Add celery, onion and green pepper; cook, stirring often, for 3 to 5 minutes or until onion is translucent. Add garlic, chili powder and cumin; cook, stirring, for 1 minute or until fragrant. Cancel cooking.

2. Add lentils, sugar, tomato sauce, water, tomato paste, Worcestershire sauce and Sriracha (if using), stirring well. Close and lock the lid. Cook on high pressure for 12 minutes. Let stand, covered, until the float valve drops down. Check to make sure the lentils are tender but firm; if more cooking time is needed, reset to high pressure for 2 minutes. Season to taste with salt.

3. Spoon lentil mixture onto toasted buns. Serve with any of the toppings, as desired.

TIPS
Green lentils do not need to be presoaked.

In place of the homemade tomato sauce, you can substitute a 28-oz (796 mL) can of tomato sauce.

Lentil and Quinoa Tacos

When it's taco Tuesday (or any night you are craving tacos — which for me is just about any night), dive into this quick and easy recipe that is both vegan and gluten-free. You'll love this spicy and smoky treatment for lentils and quinoa.

MAKES 8 SERVINGS

2 tbsp	vegetable oil	30 mL
1	onion, finely chopped	1
3	cloves garlic, minced	3
1 cup	dried green (Puy) lentils, rinsed	250 mL
½ cup	quinoa, rinsed	125 mL
1 tbsp	ground cumin	15 mL
1 tsp	chipotle chile powder	5 mL
1	can (4 oz/114 mL) diced green chiles	1
2¼ cups	low-sodium vegetable stock (page 204) or ready-to-use vegetable broth	550 mL
¼ cup	tomato paste	60 mL
8	taco-size (6-inch/15 cm) corn tortillas	8
1	tomato, finely chopped	1
1½ cups	chopped lettuce	375 mL
	Sliced avocado (optional)	
	Sliced green onions (optional)	

1. Heat the pressure cooker on High/Sauté/Brown. Add oil and heat until shimmering. Add onion and cook, stirring often, for 3 to 5 minutes or until translucent. Add garlic and cook, stirring, for 1 minute or until fragrant. Cancel cooking.

2. Add lentils, quinoa, cumin, chipotle powder, chiles, stock and tomato paste, stirring well. Close and lock the lid. Cook on high pressure for 10 minutes. Let stand, covered, until the float valve drops down. Check to make sure the lentils are tender but firm; if more cooking time is needed, reset to high pressure for 2 minutes.

3. Spoon taco mixture onto tortillas and top with tomato and lettuce. Serve garnished with avocado and green onions, if desired.

TIPS

If you need to eat gluten-free, check the packaging of the tortillas to make sure they were processed in a gluten-free environment.

In place of the tortillas, you can spoon this mixture into large lettuce leaves.

Vegetable and Tempeh Shepherd's Pie

Loaded with vegetables and ground tempeh, and seasoned just right, this delightful, mouthwatering dish is vegan and gluten-free.

- Steamer basket
- Steam rack
- 4-cup (1 L) round casserole dish, sprayed with nonstick cooking spray

4	medium potatoes (about 1½ lbs/750 g)	4
2 tbsp	vegetable oil	30 mL
1 lb	tempeh, crumbled	500 g
1	onion, chopped	1
2	large carrots, peeled and coarsely chopped	2
1	sprig fresh thyme	1
1½ tsp	kosher salt, divided	7 mL
¼ tsp	freshly ground black pepper	1 mL
1 cup	salt-free vegetable stock (page 205) or ready-to-use vegetable broth	250 mL
1 tbsp	tomato paste	15 mL
1 tbsp	tamari or soy sauce	15 mL
½ cup	frozen peas	125 mL
½ cup	frozen corn kernels	125 mL
½ cup	coconut milk	125 mL
½ cup	slivered almonds (optional)	125 mL

TIP

When releasing pressure quickly, keep your hands and face away from the hole on top of the steam release handle so you don't get scalded by the escaping steam.

1. Cut potatoes into 2-inch (5 cm) thick slices. Place in steamer basket and set aside.

2. Heat the pressure cooker on High/Sauté/Brown. Add oil and heat until shimmering. Add tempeh and onion; cook, stirring often, for 3 to 5 minutes or until onion is translucent. Stir in carrots, thyme, 1 tsp (5 mL) salt, pepper, stock, tomato paste and tamari. Cancel cooking.

3. Place steam rack over the tempeh mixture. Place the steamer basket on the rack. Close and lock the lid. Cook on high pressure for 12 minutes. Quickly release the pressure. Check to make sure the potatoes are fork-tender; if more cooking time is needed, reset to high pressure for 2 minutes. Remove basket and transfer potatoes to a bowl. Discard thyme sprig.

4. Preheat oven to 400°F (200°C).

5. Add peas and corn to the tempeh mixture, stirring well. Cover and let stand for 3 to 5 minutes or until peas and corn are heated through. Spoon into prepared casserole dish.

6. Carefully pull off and discard potato skins. Add milk and the remaining salt to the potatoes and mash until fluffy.

7. Spoon mashed potatoes over tempeh mixture. Using the back of a fork, spread potatoes into an even layer, completely covering tempeh mixture. Sprinkle with almonds (if using).

8. Bake for 20 to 25 minutes or until peaks of potatoes are browned. Let stand for 5 minutes, then cut into wedges. Serve immediately.

One-Pot Barbecue Curry Tofu with Jasmine Rice

This recipe takes advantage of a wonderful technique that enables you to cook your main dish in the bottom of the pot and steam your rice in a dish on top. You get the advantage of a delicious vegan main dish and a side of rice all in one pot.

MAKES 6 SERVINGS

- Tall steam rack
- 6-inch (15 cm) round metal cake pan

2 tbsp	grapeseed oil	30 mL
1	onion, chopped	1
1	green bell pepper, chopped	1
1	yellow or orange bell pepper, chopped	1
1½ lbs	extra-firm tofu, cut into 1-inch (2.5 cm) cubes	750 g
3	cloves garlic, minced	3
¼ tsp	curry powder	1 mL
1½ cups	barbecue sauce	375 mL
	Kosher salt	
1½ cups	jasmine rice, rinsed	375 mL
1½ cups	low-sodium vegetable stock (page 204) or ready-to-use vegetable broth	375 mL

> **TIP**
> For homemade barbecue sauce, see the recipe on page 211.

1. Heat the pressure cooker on High/Sauté/Brown. Add oil and heat until shimmering. Add onion, green pepper and yellow pepper; cook, stirring often, for 3 to 5 minutes or until onion is translucent. Add tofu and cook, stirring often, for 5 minutes or until lightly browned. Add garlic and curry powder; cook, stirring, for 1 minute or until fragrant. Stir in barbecue sauce and season with salt. Cancel cooking.

2. Place the steam rack on top of the tofu mixture. In the cake pan, combine rice and stock. Keeping the pan level, lower it onto the rack. Close and lock the lid. Cook on high pressure for 6 minutes. Let stand, covered, for 10 minutes, then release any remaining pressure. Remove pan and fluff rice with a fork.

3. Spoon rice onto individual serving plates and serve with barbecue curry tofu.

Thai Tofu, Carrots, Broccoli and Cauliflower with Peanut Sauce

The distinctive combination of tofu, vegetables and a sweet and spicy peanut sauce gives this dish a rich and highly pleasing flavor. It also stores perfectly for a few days, so you can eat it later in the week.

MAKES 2 SERVINGS

- Tall steam rack
- Steamer basket

2½ tbsp	toasted sesame oil, divided	37 mL
1	small onion, finely chopped	1
3	cloves garlic, minced	3
2 tbsp	sesame seeds, divided	30 mL
12 oz	extra-firm tofu, cut into 1-inch (2.5 cm) cubes	375 g
¾ cup	salt-free vegetable stock (page 205) or ready-to-use vegetable broth	175 mL
¼ cup	tamari, divided	60 mL
1 tbsp	unseasoned rice vinegar	15 mL
1	bag (12 oz/375 g) frozen broccoli, cauliflower and carrot blend	1
2½ tbsp	peanut butter	37 mL
2 tbsp	pure maple syrup	30 mL
1 tbsp	chili garlic sauce	15 mL
1	green onion, sliced	1

TIPS

You can serve this dish on its own or over rice or grains.

This dish can be stored in an airtight container in the refrigerator for up to 3 days.

1. Heat the pressure cooker on High/Sauté/Brown. Add 1 tbsp (15 mL) oil and heat until shimmering. Add onion and cook, stirring often, for 3 to 5 minutes or until translucent. Add garlic and 1 tbsp (15 mL) sesame seeds; cook, stirring, for 1 minute or until fragrant. Stir in tofu, stock, 2 tbsp (30 mL) tamari and vinegar. Cancel cooking.

2. Place the steam rack on top of the tofu mixture. Add vegetable blend to the steamer basket and place basket on the rack. Close and lock the lid. Cook on high pressure for 4 minutes. Quickly release the pressure. Remove basket and rack.

3. Using a slotted spoon, transfer tofu mixture to individual serving bowls. Arrange half the steamed vegetables in each bowl.

4. In a small bowl, whisk together peanut butter, maple syrup, chili garlic sauce and the remaining tamari and oil. Drizzle over tofu and vegetables. Serve garnished with green onions and the remaining sesame seeds.

VARIATION

Substitute frozen green beans, wax beans or Brussels sprouts for the vegetable blend.

Tofu and Cabbage Wontons

These delightful little dumplings may be vegan, but they are also a treat for meat lovers. They make a great appetizer, lunch, snack or light dinner. Did I mention I could eat these just about any time? I think you will find them just as enticing.

MAKES 36 WONTONS

- Steam rack

8 oz	firm tofu	250 g
4	green onions, finely sliced, divided	4
2	cloves garlic, minced	2
½ cup	grated carrots	125 mL
½ cup	shredded napa cabbage	125 mL
1 tbsp	minced gingerroot	15 mL
1 tbsp	chopped fresh cilantro leaves	15 mL
1 tsp	kosher salt	5 mL
1 tbsp	soy sauce or tamari	15 mL
1 tbsp	hoisin sauce	15 mL
2 tsp	sesame oil	10 mL
36	3-inch (7.5 cm) square wonton wrappers	36

TIPS

Wonton wrappers can be found in the frozen or produce section of well-stocked grocery stores or at Asian markets. If frozen, let thaw in the refrigerator overnight before using.

Serve with additional soy sauce, hoisin sauce or your favorite sauce for dipping.

1. Cut tofu in half horizontally and place in between paper towels. Cover with a plate and top with a heavy saucepan or unopened cans to weigh down. Let stand for 20 minutes. Remove tofu and cut into ¼-inch (0.5 cm) cubes.

2. Place tofu in a large bowl and add half the green onions, garlic, carrots, cabbage, ginger, cilantro, salt, soy sauce, hoisin sauce and sesame oil. Gently stir to combine.

3. Working in batches, place wonton wrappers on a plate and add about 1 tbsp (15 mL) tofu mixture to the center of each. Using your fingers, brush the edges of the wrappers with water and fold into a triangle, squeezing out air and pressing down edges to seal. Repeat until all wrappers are filled.

4. Add 1 cup (250 mL) water (or the amount required by your cooker to reach pressure) to the pressure cooker and place the steam rack in the pot. Place about 12 filled wontons on the rack, overlapping them slightly. Close and lock the lid. Cook on high pressure for 7 minutes. Quickly release the pressure. Check to make sure the wontons are hot and steaming; if more cooking time is needed, reset to high pressure for 1 minute.

5. Transfer wontons to a serving platter, cover with foil and keep warm. Add water as necessary to maintain the minimum amount of water needed in the pot. Repeat with the remaining wontons. Serve sprinkled with the remaining green onions.

Tex-Mex Stuffed Peppers

With slightly crunchy millet, the pleasant textures of lentils and corn, and Tex-Mex-inspired seasonings, these stuffed peppers, full of flavor and fiber, make a tantalizing, filling main dish or side.

MAKES 4 SERVINGS

- Steam rack

1 tbsp	virgin olive oil	15 mL
1	onion, finely chopped	1
1 cup	millet, rinsed	250 mL
½ cup	dried green (Puy) lentils, rinsed	125 mL
2¼ cups	low-sodium vegetable stock (page 204) or ready-to-use vegetable broth	550 mL
4	bell peppers (any color)	4
1 cup	frozen corn kernels	250 mL
½ cup	shredded Monterey Jack cheese, divided	125 mL
½ cup	shredded mozzarella cheese	125 mL
2 tbsp	chopped fresh cilantro	30 mL
1 tsp	ground cumin	5 mL
½ tsp	hot pepper flakes	2 mL
1 cup	salsa	250 mL
	Kosher salt and freshly ground black pepper	
1	green onion, sliced	1
	Cilantro leaves	

1. Heat the pressure cooker on High/Sauté/Brown. Add oil and heat until shimmering. Add onion and cook, stirring often, for 3 to 5 minutes or until translucent. Add millet and lentils; cook, stirring, for 1 minute or until lightly toasted. Cancel cooking.

2. Add stock, stirring well. Close and lock the lid. Cook on high pressure for 10 minutes. Let stand, covered, until the float valve drops down. Check to make sure the lentils are tender; if more cooking time is needed, reset to high pressure for 2 minutes. Transfer millet mixture to a large bowl.

3. Cut the tops off the peppers and remove the seeds and ribs. Finely chop the tops.

4. To the millet mixture, add finely chopped bell pepper, corn, ¼ cup (60 mL) Monterey Jack, mozzarella, chopped cilantro, cumin, hot pepper flakes and salsa. Season with salt and black pepper, stirring well. Spoon mixture into bell pepper shells, dividing evenly.

5. Add 1 cup (250 mL) water (or the amount required by your cooker to reach pressure) to the pressure cooker and place the steam rack in the pot. Arrange the peppers on the rack. Close and lock the lid. Cook on high pressure for 15 minutes. Let stand, covered, for 10 minutes, then release any remaining pressure. Check to make sure the bell peppers are tender and the stuffing is heated through; if more cooking time is needed, reset to high pressure for 2 minutes.

6. Transfer peppers to individual serving plates. Serve garnished with the remaining Monterey Jack, green onion and cilantro leaves.

VARIATION

Slow Cooker Tex-Mex Stuffed Peppers: For step 5, spray the inner cooking pot with cooking spray. Arrange stuffed peppers upright in pot. Close and lock the lid, making sure the steam vent is open. Press Slow Cook and adjust the temperature to the lowest setting. Cook for 5 to 5½ hours or until bell peppers are tender and stuffing is heated through.

Root Vegetable Gratin

This riff on scalloped potatoes adds celery root, parsnips and turnips to the potatoes for a cornucopia of fall harvest vegetables in a creamy, flavorful sauce.

MAKES 8 SERVINGS

- Steamer basket
- Steam rack
- 13- by 9-inch (33 by 23 cm) glass baking dish, sprayed with nonstick cooking spray

4	parsnips (about 1 lb/500 g total)	4
3	large turnips (about 1 lb/500 g total)	3
2	russet potatoes (about 1 lb/500 g total)	2
1	small celery root (about 1 lb/500 g)	1
2 tbsp	butter or ghee	30 mL
1	onion, chopped	1
1 tsp	kosher salt	5 mL
1/8 tsp	freshly ground black pepper	0.5 mL
1 cup	low-sodium vegetable stock (page 204) or ready-to-use vegetable broth	250 mL
1 cup	panko	250 mL
3 tbsp	butter or ghee, melted	45 mL
1/2 cup	sour cream or plain yogurt	125 mL
1 cup	shredded Monterey Jack cheese	250 mL

TIP

You can change the amount of any of the root vegetables in the list. Just make sure you end up with a total of 6 cups (1.5 L) sliced vegetables.

1. Peel parsnips, turnips, potatoes and celery root and cut into 1/8-inch (3 mm) thick slices. Place vegetables in the steamer basket. Set aside.

2. Heat the pressure cooker on High/Sauté/Brown. Add 2 tbsp (30 mL) butter and heat until melted. Add onion and cook, stirring often, for 3 to 5 minutes or until translucent. Stir in salt, pepper and stock. Cancel cooking.

3. Place the steam rack in the pot and place the steamer basket on the rack. Close and lock the lid. Cook on high pressure for 5 minutes.

4. Meanwhile, preheat broiler.

5. In a small bowl, combine panko and melted butter. Set aside.

6. When the cooking time is done, quickly release the pressure. Check to make sure the vegetables are fork-tender; if more cooking time is needed, close the lid and let stand for 3 minutes. Remove basket and transfer vegetables to the prepared baking dish.

7. Add sour cream and cheese to the liquid in the cooker, stirring well. Pour over vegetable mixture. Using a fork, move vegetables around slightly so the sauce gets mixed in. Sprinkle with panko mixture.

8. Broil for 5 to 7 minutes or until golden brown. Let stand for 10 minutes before serving.

Hearty Mushroom Bolognese

Cremini and shiitake mushrooms paired up with sautéed vegetables and Italian seasonings develop into a deep, healthy Bolognese sauce. Serve it over your favorite pasta — either whole wheat or gluten-free — or over zucchini noodles.

MAKES 6 SERVINGS

1 tbsp	olive oil	15 mL
1	onion, chopped	1
1	carrot, chopped	1
2 tbsp	butter or virgin coconut oil	30 mL
1½ lbs	cremini mushrooms, trimmed and quartered	750 g
12 oz	shiitake mushrooms, stems discarded, caps finely chopped	375 g
3	cloves garlic, minced	3
1 cup	dry red wine	250 mL
3	bay leaves	3
¼ cup	finely chopped fresh sage	60 mL
¼ cup	finely chopped fresh basil	60 mL
1 tbsp	kosher salt	15 mL
1 tsp	granulated sugar	5 mL
1	can (28 oz/796 mL) whole tomatoes, with juice	1
1½ cups	salt-free vegetable stock (page 205) or ready-to-use vegetable broth	375 mL
3 tbsp	tomato paste	45 mL
2 tsp	coconut amino acids	10 mL
3 tbsp	heavy cream, whipping (35%) cream or coconut cream	45 mL

TIP

When releasing pressure quickly, keep your hands and face away from the hole on top of the steam release handle so you don't get scalded by the escaping steam.

1. Heat the pressure cooker on High/Sauté/Brown. Add oil and heat until shimmering. Add onion and carrot; cook, stirring, for 3 to 5 minutes or until onion is translucent. Add butter and heat until melted. Add cremini and shiitake mushrooms; cook, stirring often, for 7 to 9 minutes or until mushrooms have released most of their liquid. Add garlic and cook, stirring, for 1 minute or until fragrant. Add wine and cook, stirring and scraping up any browned bits from the bottom of the pot, for 5 to 7 minutes or until wine is almost evaporated. Cancel cooking.

2. Add bay leaves, sage, basil, salt, sugar, tomatoes, stock, tomato paste and amino acids, stirring well. Close and lock the lid. Cook on high pressure for 20 minutes. Quickly release the pressure. Discard bay leaves.

3. Using a potato masher, mash the tomatoes. Heat the cooker on High/Sauté/Brown. Cook, stirring, for 5 to 10 minutes or until sauce is thickened to your liking. Stir in cream.

Asparagus and Lemon Risotto with Arugula

Nothing beats a good risotto, and this is one of my favorites. No more messing around with stirring your risotto on the stove; the pressure cooker gives perfect results without extra effort.

- 6-cup (1.5 L) measuring cup

1 lb	fresh asparagus, ends trimmed	500 g
4 cups	water	1 L
1 tbsp	virgin olive oil	15 mL
1	large shallot, minced (about $1/3$ cup/75 mL)	1
$1\frac{1}{2}$ cups	Arborio rice	375 mL
$\frac{1}{2}$ cup	dry white wine	125 mL
2 tsp	kosher salt	10 mL
$\frac{1}{2}$ cup	packed arugula leaves, shredded	125 mL
$\frac{1}{3}$ cup	grated Parmigiano-Reggiano cheese	75 mL
	Grated zest and juice of $\frac{1}{2}$ lemon	
1 tbsp	butter or extra virgin olive oil (optional)	15 mL
	Kosher salt and freshly ground black pepper	

TIPS

Using authentic, full-flavored Parmigiano-Reggiano cheese creates a complex, yet subtle tango of flavors. If you can't find it, you can use regular Parmesan.

Serve with a fresh lettuce salad with a tangy vinaigrette for a complete meal.

1. Cut off the tips of the asparagus and set aside. Cut the spears into $3/4$-inch (2 cm) slices.

2. In the pressure cooker, combine asparagus slices and water. Close and lock the lid. Cook on high pressure for 12 minutes. Quickly release the pressure. Check to make sure the asparagus is tender but firm; if more cooking time is needed, reset to high pressure for 2 minutes.

3. Using a slotted spoon, transfer asparagus to the measuring cup. Pour in enough cooking liquid to measure $4\frac{1}{4}$ cups (1.05 L) total volume, adding more water if needed.

4. Heat the cooker on High/Sauté/Brown. Add oil and heat until shimmering. Add shallot and cook, stirring, for 2 to 3 minutes or until softened. Add rice, stirring to coat with oil. Add wine and cook, stirring constantly, for 2 to 3 minutes or until absorbed. Cancel cooking.

5. Add asparagus mixture, the reserved asparagus tips and salt, stirring well. Close and lock the lid. Cook on high pressure for 6 minutes. Quickly release the pressure. Check to make sure the rice is al dente; if more cooking time is needed, close the lid and let stand for 2 minutes. Set the cooker to Warm/Keep Warm.

6. Add arugula, cheese, lemon zest, lemon juice and butter (if using), stirring vigorously to combine. Season to taste with salt and pepper. Serve immediately.

Layered Tortilla and Black Bean Pie

A riff on enchiladas, this black bean pie is the ultimate comfort food. When you taste its blend of Southwestern flavors, you'll be saying "Yum!" over and over again.

MAKES 6 SERVINGS

2 cups	dried black beans, rinsed	500 mL
	Water	
1	red onion, finely chopped	1
1	bay leaf	1
1 tbsp	virgin olive oil	15 mL
2	tomatoes, diced	2
1 cup	corn kernels	250 mL
½ cup	sliced black olives	125 mL
1 tbsp	chopped fresh cilantro	15 mL
1	can (4 oz/114 mL) diced green chiles	1
1	jar (16 oz/473 mL) salsa verde	1
12	taco-size (6-inch/15 cm) corn tortillas	12
1½ cups	shredded Mexican cheese blend	375 mL
	Sour cream (optional)	

TIP

When pressure-cooking beans of any type, make sure to fill the pot no more than halfway full. Do not attempt to double or triple the recipe, or the exhaust valve may become clogged as the beans froth up under pressure. Adding oil with the beans helps to reduce the amount of froth.

1. Place beans in a large bowl, add 8 cups (2 L) cold water and let soak at room temperature for 8 hours or overnight. Drain and rinse beans.

2. In the pressure cooker, combine beans, red onion, bay leaf, 4 cups (1 L) water and oil. Close and lock the lid. Cook on high pressure for 5 minutes. Let stand, covered, until the float valve drops down. Check to make sure the beans are tender; if more cooking time is needed, reset to high pressure for 1 minute. Discard bay leaf. Drain and rinse beans.

3. Transfer beans to a large bowl and stir in tomatoes, corn, olives, cilantro, chiles and salsa verde.

4. Add ¼ inch (0.5 cm) water to the cooker and spoon in one-fifth of the bean mixture. Arrange 3 tortillas on top, overlapping them as needed. Repeat layers three more times and top with the remaining bean mixture. Close and lock the lid. Cook on high pressure for 5 minutes. Quickly release the pressure.

5. Sprinkle with cheese, cover and let stand for 10 minutes. Cut into wedges and, if desired, dollop with sour cream.

Crustless Tomato Spinach Quiche

This light quiche, filled with tomatoes, baby spinach and green onions, is perfect for breakfast or lunch, or when you are craving breakfast for dinner.

- 6-cup (1.5 L) round casserole dish
- Steam rack

12	large eggs	12
1/2 cup	milk or almond milk	125 mL
1/2 tsp	kosher salt	2 mL
1/4 tsp	freshly ground black pepper	1 mL
1	tomato, seeded and diced	1
3	green onions, sliced	3
3 cups	packed baby spinach, coarsely chopped	750 mL
1/4 cup	freshly grated Parmesan cheese or nutritional yeast	60 mL

TIPS

The quiche is good served hot, cool or cold. Leftovers can be covered and refrigerated for up to 5 days.

A slice of quiche is perfect for lunch. Serve it with a small bowl of fruit for a satisfying complement. If packing the quiche to go, make sure you can keep it cold until you're ready to eat.

1. In a large bowl, whisk together eggs, milk, salt and pepper. Stir in tomato, green onions and spinach. Transfer to the casserole dish and sprinkle with Parmesan.

2. Add 1 cup (250 mL) water (or the amount required by your cooker to reach pressure) to the pressure cooker and place the steam rack in the pot. Keeping the casserole dish level, lower it onto the rack. Close and lock the lid. Cook on high pressure for 20 minutes. Let stand, covered, for 10 minutes, then release any remaining pressure. Remove dish from pot and let stand for 5 minutes, then cut into wedges.

Eggplant Parmigiana

Eggplant can take some prep work to eliminate its rather strong and bitter liquids. The pressure cooker eliminates this step with a quick steam. Then all you need to do is assemble your dish and bake it in the oven for a hearty, satisfying dish in much less time.

MAKES 6 SERVINGS

- Steam rack
- Steamer basket
- 13- by 9-inch (33 by 23 cm) glass baking dish, sprayed with nonstick cooking spray

2 lbs	eggplant (about 1 large), cut into 1/4-inch (0.5 cm) slices	1 kg
1	large egg	1
2 tsp	kosher salt	10 mL
1 tbsp	water	15 mL
2 2/3 cups	tomato sauce	650 mL
1 1/2 cups	panko	375 mL
2 cups	shredded mozzarella cheese	500 mL
1/4 cup	grated Parmigiano-Reggiano cheese	60 mL
	Virgin olive oil	
	Finely sliced basil leaves	

TIP

Using authentic, full-flavored Parmigiano-Reggiano cheese creates a complex, yet subtle tango of flavors. If you can't find it, you can use regular Parmesan cheese.

1. Add 1 cup (250 mL) water (or the amount required by your cooker to reach pressure) to the pressure cooker and place the steam rack in the pot. Arrange eggplant slices in the steamer basket and place basket on the rack. Close and lock the lid. Cook on high pressure for 5 minutes. Quickly release the pressure. Check to make sure the eggplant is tender but firm; if more cooking time is needed, reset to high pressure for 1 minute. Transfer eggplant slices to a cutting board.

2. Preheat oven to 350°F (180°C).

3. In a small bowl, whisk together egg, salt and water.

4. Drizzle 3 tbsp (45 mL) tomato sauce over bottom of prepared baking dish. Arrange one-quarter of the eggplant in the dish, overlapping slices to cover the bottom. Brush eggplant with egg mixture and sprinkle with one-quarter of the panko. Drizzle with 2/3 cup (150 mL) tomato sauce and sprinkle with 1/2 cup (125 mL) mozzarella. Starting with another layer of eggplant, repeat layers three more times, then sprinkle Parmigiano-Reggiano on top. Drizzle with oil.

5. Bake for 20 minutes. Transfer to a wire rack and let cool for 10 minutes. Cut into sections and serve garnished with basil.

Savory Vegetable Loaf

Don't be daunted by the list of ingredients; this mouthwatering loaf is packed with so much flavor, even dedicated meat lovers will want in on the action.

MAKES 4 TO 6 SERVINGS

- 1 sheet of heavy-duty foil, edges turned up and folded to form a loaf-like pan
- Steam rack

Loaf

4 oz	sun-dried tomatoes	125 g
1 cup	warm water	250 mL
2	large eggs	2
1 cup	panko	250 mL
1 cup	chopped walnuts	250 mL
1 tbsp	butter or ghee	15 mL
1 lb	cremini mushrooms, finely chopped	500 g
1 tbsp	virgin olive oil	15 mL
1	small onion, finely chopped	1
1 cup	½-inch (1 cm) asparagus pieces	250 mL
2	cloves garlic, minced	2
½ cup	freshly grated Parmesan cheese	125 mL
2 tbsp	chopped fresh basil	30 mL
1 tsp	kosher salt	5 mL
½ tsp	freshly ground black pepper	2 mL
1 tbsp	ketchup	15 mL
2 tsp	Worcestershire sauce	10 mL
1 tsp	Dijon mustard	5 mL

Topping

2 tbsp	ketchup	30 mL
1 tbsp	low-sodium vegetable stock (page 204) or ready-to-use vegetable broth	15 mL
½ tsp	Dijon mustard	2 mL

1. *Loaf:* In a small bowl, combine sun-dried tomatoes and water. Let stand for 15 minutes or until soft. Drain, reserving soaking water. Coarsely chop tomatoes and set aside.

2. In a medium bowl, whisk together eggs and the reserved soaking water. Stir in panko. Set aside.

3. Heat the pressure cooker on High/Sauté/Brown. Add walnuts and cook, stirring, for 2 minutes or until lightly toasted and fragrant. Transfer to a plate to cool.

4. Add butter to the cooker and heat until melted. Add tomatoes and mushrooms; cook, stirring often, for 8 to 10 minutes or until mushrooms have released their liquid. Transfer mixture to another plate to cool.

5. Add oil to the cooker and heat until shimmering. Add onion and cook, stirring often, for 3 to 5 minutes or until translucent. Add asparagus and cook, stirring, for 2 minutes or until slightly softened. Add garlic and cook, stirring, for 1 minute or until fragrant. Transfer mixture to a large bowl to cool.

6. Add panko mixture, walnuts, mushroom mixture, Parmesan, basil, salt, pepper, ketchup, Worcestershire sauce and mustard to the cooled asparagus mixture. Using your hands, combine well. Transfer to prepared foil and form into an oblong loaf that will fit in the cooker.

7. *Topping:* In a small bowl, combine ketchup, stock and mustard. Spread over top of loaf.

8. Add 2 cups (500 mL) water (or the amount required by your cooker to reach pressure) to the cooker. Use the foil to lift the loaf onto the steam rack. Lower the rack into the pot. Close and lock the lid. Cook on high pressure for 9 minutes. Quickly release the pressure. Carefully transfer loaf to a cutting board, cover with foil and let stand for 5 minutes before slicing.

Desserts

Classic Cheesecake

You have probably heard about the amazing cheesecake you can make in a pressure cooker. Well, cheesecake lovers, here it is. This lovely little gem is so easy and so delicious, and it consistently turns out firm and flavorful every time I make it.

MAKES 8 SERVINGS

- 6-inch (15 cm) springform pan, buttered
- Food processor
- Steam rack

1¼ cups	graham cracker crumbs	300 mL
¼ cup	unsalted butter, melted	60 mL
1 lb	brick-style cream cheese, softened	500 g
½ cup	granulated sugar	125 mL
2	large eggs, at room temperature	2
1½ tbsp	all-purpose flour	22 mL
¼ cup	cottage cheese (preferably small-curd)	60 mL
	Grated zest and juice of ½ lemon	
½ tsp	vanilla extract	2 mL

TIPS

Make sure your cream cheese is softened (at least 1 to 2 hours at room temperature) and your eggs are at room temperature. Your cheesecake will be smooth and creamy, not lumpy.

You can substitute an equal amount of full-fat sour cream for the cottage cheese, if you prefer.

1. In a small bowl, combine graham cracker crumbs and butter until evenly moist. Press into the bottom and halfway up the sides of the prepared pan.

2. In food processor, process cream cheese and sugar until smooth, scraping down the sides of the bowl as needed. With the motor running, add eggs through the feed tube and process until smooth. Add flour, cottage cheese, lemon zest, lemon juice and vanilla; process for 2 minutes or until smooth and creamy. Pour batter into the pan.

3. Add 2 cups (500 mL) water (or the amount required by your cooker to reach pressure) to the pressure cooker and place the steam rack in the pot. Place the pan on the rack. Close and lock the lid. Cook on high pressure for 25 minutes. Let stand, covered, until the float valve drops down. Check to make sure a tester inserted in the center of the cheesecake comes out clean; if more cooking time is needed, reset to high pressure for 5 minutes. Carefully remove pan and rack; let stand on rack for 1 hour.

4. Remove the ring of the pan, cover and refrigerate cheesecake for at least 6 hours or up to 2 days before slicing.

VARIATION

Instead of the graham cracker crumbs, use crushed vanilla or chocolate wafers, shortbread cookies or gingersnaps.

Chocolate Marble Cheesecake

What makes cheesecake even better? Chocolate, of course! This dreamy little cheesecake is swirled with chocolate for a decadent taste experience. Its lovely presentation makes it perfect for special occasions. You can even drizzle it with caramel topping and grated bittersweet chocolate for extra pizzazz.

MAKES 8 SERVINGS

- 6-inch (15 cm) springform pan, buttered
- Food processor
- Steam rack

1¼ cups	chocolate graham cracker crumbs	300 mL
¼ cup	unsalted butter, melted	60 mL
1 lb	brick-style cream cheese, softened	500 g
½ cup	granulated sugar	125 mL
2	large eggs, at room temperature	2
1½ tbsp	all-purpose flour	22 mL
¼ cup	cottage cheese (preferably small-curd)	60 mL
½ tsp	vanilla extract	2 mL
3 tbsp	unsweetened cocoa powder	45 mL
¼ cup	hot water	60 mL
3 tbsp	dark (bittersweet) chocolate chips	45 mL
	Caramel ice cream topping (optional)	
	Grated bittersweet chocolate (optional)	

1. In a small bowl, combine graham cracker crumbs and butter until evenly moist. Press into the bottom and halfway up the sides of the prepared pan.

2. In food processor, process cream cheese and sugar until smooth, scraping down the sides of the bowl as needed. With the motor running, add eggs through the feed tube and process until smooth. Add flour, cottage cheese and vanilla; process for 2 minutes or until smooth and creamy.

3. In a medium bowl, whisk together cocoa and hot water. Stir in chocolate chips. Add 1 cup (250 mL) cream cheese mixture, stirring well. Set aside.

4. Pour the remaining batter into the pan. Drizzle chocolate mixture in a circular pattern over the plain filling. Using a knife, make circular strokes in the batter to create swirls.

5. Add 2 cups (500 mL) water (or the amount required by your cooker to reach pressure) to the pressure cooker and place the steam rack in the pot. Place the pan on the rack. Close and lock the lid. Cook on high pressure for 25 minutes. Let stand, covered, until the float valve drops down. Check to make sure a tester inserted in the center of the cheesecake comes out clean; if more cooking time is needed, reset to high pressure for 5 minutes. Carefully remove pan and rack; let stand on rack for 1 hour.

6. Remove the ring of the pan, cover and refrigerate cheesecake for at least 6 hours or up to 2 days before slicing. Just before serving, drizzle with caramel topping and grated chocolate, if desired.

VARIATION

Instead of the graham cracker crumbs, use crushed vanilla wafers, chocolate wafers or shortbread cookies.

TIP

Make sure not to overprocess the mixture in step 2, or the cheesecake will become too firm and not as creamy.

Strawberry Mini Cheesecakes

These scrumptious cheesecakes are a fun treat. Once cooled, they are topped with glazed strawberries for a mouthwatering presentation.

- Four 4-oz (125 mL) ovenproof custard cups (see tip)
- Food processor
- Steam rack

1 cup	graham cracker crumbs	250 mL
3 tbsp	unsalted butter, melted	45 mL
8 oz	brick-style cream cheese, softened	250 g
1/4 cup	granulated sugar	60 mL
1	large egg, at room temperature	1
2 tsp	all-purpose flour	10 mL
2 tbsp	sour cream	30 mL
2 tsp	freshly squeezed lemon juice	10 mL
1/2 tsp	vanilla extract	2 mL
	Water	
1/4 cup	strawberry jelly	60 mL
12	small whole strawberries	12

TIPS

I like using custard cups, as you can see your yummy cheesecakes through them. But you can use 3½-inch (8.5 cm) ramekins; just increase the pressure cooking time to 9 minutes. If you want to remove the cheesecakes from the ramekins to serve, line the ramekins with foil.

Monitor the jelly closely while heating it, as you do not want it to start bubbling.

Hull the strawberries just before serving, as the juice from the berries can bleed down into the cheesecake.

1. In a small bowl, combine graham cracker crumbs and butter until evenly moist. Press into the bottom of the custard cups.

2. In food processor, process cream cheese and sugar until smooth, scraping down the sides of the bowl as needed. With the motor running, add egg through the feed tube and process until smooth. Add flour, sour cream, lemon juice and vanilla; process for 2 minutes or until smooth and creamy. Pour batter into the custard cups, dividing evenly.

3. Add 1 cup (250 mL) water (or the amount required by your cooker to reach pressure) to the pressure cooker and place the steam rack in the pot. Place the cups on the rack. Close and lock the lid. Cook on high pressure for 7 minutes. Let stand, covered, until the float valve drops down. Check to make sure a tester inserted in the center of a cheesecake comes out clean; if more cooking time is needed, reset to high pressure for 1 minute. Carefully remove cups and rack; let stand on rack for 1 hour. Refrigerate cups for at least 4 hours or up to 12 hours.

4. Add strawberry jelly to a small glass bowl and microwave on High for 20 seconds or until liquefied.

5. Hull strawberries and arrange 3 berries, stem side down, on top of each cheesecake. Using a pastry brush, brush berries with strawberry glaze.

Molten Chocolate Cakes

If you are in the mood for chocolate indulgence, this is the cake for you. When you dive in with your fork, you will experience sheer bliss as the gooey, pudding-like center flows out of the cake dome. True chocolate lovers can even top it with a chocolate shell topping.

- Four 6-oz (175 mL) ovenproof custard cups, sprayed with nonstick cooking spray
- Steam rack

1 cup	semisweet chocolate chips	250 mL
½ cup	unsalted butter	125 mL
1 cup	confectioners' (icing) sugar	250 mL
3	large eggs	3
1	large egg yolk	1
1 tbsp	vanilla extract	15 mL
6 tbsp	all-purpose flour	90 mL

Optional Toppings

Chocolate shell topping (see tip)
or caramel sauce
Vanilla ice cream

1. In a medium heavy-bottom saucepan, heat chocolate chips and butter over low heat, stirring until just melted and combined. Remove from heat and stir in confectioners' sugar until smooth.

2. In a small bowl, whisk together eggs, egg yolk and vanilla. Whisk in flour. Pour into chocolate mixture, stirring well. Pour batter into custard cups, dividing evenly.

3. Add 1 cup (250 mL) water (or the amount required by your cooker to reach pressure) to the pressure cooker and place the steam rack in the pot. Arrange cups on rack, stacking them in alternating layers (like stacking bricks), if needed. Close and lock the lid. Cook on high pressure for 10 minutes. Quickly release the pressure. If you like a pudding-like center, check to make sure the top is firm and dry. If you prefer a more cake-like center, use a fork to make sure the inside is firm. If more cooking time is needed, reset to high pressure for 5 minutes.

4. Carefully remove cups and invert onto dessert plates. If desired, drizzle with chocolate shell topping or caramel sauce and/or serve with ice cream.

TIPS

Chocolate Shell Topping: In a 2-cup (500 mL) glass measuring cup, combine 1 cup (250 mL) chopped dark (bittersweet) chocolate and 2 tbsp (30 mL) virgin coconut oil. Microwave on High in 30-second increments until completely melted. Stir well. Pour over cakes and let stand for 30 seconds or until hardened. (The topping will harden faster if the cake has been cooled slightly.) Makes 1 cup (250 mL).

In step 1, instead of melting the chocolate and butter on the stovetop, you can put them in a medium microwave-safe container and microwave on High, stirring occasionally, for 1 to 2 minutes or until melted.

Chocolate, Peanut Butter and Marshmallow Brownies

Chocolate, peanut butter and marshmallows are the magic trio in these gooey, moist brownies. Serve them warm or at room temperature; either way, they are sure to be a hit.

- 6-inch (15 cm) springform pan, sprayed with nonstick cooking spray
- Steam rack

²⁄₃ cup	unsweetened cocoa powder	150 mL
¼ cup	all-purpose flour	60 mL
¾ cup	granulated sugar	175 mL
2	large eggs	2
½ cup	unsalted butter, melted	125 mL
½ tsp	vanilla extract	2 mL
½ cup	chopped walnuts	125 mL
3 tbsp	peanut butter chips	45 mL
	Marshmallow fluff	

TIPS

You can also use a 6-inch (15 cm) round metal cake pan in this recipe. To make it easier to release your brownies from the pan, line the bottom of the pan with waxed paper or parchment paper lightly coated with nonstick cooking spray.

You can use any variety of nuts and chips in this recipe; just keep the measurements the same.

1. In a large bowl, whisk together cocoa and flour.

2. In a medium bowl, whisk together sugar, eggs, butter and vanilla. Add to the cocoa mixture, whisking well. Fold in walnuts and peanut butter chips. Pour batter into prepared pan.

3. Add 2 cups (500 mL) water (or the amount required by your cooker to reach pressure) to the pressure cooker and place the steam rack in the pot. Place pan on the rack. Close and lock the lid. Cook on high pressure for 25 minutes. Let stand, covered, for 10 minutes, then release any remaining pressure. Check to make sure a tester inserted in the center of the brownie comes out clean; if more cooking time is needed, reset to high pressure for 3 minutes. Carefully remove pan and rack; let stand on rack for 10 minutes.

4. Remove the ring of the pan and cut brownie into 6 wedges to serve warm, or let cool to room temperature before cutting. Serve with dollops of marshmallow fluff.

Poppy Seed, Lemon and Peach Crisp

My first experience with the marriage of peaches and poppy seeds was at my local produce market, where they were giving out samples of chin-dripping peaches with a poppy seed dressing. It was heavenly. This crumb-topped dessert is a tribute to that light and refreshing taste.

MAKES 6 SERVINGS

- 4-cup (1 L) casserole dish
- Steam rack

Streusel

2 tbsp	all-purpose flour	30 mL
1 tbsp	large-flake (old-fashioned) rolled oats	15 mL
1 tbsp	packed light brown sugar	15 mL
1 tsp	poppy seeds	5 mL
1/8 tsp	ground cardamom	0.5 mL
Pinch	kosher salt	Pinch
3 tbsp	cold unsalted butter, cut into small pieces	45 mL

Filling

2 lbs	peaches (3 to 4 medium), diced	1 kg
1/2 cup	dry bread crumbs	125 mL
1/2 cup	superfine sugar (see tip, page 198)	125 mL
1 1/2 tbsp	poppy seeds	22 mL
1/2 tsp	ground cardamom	2 mL
1/2 cup	plain yogurt	125 mL
	Grated zest of 1 lemon	
2 tbsp	freshly squeezed lemon juice	30 mL

1. *Streusel:* In a small bowl, combine flour, oats, brown sugar, poppy seeds, cardamom and salt, mixing well. Using a fork, cut in butter until streusel is in small bits. Set aside.

2. *Filling:* In a medium bowl, combine peaches, bread crumbs, sugar, poppy seeds, cardamom, yogurt, lemon zest and lemon juice. Pour into casserole dish.

3. Add 2 cups (500 mL) water (or the amount required by your cooker to reach pressure) to the pressure cooker and place the steam rack in the pot. Place the casserole dish on the rack. Close and lock the lid. Cook on high pressure for 12 minutes.

4. Meanwhile, preheat broiler with the rack on the second-highest rung.

5. When the cooking time is done, quickly release the pressure. Check to make sure the peaches are tender; if more cooking time is needed, reset to high pressure for 3 minutes.

6. Carefully remove dish and sprinkle with streusel. Broil for 3 to 5 minutes or until streusel is golden brown and caramelized. Let stand for 5 minutes before serving.

TIPS

If desired, you can toast the bread crumbs in a skillet over medium-high heat, tossing until golden brown.

Leftover crisp can be covered tightly and stored in the refrigerator for up to 3 days or in the freezer for up to 2 months.

Crustless Pumpkin Pies

My grandmother discovered crustless pumpkin pie when the concept was first introduced. I was ecstatic, since I am not a crust lover. Her creation was creamy, light and scrumptious — the best pumpkin pie ever. These mini pies take it a step further and are amazingly quick and easy.

MAKES 8 SERVINGS

- Steamer basket
- Steam rack
- Food processor or blender
- Fine-mesh sieve, lined with cheesecloth
- Eight 4-oz (125 mL) ramekins

2 to 3 lb	pie (sugar) pumpkin	1 to 1.5 kg
2	large eggs	2
1 tbsp	cornstarch	15 mL
1 tsp	ground cinnamon	5 mL
½ tsp	ground ginger	2 mL
½ tsp	ground allspice	2 mL
½ tsp	kosher salt	2 mL
¼ tsp	ground cloves	1 mL
1 cup	heavy or whipping (35%) cream	250 mL
¾ cup	pure maple syrup	175 mL
	Whipped cream	
	Ground nutmeg	

1. Remove the stem from the pumpkin and cut the pumpkin into 6 wedges. Remove and discard seeds and stringy pulp. Arrange pumpkin wedges in the steamer basket.

2. Add 1 cup (250 mL) water (or the amount required by your cooker to reach pressure) to the pressure cooker and place the steam rack in the pot. Place basket on the rack. Close and lock the lid. Cook on high pressure for 7 minutes. Quickly release the pressure. Check to make sure the pumpkin is fork-tender and easily pulls away from the skin; if more cooking time is needed, reset to high pressure for 2 minutes. Remove pumpkin and let stand until cool enough to handle.

3. Peel skin from pumpkin and discard. Transfer pulp to food processor, in batches, as necessary, and purée pumpkin until smooth (or your desired consistency). Transfer pumpkin to the lined sieve; let drain, then squeeze out any remaining liquid with the cheesecloth.

4. Measure 2 cups (500 mL) drained pumpkin purée (transfer the remaining purée to an airtight container and refrigerate or freeze to use in another dish).

5. In a large bowl, whisk eggs. Whisk in cornstarch, cinnamon, ginger, allspice, salt, cloves, cream and maple syrup until well combined. Stir in pumpkin purée until thoroughly combined. Pour into ramekins, dividing evenly.

6. Replenish the water in the cooker as needed and place the steam rack in the pot. Arrange ramekins on the rack, stacking them in alternating layers (like stacking bricks). Close and lock the lid. Cook on high pressure for 9 minutes. Let stand, covered, for 10 minutes, then release any remaining pressure. Check to make sure a tester inserted in the center of a pie comes out clean; if more cooking time is needed, reset to high pressure for 2 minutes. Carefully remove ramekins and let stand for 5 minutes. Serve warm, with a dollop of whipped cream, sprinkled with nutmeg.

Lemon and Rosemary Stuffed Apples

In this unique and refreshing dessert, firm apples are stuffed with a fusion of lemon marmalade, almond biscuits, walnuts and fresh rosemary for a treat that is tart, sweet and savory, all in one bundle.

MAKES 4 SERVINGS

• Steam rack

4	small tart cooking apples (such as Granny Smith or Cameo)	4
¼ cup	lemon marmalade	60 mL
2 tsp	minced fresh rosemary	10 mL
1¼ cups	crumbled almond biscuits or amaretti cookies, divided	300 mL
½ cup	finely chopped walnuts	125 mL
1 tbsp	granulated sugar	15 mL
¼ cup	cold unsalted butter, cut into small pieces	60 mL
	Vanilla ice cream	

TIPS

This recipe is suitable for 6- to 8-quart (6 to 8 L) pressure cookers. You can cut it in half for smaller cookers.

When quickly releasing the pressure, keep your hands and face away from the hole on top of the steam release handle, so you don't get scalded by the escaping steam.

1. Cut apples in half lengthwise. Using a melon baller or spoon, scoop out the center of the apple halves, leaving about ¾ inch (2 cm) flesh. Brush cut surface of apples with marmalade. Sprinkle with rosemary. Set aside.

2. In a small bowl, combine 1 cup (250 mL) crumbled biscuits, walnuts and sugar. Using a fork, cut in butter until crumbly. Spoon mixture into the center of the apples, filling the hole and covering the top.

3. Add 2 cups (500 mL) water (or the amount required by your cooker to reach pressure) to the pressure cooker and place the steam rack in the pot. Place apples on the rack, stacking them in alternating layers (like stacking bricks), if needed. Close and lock the lid. Cook on high pressure for 5 minutes. Quickly release the pressure. Check to make sure the apples are tender; if more cooking time is needed, reset to high pressure for 1 minute.

4. Using two large spoons, transfer apples to individual serving plates. Serve each with a scoop of ice cream sprinkled with the remaining biscuits.

VARIATION

In place of fresh rosemary, try minced fresh thyme, mint or basil.

Cherries Jubilee

This surprisingly simple version of the classic dessert doesn't feature a burst of flames, but you'll fall in love with its easy elegance and scrumptious flavor.

MAKES 4 SERVINGS		
1	lemon	1
1 lb	frozen sweet cherries (such as Bing)	500 g
½ cup	granulated sugar	125 mL
⅓ cup	white grape juice	75 mL
6 tbsp	water, divided	90 mL
2 tsp	cherry extract	10 mL
¼ tsp	almond extract	1 mL
1 tbsp	cornstarch	15 mL
1 pint	vanilla ice cream	500 mL

TIP

You can use fresh sweet cherries instead of frozen; just increase the cooking time in step 2 to 8 minutes. Wash and dry the cherries, then remove the pits. You will want to use kitchen gloves so the cherries do not stain your hands. It is best to pit cherries in a bowl in the bottom of your sink, as they will squirt staining juices when they are pitted.

1. Peel 2 wide strips of zest from the lemon and squeeze the juice from ½ lemon.

2. In the pressure cooker, combine lemon zest, lemon juice, cherries, sugar, grape juice, 4 tbsp (60 mL) water, cherry extract and almond extract, stirring well. Close and lock the lid. Cook on low pressure for 7 minutes. Quickly release the pressure. Check to make sure the cherries give easily when pressed with a wooden spoon; if more cooking time is needed, reset to low pressure for 2 minutes.

3. In a small bowl, whisk together cornstarch and the remaining water. Heat the cooker on High/Sauté/Brown. Stir in cornstarch mixture and cook, stirring often, for 3 to 4 minutes or until sauce is thickened.

4. Scoop ice cream into serving bowls and top with cherry sauce.

Bananas Foster Flan

This rich flan recipe is inspired by the flavors of bananas Foster, but it's so versatile you can easily change it up to make almond, coconut or crème de menthe flan instead.

MAKES 6 SERVINGS

- 4-cup (1 L) round soufflé dish, bottom and sides buttered
- Steam rack

Sauce

¾ cup	granulated sugar	175 mL
½ cup	water, divided	125 mL
½ tsp	banana or vanilla extract	2 mL

Flan

3	large eggs	3
2	large egg yolks	2
⅓ cup	granulated sugar	75 mL
2 tbsp	banana-flavored syrup	30 mL
½ tsp	vanilla extract	2 mL
2 cups	milk	500 mL
½ cup	half-and-half (10%) cream	125 mL

1. *Sauce:* In a small saucepan, combine sugar and ¼ cup (60 mL) water. Bring to a boil over medium-high heat, stirring to dissolve sugar. Boil, moving pan frequently but without stirring, for 5 to 7 minutes or until mixture becomes a light brown caramel color. Pour ¼ cup (60 mL) of the caramel into the prepared soufflé dish, tilting the dish so the caramel coats the bottom.

2. Add the remaining water to the caramel in the pan and boil, stirring, for 2 minutes or until mixture is smooth. Transfer caramel sauce to a heatproof bowl and let stand until it becomes a heavy syrup. When caramel is cool, add banana extract, stirring well. Cover tightly and store at room temperature until ready to use.

3. *Flan:* In a medium bowl, whisk together eggs and egg yolks. Whisk in sugar, banana syrup and vanilla. Gradually whisk in milk and cream. Strain through a fine-mesh sieve into the soufflé dish.

4. Add 1½ cups (375 mL) water (or the amount required by your cooker to reach pressure) to the pressure cooker and place the steam rack in the pot. Keeping the soufflé dish level, lower it onto the rack. Close and lock the lid. Cook on high pressure for 15 minutes. Let stand, covered, for 10 minutes, then release any remaining pressure. Check to make sure a tester inserted in the center of the flan comes out clean; if more cooking time is needed, reset to high pressure for 2 minutes. Carefully remove pan and rack; let stand on rack until cool. Cover and refrigerate flan for at least 6 hours, until chilled, or up to 3 days.

5. Run a knife around the edges of the flan. Place a serving platter on top of the dish and invert both platter and dish, transferring the flan to the platter. Drizzle some of the caramel sauce over top. Serve any remaining sauce on the side.

TIP

Banana-flavored syrup can be found in well-stocked grocery stores, online and in specialty coffee shops. If you cannot find it, use 1½ tsp (7 mL) banana extract and 5 tsp (25 mL) liquid honey.

Crème Brûlée

Although crème brûlée is one of my favorite desserts, I always used to find making it at home too finicky, so I only really indulged while dining out. But this simple version of the gourmet dessert allows us all to enjoy it whenever we like!

MAKES 6 SERVINGS

- Six 4-oz (125 mL) ramekins
- Steam rack

⅓ cup	granulated sugar	75 mL
6	large egg yolks	6
1 cup	heavy or whipping (35%) cream	250 mL
1 cup	half-and-half (10%) cream	250 mL
2 tsp	vanilla extract	10 mL
⅓ cup	superfine sugar (see tip)	75 mL

TIPS

Leftover egg whites can be stored in an airtight container in the freezer for up to 3 months. Use them to make meringues and other desserts.

Superfine sugar is often called baker's sugar. If you cannot find it, you can pulse granulated sugar in a blender or grinder until fine.

You can prepare these through step 4 ahead of time (omit step 3). Let cool, then cover and refrigerate for up to 3 days. Bring flan to room temperature before adding sugar and broiling.

1. In a large bowl, whisk together granulated sugar and egg yolks. Whisk in heavy cream, half-and-half and vanilla until just combined. Strain through a fine-mesh sieve into a container with a spout. Pour into ramekins, dividing evenly. Cover each ramekin with foil, pinching tightly around the sides.

2. Add 1½ cups (375 mL) water (or the amount required by your cooker to reach pressure) to the pressure cooker and place the steam rack in the pot. Stack ramekins like bricks on the rack, making sure they are level. Close and lock the lid. Cook on high pressure for 6 minutes.

3. Meanwhile, preheat broiler with the rack 4 inches (10 cm) from the heat source.

4. When the cooking time is done, let stand, covered, for 10 minutes, then release any remaining pressure. Check to make sure a tester inserted in the center of a custard comes out clean; if more cooking time is needed, reset to high pressure for 2 minutes.

5. Transfer ramekins to a baking sheet and remove foil. Sprinkle superfine sugar evenly over each custard. Broil for 2 to 3 minutes, watching carefully and rotating as needed, until sugar has evenly melted and caramelized. Serve warm.

VARIATION

Omit the superfine sugar and steps 3 and 5. Top the custards with your favorite berries.

Almond Chocolate Pots de Crème

These decadent little cups are a masterpiece of flavor in individual servings of rich, chocolaty custard. Cocoa, cream and almond butter coalesce into a memorable, satisfying dessert.

MAKES 4 SERVINGS

- Four 4-oz (125 mL) ramekins
- Steam rack

⅓ cup	unsweetened cocoa powder	75 mL
1 cup	almond butter	250 mL
⅔ cup	heavy or whipping (35%) cream	150 mL
⅔ cup	milk	150 mL
½ cup	granulated sugar	125 mL
4	large egg yolks	4
1 tsp	vanilla extract	5 mL
	Whipped cream	

TIPS

Leftover egg whites can be stored in an airtight container in the freezer for up to 3 months. Use them to make meringues and other desserts.

You can serve the pots de crème warm instead of cooled, if you prefer. They can also be covered and refrigerated for up to 2 days before serving.

1. In a small saucepan, combine cocoa, almond butter, cream and milk. Cook over low heat, stirring, for 3 minutes or until almond butter is melted and the mixture is combined. Let cool completely.

2. Meanwhile, in a medium bowl, whisk together sugar, egg yolks and vanilla. Slowly whisk in cooled cream mixture until just combined. Strain through a fine-mesh sieve into a container with a spout. Pour into ramekins, dividing evenly. Cover each ramekin with foil, pinching tightly around the sides.

3. Add 1 cup (250 mL) water (or the amount required by your cooker to reach pressure) to the pressure cooker and place the steam rack in the pot. Place ramekins on the rack. Close and lock the lid. Cook on high pressure for 5 minutes. Let stand, covered, until the float valve drops down. Check to make sure a tester inserted in the center of a custard comes out clean; if more cooking time is needed, reset to high pressure for 2 minutes.

4. Remove ramekins from pot, remove foil and let cool. Serve with dollops of whipped cream.

Southern-Style Bread Pudding with Bourbon Sauce

I had never heard of bread pudding when I was growing up, and when I first learned of it, it didn't sound all that appealing. But once I indulged in this rich version, interspersed with pecans and peaches and dripping with sweet bourbon sauce, I was sold. You can halve this recipe, but don't double it.

MAKES 6 SERVINGS

- 4-cup (1 L) casserole dish, buttered
- Steam rack

Bread Pudding

¾ cup	finely chopped dried peaches	175 mL
	Boiling water	
1 cup	granulated sugar	250 mL
2	large eggs	2
½ tsp	ground cinnamon	2 mL
¼ tsp	ground nutmeg	1 mL
¼ tsp	ground cardamom	1 mL
¼ tsp	ground allspice	1 mL
2 cups	milk	500 mL
3 cups	torn stale or dried French bread (1-inch/2.5 cm pieces)	750 mL
¼ cup	chopped pecans	60 mL
2 tbsp	unsalted butter, cut into small pieces	30 mL

Bourbon Sauce

2 tbsp	unsalted butter	30 mL
2 tbsp	all-purpose flour	30 mL
3 tbsp	granulated sugar	45 mL
1 cup	milk	250 mL
3 tbsp	bourbon	45 mL

1. *Pudding:* Place peaches in a small bowl and cover with boiling water. Let stand for 10 minutes. Drain peaches.

2. In a large bowl, whisk together sugar and eggs until sugar has dissolved and mixture is pale yellow. Whisk in peaches, cinnamon, nutmeg, cardamom, allspice and milk until blended. Add bread cubes and stir to cover bread with liquid. Let stand for 30 minutes, stirring occasionally. Stir in pecans.

3. Spoon mixture into prepared casserole dish and dot butter on top.

4. Add 2 cups (500 mL) water (or the amount required by your cooker to reach pressure) to the pressure cooker and place the steam rack in the pot. Place casserole dish on the rack. Close and lock the lid. Cook on high pressure for 15 minutes. Let stand, covered, for 10 minutes, then release any remaining pressure. Check to make sure the pudding is firm and a tester inserted in the center comes out clean; if more cooking time is needed, reset to high pressure for 2 minutes. Carefully remove dish and rack; keep dish on rack and cover with foil.

5. *Sauce:* In a small saucepan, melt butter over medium heat. Whisk in flour and cook, whisking, for 1 minute or until golden. Whisk in sugar and milk; cook, whisking, for 5 minutes or until thickened. Remove from heat and stir in bourbon.

6. Remove foil from casserole dish and pour sauce over pudding. Spoon pudding into individual serving bowls. Serve warm.

VARIATION

Substitute a sweet egg bread, such as challah, for the French bread.

Chocolate Chunk Bread Pudding

Here's a perfect way to use up leftover bread: just convert it into a decadent dessert! Add in some chocolate chunks, and you have a rich, hassle-free bread pudding with lots of chocolate.

MAKES 6 SERVINGS

- 4-cup (1 L) round soufflé dish, bottom and sides buttered
- Steam rack

3 tbsp	unsalted butter, softened	45 mL
6	slices stale French or Italian bread	6
3	large eggs	3
1/3 cup	granulated sugar	75 mL
1 1/2 cups	half-and-half (10%) cream	375 mL
2 tsp	vanilla extract	10 mL
2 tsp	grated orange zest	10 mL
2/3 cup	dark chocolate chunks	150 mL
1/2 cup	chopped walnuts	125 mL
	Whipped cream	
1/2 tsp	ground nutmeg	2 mL

1. Butter both sides of bread and cut into 2-inch (5 cm) square pieces. You should have about 6 cups (1.5 L).

2. In a large bowl, whisk eggs. Whisk in sugar, cream, vanilla and orange zest.

3. Add half the bread pieces to the prepared soufflé dish. Pour half the egg mixture on top. Sprinkle with half each of the chocolate chunks and walnuts. Repeat layers. Press bread down into liquid and let stand for 10 minutes. Cover dish with foil, pinching tightly around the sides.

4. Add 2 cups (500 mL) water (or the amount required by your cooker to reach pressure) to the pressure cooker and place the steam rack in the pot. Place the dish on the rack. Close and lock the lid. Cook on high pressure for 15 minutes. Let stand, covered, for 10 minutes, then release any remaining pressure. Check to make sure a tester inserted in the center of the pudding comes out clean; if more cooking time is needed, reset to high pressure for 5 minutes. Carefully remove dish, remove foil and let stand for at least 10 minutes or until ready to serve.

5. Top pudding with dollops of whipped cream and sprinkle with nutmeg.

VARIATION

Cranberry Almond Bread Pudding: Substitute dried cranberries for the chocolate chunks, and slivered almonds for the walnuts. Soak the dried cranberries in hot water for 10 minutes, then drain before adding them in step 3.

Nutmeg Rum Raisin Rice Pudding

This rich and creamy dessert is not only warm and comforting, but is also laden with raisins, rum, honey and nutmeg. The hardest part about making it is waiting until you can open the cooker and experience the magical aroma.

MAKES 6 SERVINGS

2 tbsp	unsalted butter	30 mL
1 cup	Arborio or other short-grain white rice	250 mL
2 cups	water	500 mL
1 tsp	rum extract	5 mL
1/3 cup	raisins	75 mL
1 1/2 cups	milk	375 mL
1/3 cup	liquid honey	75 mL
1/2 tsp	ground nutmeg	2 mL

TIP

When quickly releasing the pressure, keep your hands and face away from the hole on top of the steam release handle, so you don't get scalded by the escaping steam.

1. Heat the pressure cooker on High/Sauté/Brown. Add butter and heat until melted. Add rice and cook, stirring, for 1 to 2 minutes or until coated and starting to crackle. Cancel cooking.

2. Add water and rum extract, stirring well. Close and lock the lid. Cook on high pressure for 7 minutes. Quickly release the pressure. Check to make sure the rice is tender; if more cooking time is needed, reset to high pressure for 2 minutes.

3. Stir in raisins, milk and honey. Heat the cooker on High/Sauté/Brown. Cook, stirring often, for 4 to 6 minutes or until pudding is your desired consistency. (Note: it will continue to thicken after it is removed from the heat.) Sprinkle with nutmeg.

VARIATION

Cranberry Rice Pudding: In place of the rum extract, use vanilla extract. Replace the raisins with dried cranberries, and substitute 1/2 cup (125 mL) granulated sugar for the honey. Garnish with ground cardamom instead of nutmeg, if desired.

Bonus Recipes: Stocks and Sauces

Low-Sodium Vegetable Stock

Homemade vegetable stock works so well in many recipes where you want a homemade stock. This low-sodium version is wonderful for vegetarian and vegan recipes.

MAKES ABOUT 8 CUPS (2 L)

3	stalks celery, roughly chopped	3
3	cloves garlic, smashed	3
2	leeks (middle green parts only), thickly sliced	2
1	large onion, quartered	1
1	large carrot, roughly chopped	1
½ oz	dried shiitake mushrooms	15 g
10	sprigs fresh parsley	10
6	sprigs fresh thyme	6
3	bay leaves	3
1 tbsp	whole black peppercorns	15 mL
8 cups	water	2 L
2 tsp	coconut amino acids	10 mL

TIPS

You can also use the white and light green parts of the leek, but they are a common addition to other recipes, and stock is a great use for the leftover middle green parts. The darker green parts add a sulfuric taste that is intensified in the pressure cooker.

In addition to the vegetables listed, you can add leftover broccoli stems, chopped celery root or corn cobs for added flavor and texture, and to use up leftover ingredients.

The stock can be refrigerated for up to 3 days or frozen for up to 3 months.

1. In the pressure cooker, combine celery, garlic, leeks, onion, carrot, mushrooms, parsley, thyme, bay leaves, peppercorns, water and amino acids. Close and lock the lid. Cook on high pressure for 15 minutes. Let stand, covered, until the float valve drops down.

2. Strain stock through a fine-mesh sieve into a large container, pressing on solids to extract more liquid. Discard solids. Let stand at room temperature until cool.

Salt-Free Vegetable Stock

This salt-free vegetable stock is a classic addition to many recipes. Use it when you want to control the amount of salt in your recipe.

MAKES ABOUT 8 CUPS (2 L)

3	stalks celery, roughly chopped	3
3	cloves garlic, smashed	3
2	leeks (middle green parts only), thickly sliced	2
1	large onion, quartered	1
1	large carrot, roughly chopped	1
½ oz	dried shiitake mushrooms, rinsed	15 g
10	sprigs fresh parsley	10
6	sprigs fresh thyme	6
3	bay leaves	3
1	2-inch (5 cm) piece kombu (optional)	1
1 tbsp	whole black peppercorns	15 mL
8 cups	water	2 L

1. In the pressure cooker, combine celery, garlic, leeks, onion, carrot, mushrooms, parsley, thyme, bay leaves, kombu (if using), peppercorns and water. Close and lock the lid. Cook on high pressure for 15 minutes. Let stand, covered, until the float valve drops down.

2. Strain stock through a fine-mesh sieve into a large container, pressing on solids to extract more liquid. Discard solids. Let stand at room temperature until cool.

TIPS

Kombu is a dried sea kelp that is used in many Asian dishes. It is also used to make dashi, an essential broth for Japanese dishes. You can find it in Asian markets and online. Kombu adds umami and a slightly salty taste without adding salt. It does contain relatively small amounts of sodium, and is a good source of other nutrients.

The stock can be refrigerated for up to 3 days or frozen for up to 3 months.

Low-Sodium Chicken Stock

The flavor of homemade chicken stock is noticeably richer than store-bought broth, and you know exactly what ingredients were used. The pressure cooker cuts the preparation time significantly and does an exceptional job of extracting flavor.

MAKES ABOUT 8 CUPS (2 L)

3 lbs	chicken wings or other parts (see tip)	1.5 kg
1	large onion, coarsely chopped	1
5	sprigs fresh parsley	5
3	bay leaves	3
½ tsp	salt	2 mL
8 cups	water	2 L

TIPS

You can use any chicken parts or bony scraps you have on hand, but parts such as wings, backs and feet will produce stocks that are much richer and thicker.

For deeper flavor, brown the chicken parts before use. Use 2 tbsp (30 mL) vegetable oil or schmaltz (rendered chicken fat) and follow step 1 on page 207.

The stock can be refrigerated for up to 2 days or frozen for up to 7 months. It will gel in the refrigerator. Measure out as directed in the recipe or reheat to liquefy.

1. In the pressure cooker, combine wings, onion, parsley, bay leaves, salt and water. Close and lock the lid. Cook on high pressure for 55 minutes. Let stand, covered, until the float valve drops down.

2. Strain stock through a fine-mesh sieve into a large container, pressing on solids to extract more liquid. Discard solids. Skim fat from stock before use (you can use immediately or, to make skimming the fat easier, cover and refrigerate for 8 hours, until chilled).

Salt-Free Chicken Stock

This version of chicken stock gets its added flavor from vegetables instead of salt. Sautéing the chicken before pressure cooking also adds flavor and color to the stock.

MAKES ABOUT 8 CUPS (2 L)

2 tbsp	vegetable oil or schmaltz	30 mL
3 lbs	chicken wings or other parts (see tip)	1.5 kg
3	stalks celery, with leaves, sliced	3
1	large carrot, coarsely chopped	1
1	onion, coarsely chopped	1
5	sprigs fresh parsley	5
2	sprigs fresh thyme	2
1	bay leaf	1
8 cups	water	2 L

TIPS

Schmaltz is rendered chicken fat. It can be found in the kosher section of well-stocked grocery stores or online.

You can use any chicken parts or bony scraps you have on hand, but parts such as wings, backs and feet will produce stocks that are much richer and thicker.

If you have leftover roasted chicken parts, you can use them in this stock. Skip step 1, and heat the cooker with 1 tbsp (15 mL) vegetable oil or schmaltz at the beginning of step 2.

The stock can be refrigerated for up to 2 days or frozen for up to 7 months. It will gel in the refrigerator. Measure out as directed in the recipe or reheat to liquefy.

1. Heat the pressure cooker on High/ Sauté/Brown. Add oil and heat until shimmering. Working in batches, add chicken parts and cook, turning often, for 5 to 7 minutes or until browned on all sides. Using tongs, transfer chicken to a bowl. Discard all but 1 tbsp (15 mL) oil from the pot.

2. Add celery, carrot and onion to the cooker and cook, stirring often, for 7 minutes or until browned. Add 1 cup (250 mL) water, scraping up any browned bits from the bottom of the pot. Cancel cooking.

3. Return chicken and any accumulated juices to the cooker. Add parsley, thyme, bay leaf, salt and the remaining water, stirring well. Close and lock the lid. Cook on high pressure for 55 minutes. Let stand, covered, until the float valve drops down.

4. Strain stock through a fine-mesh sieve into a large container, pressing on solids to extract more liquid. Discard solids. Skim fat from stock before use (you can use immediately or, to make skimming the fat easier, cover and refrigerate for 8 hours, until chilled).

Low-Sodium Beef Bone Broth

This delicious homemade bone broth imparts rich flavor to many dishes. You can also drink it for a satisfying, nutrient-rich paleo treat. The pressure cooker reduces the hours of stovetop simmering that is usually required, and intensifies the flavor.

MAKES ABOUT 8 CUPS (2 L)

2 tbsp	vegetable oil (approx.)	30 mL
4 lbs	beef shanks, oxtails or short ribs	2 kg
2	leeks (middle green parts only), thickly sliced	2
½ oz	dried shiitake mushrooms	15 g
3	bay leaves	3
1 tbsp	whole black peppercorns	15 mL
8 cups	water	2 L
1 tsp	apple cider vinegar or dry red wine (optional)	5 mL

TIPS

Instead of browning the beef in the pressure cooker, you can roast it in the oven. Arrange beef on a foil-lined baking sheet and drizzle with oil. Bake at 400°F (200°C) for 1 hour, turning once. Add beef and any accumulated juices to the cooker and continue with step 2.

After cooking the broth, you can add salt to taste, if desired. Just be aware that the beef already contributes some sodium.

The broth can be refrigerated for up to 3 days or frozen for up to 6 months.

1. Heat the pressure cooker on High/Sauté/Brown. Add 1 tbsp (15 mL) oil and heat until shimmering. Working in batches, add beef and cook, turning often, for 5 to 7 minutes or until browned on all sides, adding more oil as needed between batches. Using tongs, transfer beef to a plate as it is browned. Cancel cooking.

2. Return all beef and any accumulated juices to the cooker. Add leeks, mushrooms, bay leaves, peppercorns, water and vinegar (if using), stirring well. Close and lock the lid. Cook on high pressure for 90 minutes. Let stand, covered, until the float valve drops down.

3. Strain broth through a fine-mesh sieve into a large container. Remove and discard bones. Press on the remaining solids to extract more liquid. Discard solids. To use immediately, skim fat from broth and serve. If using later, let stand at room temperature until cool, then cover and refrigerate for 8 hours, until chilled. Skim congealed fat from top of broth.

Traditional Tomato Sauce

This classic foundational tomato sauce recipe is streamlined with simple ingredients and relatively quick pressure cooking time, for a rich tomato sauce that tastes like it took all day to prepare.

MAKES ABOUT 8 CUPS (2 L)

2	cans (each 28 oz/796 mL) whole tomatoes (preferably San Marzano), with juice	2
3 tbsp	virgin olive oil, divided	45 mL
2 tbsp	butter (preferably unsalted)	30 mL
4	cloves garlic, minced	4
1½ tsp	dried oregano	7 mL
1	carrot, cut into large chunks	1
1	small onion, cut in half	1
½ cup	water	125 mL
2 tsp	Worcestershire sauce (optional)	10 mL
	Kosher salt and freshly ground black pepper	
2 tbsp	minced fresh parsley	30 mL
2 tbsp	minced fresh basil	30 mL

1. Pour tomatoes into a large bowl. Using your hands, crush tomatoes until pieces are about ½ inch (1 cm).

2. Heat the pressure cooker on High/Sauté/Brown. Add 2 tbsp (30 mL) oil and the butter; heat until oil is shimmering. Add garlic and cook, stirring, for 1 minute or until fragrant. Add oregano and cook, stirring, for 1 minute or until fragrant. Cancel cooking.

3. Add tomatoes, carrot, onion, water and Worcestershire sauce (if using), stirring well. Season with salt and pepper. Close and lock the lid. Cook on high pressure for 45 minutes. Quickly release the pressure. Using tongs, remove and discard carrots chunks and onion halves. Stir in parsley, basil and the remaining oil.

VARIATIONS

To make this sauce a little spicier, add ½ tsp (2 mL) hot pepper flakes with the oregano.

Reserve 1 cup (250 mL) of the crushed tomatoes and stir them in with the fresh herbs in step 3. This imparts an even fresher flavor to the sauce.

TIPS

Use the best canned tomatoes you can find. San Marzano tomatoes are known for their quality, but any high-quality brand will work.

You can use fresh, in-season tomatoes in place of canned. You will need about 20 to 24 peeled plum (Roma) tomatoes for this recipe. To quickly peel tomatoes, score one end of each tomato and add them to a pot of boiling water for 45 seconds or until the skin begins to wrinkle. Using tongs, quickly transfer the tomatoes to a bowl of ice water, then peel off the skins.

The sauce can be refrigerated for up to 3 days or frozen for up to 3 months. Before freezing tomato sauce, divide it into measured amounts and label each container with the amount and date.

Ragù Bolognese

This delectable Bolognese is so quick and easy, it may just become your go-to sauce. Lightly coat your pasta with this inspired sauce and add a sprinkling of Parmigiano-Reggiano, and you will swoon with delight. You can use this sauce to make lasagna.

MAKES ABOUT 5½ CUPS (1.375 L)

2 tbsp	butter	30 mL
1 tbsp	virgin olive oil	15 mL
2	carrots, chopped	2
1	small onion, chopped	1
1	stalk celery, chopped	1
12 oz	ground beef	375 g
½ cup	dry white wine	125 mL
½ cup	low-sodium beef bone broth (page 208) or ready-to-use beef broth	125 mL
2 tbsp	tomato paste	30 mL
1	can (14 oz/398 mL) diced or crushed tomatoes, with juice	1
1	bay leaf	1
⅛ tsp	ground nutmeg	0.5 mL
1½ cups	hot water	375 mL
2 tbsp	heavy or whipping (35%) cream	30 mL
	Kosher salt and freshly ground black pepper	

TIPS

This recipe makes enough sauce for 1¼ to 1½ lbs (625 to 750 g) of pasta such as fettuccine, spaghetti or penne.

The sauce can be refrigerated for up to 3 days or frozen for up to 3 months.

1. Heat the pressure cooker on High/Sauté/Brown. Add butter and oil; heat until oil is shimmering. Add carrots, onion and celery; cook, stirring often, for 3 to 5 minutes or until onion is translucent. Add beef and cook, breaking it up with a spoon, for 8 to 10 minutes or until beef is no longer pink and liquid has evaporated. Add wine and cook, stirring and scraping up any browned bits from the bottom of the pot, for 5 to 7 minutes or until wine is almost evaporated. Cancel cooking.

2. In a medium bowl, combine broth and tomato paste, mixing well.

3. Add broth mixture, tomatoes, bay leaf and nutmeg to the cooker, mixing well. Close and lock the lid. Cook on high pressure for 10 minutes. Quickly release the pressure.

4. Add hot water and stir well, scraping up any browned bits from the bottom of the pot. Close and lock the lid. Cook on high pressure for 10 minutes. Quickly release the pressure. Discard bay leaf.

5. Stir in cream and season to taste with salt and pepper.

Sweet and Sassy Barbecue Sauce

Create your own barbecue sauce with your own ingredients in no time in the pressure cooker. What I really love about this recipe is that you can adjust the level of spiciness, sweetness or tanginess to make it your own.

MAKES ABOUT 3 CUPS (750 ML)

- Immersion blender or blender

1	chipotle pepper in adobo sauce, drained and minced	1
2 tsp	kosher salt	10 mL
2 tsp	garlic powder	10 mL
1 tsp	smoked paprika	5 mL
½ tsp	dry mustard	2 mL
¼ tsp	ground cloves	1 mL
¾ cup	tomato purée	175 mL
¾ cup	water	175 mL
¼ cup	liquid honey	60 mL
¼ cup	light (fancy) molasses	60 mL
¼ cup	apple cider vinegar	60 mL
5 tsp	grapeseed or sesame oil	25 mL
2	small onions, chopped	2

TIPS

Fully drain the chipotle pepper, as the adobo sauce will make the barbecue sauce too thick.

This recipe can be made in 6-quart (6 L) or larger pressure cookers, as long as your cooker does not require more than 3 cups (750 mL) liquid to reach pressure. You can cut the recipe in half or double it, as long as you have enough liquid as required by your cooker.

The sauce can be refrigerated for up to 3 days or frozen for up to 3 months.

1. In a medium bowl, combine chipotle, salt, garlic powder, paprika, mustard, cloves, tomato purée, water, honey, molasses and vinegar, stirring well. Set aside.

2. Heat the pressure cooker on High/ Sauté/Brown. Add oil and heat until shimmering. Add onions and cook, stirring, for 7 to 9 minutes or until lightly browned. Cancel cooking.

3. Stir in tomato mixture, scraping up any browned bits from the bottom of the pot. Close and lock the lid. Cook on high pressure for 10 minutes. Quickly release the pressure.

4. Using the immersion blender (or transferring sauce in batches to a blender), purée sauce until smooth.

VARIATIONS

For a less smoky flavor, replace the chipotle pepper with hot pepper sauce, such as Sriracha, to taste.

For a smokier flavor but less spice, replace the chipotle pepper with up to 1 tsp (5 mL) liquid smoke to taste. Add hot pepper sauce to taste, if desired.

Replace the tomato purée with ¾ cup (175 mL) water and 1½ tbsp (22 mL) tomato paste.

Substitute brown sugar, pure maple syrup, chopped dates and/or chopped prunes for the molasses; just make sure the total amount is ¼ cup (60 mL).

Decrease the apple cider vinegar to taste, or substitute white vinegar or a combination of white vinegar and unsweetened apple juice.

Pressure Cooking Time Charts

The times given in these charts are general cooking times for these ingredients on their own, with the appropriate amount of cooking liquid. Cooking times may increase when ingredients are combined. When you are preparing a recipe that uses a combination of ingredients, always use the cooking time recommended in the recipe.

Where a range of cooking times is given, stop cooking at the shortest time and check the doneness before continuing. Once you are familiar with your pressure cooker and the recipes you are preparing, you will be able to set more precise times, though the tenderness or meats or ripeness of vegetables can also affect cooking times.

If you are cooking at altitudes above 3,000 feet (914 meters), changes in cooking times will be required. Contact your cooker's manufacturer for the required adjustments.

Beef

Cut of beef*	Cooking time	Cooking time from frozen	Pressure	Release method
Brisket	70 to 85 minutes	-	High	Natural
Chuck roast	40 to 50 minutes	-	High	Natural
Flank steak	22 to 25 minutes	30 to 33 minutes	High	Natural
Ground	5 minutes	-	High	Quick
Oxtails	45 minutes	55 to 60 minutes	High	Natural
Rib roast	60 minutes	70 to 80 minutes	High	Natural
Shanks	45 minutes	-	High	Natural
Short ribs	25 to 30 minutes	35 to 40 minutes	High	Natural
Shoulder roast	60 to 70 minutes	-	High	Natural
Sirloin steak, thin-cut	17 to 20 minutes	22 to 25 minutes	High	Quick
Stew meat, cubed	12 minutes	17 minutes	High	Natural
Top sirloin roast	45 minutes	55 to 60 minutes	High	Natural

* Always check the internal temperature of cooked meats to make sure they are done.

Lamb and Veal

Cut of lamb or veal*	Cooking time	Cooking time from frozen	Pressure	Release method
Lamb, chops (1 inch/ 2.5 cm thick)	7 minutes	12 minutes	High	Quick
Lamb, ground	12 minutes	17 minutes	High	Quick
Lamb, leg	40 minutes	50 minutes	High	Natural
Lamb, shoulder	25 to 30 minutes	-	High	Natural
Veal, chops	8 minutes	14 minutes	High	Quick
Veal, ground	6 minutes	-	High	Natural
Veal, roast	50 to 60 minutes	-	High	Natural

* Always check the internal temperature of cooked meats to make sure they are done.

Pork

Cut of pork*	Cooking time	Cooking time from frozen	Pressure	Release method
Belly	40 to 50 minutes	-	High	Natural
Chops (1 inch/2.5 cm thick)	12 to 15 minutes	22 to 25 minutes	High	Natural
Ground	5 minutes	-	High	Quick
Ham hocks	50 minutes	-	High	Natural
Loin	7 to 9 minutes	-	High	Natural
Ribs, baby back	20 minutes	-	High	Natural
Sausage, in casing (pierced)	8 to 10 minutes	-	High	Quick
Shank	35 to 40 minutes	-	High	Natural
Shoulder roast, whole	50 to 60 minutes	-	High	Natural
Shoulder roast, cubed	9 minutes	14 minutes	High	Quick
Spareribs	20 minutes	-	High	Natural

* Always check the internal temperature of cooked meats to make sure they are done.

Poultry

Cut of poultry*	Cooking time	Cooking time from frozen	Pressure	Release method
Chicken, ground	5 minutes	-	High	Quick
Chicken, whole	25 to 30 minutes	40 to 45 minutes	High	Natural
Chicken breast, bone-in	12 minutes	20 minutes	High	Quick
Chicken breast, boneless	4 minutes	11 minutes	High	Quick
Chicken leg quarters	12 minutes	20 minutes	High	Quick
Chicken thighs	12 minutes	20 minutes	High	Quick
Chicken wings	10 minutes	-	High	Quick
Cornish hen	10 minutes	20 minutes	High	Natural
Turkey breast	40 minutes	55 minutes	High	Natural
Turkey breast, sliced	9 minutes	12 minutes	High	Quick

* Always check the internal temperature of cooked poultry to make sure it is done.

Fish and Seafood

Type of fish or seafood	Cooking time	Cooking time from frozen	Pressure	Release method
Clams, fresh	5 minutes	-	High	Quick
Crab legs, small	3 minutes	-	High	Quick
Fish fillet, white, lean and firm (such as cod, haddock or halibut)	3 to 5 minutes	7 to 9 minutes	Low	Quick
Fish fillet, white, lean and flaky (such as flounder, tilapia or rainbow trout)	3 to 5 minutes	7 to 9 minutes	Low	Quick
Lobster tail	5 minutes	9 minutes	Low	Quick
Mussels	1 minute	-	Low	Quick
Perch	6 minutes	11 minutes	Low	Quick
Salmon	6 minutes	11 minutes	Low	Quick
Scallops	1 to 2 minutes	3 minutes	High	Quick
Shrimp	2 to 3 minutes	4 to 6 minutes	Low	Quick

Eggs

Desired doneness	Cooking time	Pressure	Release method
Hard-cooked	6 minutes	Low	Natural
Medium-cooked	4 minutes	Low	Quick
Soft-cooked	1 minute	Low	Quick

Legumes

Type of legume	Cooking time for soaked	Cooking time for dried	Pressure	Release method
Adzuki beans	6 minutes	18 minutes	High	Natural
Black beans	5 minutes	28 minutes	High	Natural
Black-eyed peas	4 minutes	7 minutes	High	Natural
Borlotti (cranberry) beans	8 minutes	23 minutes	High	Natural
Cannellini (white kidney) beans	7 minutes	28 minutes	High	Natural
Chickpeas (garbanzo beans)	18 minutes	38 minutes	High	Natural
Great Northern beans	7 minutes	28 minutes	High	Natural
Kidney beans, red	7 minutes	23 minutes	High	Natural
Lentils, black (beluga)	Do not soak	8 minutes	High	Natural
Lentils, brown	Do not soak	12 minutes	High	Natural
Lentils, green (Puy)	Do not soak	10 minutes	High	Natural
Lentils, split yellow or red	Do not soak	1 minute	High	Natural
Lima beans	7 minutes	13 minutes	High	Natural
Navy beans	7 minutes	20 minutes	High	Natural
Peas, green, whole	10 minutes	18 minutes	High	Natural
Peas, green, split	Do not soak	5 minutes	High	Natural
Pinto beans	8 minutes	23 minutes	High	Natural
Soy beans, yellow	18 minutes	38 minutes	High	Natural

Rice

Type of rice	Liquid per 1 cup (250 mL) rice	Cooking time	Pressure	Release method
Arborio*	2 cups (500 mL)	7 minutes	High	Quick
Basmati	1½ cups (375 mL)	3 minutes	High	10-minute
Basmati, soaked	1 cup (250 mL)	2 minutes	High	10-minute
Brown, long-grain	2 cups (500 mL)	10 minutes	High	Quick
Brown, short-grain	2 cups (500 mL)	14 minutes	High	Quick
Jasmine, rinsed	1 cup (250 mL)	1 minute	High	10-minute
Parboiled (packaged)	1½ cups (375 mL)	5 minutes	High	Quick
White, long-grain	1½ cups (375 mL)	3 minutes	High	10-minute
White, short-grain	1½ cups (375 mL)	8 minutes	High	10-minute
Wild rice	3 cups (750 mL)	22 minutes	High	10-minute

* For risotto, the amount of liquid needed may decrease depending on whether there are other ingredients in your dish that may release liquids. The recommended amount of liquid is for plain Arborio rice. Check individual recipes for the correct amount to add for perfect risotto.

Other Grains

Grain	Liquid per 1 cup (250 mL) grain	Cooking time	Pressure	Release method
Barley, pearl	2 cups (500 mL)	20 minutes	High	Natural
Bulgur	3 cups (750 mL)	8 minutes	High	10-minute
Farro	2½ cups (625 mL)	10 minutes	High	Quick
Freekeh	2½ cups (625 mL)	6 minutes	High	10-minute
Millet	1½ cups (375 mL)	1 minute	High	10-minute
Oats, large-flake (old-fashioned) rolled	4 cups (1 L)	10 minutes	High	Quick
Oats, steel-cut	3 cups (750 mL)	5 minutes	High	Quick
Quinoa	1½ cups (375 mL)	1 minute	High	10-minute

Vegetables

Vegetable	Cooking time	Pressure	Release method
Artichokes, whole	5 to 11 minutes	High	Quick
Asparagus	1 minute	High	Quick
Beet greens	2 minutes	High	Quick
Beets, whole	10 to 20 minutes	High	Quick
Bell peppers (stemmed and seeded), whole or thickly sliced	3 to 4 minutes	High	Quick
Broccoli florets	4 minutes	High	Quick
Brussels sprouts	4 minutes	High	Quick
Carrots, sliced	4 minutes	High	Quick
Carrots, whole	7 minutes	High	Quick
Cauliflower florets	3 minutes	High	Quick
Celery root (celeriac), quartered	3 minutes	High	Quick
Corn kernels, fresh	1 minute	High	Quick
Corn on the cob	3 minutes	High	Quick
Eggplant, halved lengthwise	5 minutes	High	Quick
Green or yellow beans, fresh or frozen	2 minutes	High	Quick
Kale	1 minute	High	Quick
Parsnips, whole	3 minutes	High	Quick
Peas, fresh or frozen	2 minutes	High	Quick
Potatoes, fingerling or new	5 minutes	High	Quick
Potatoes, small yellow or red	5 minutes	High	Quick
Potatoes, russet, quartered	5 minutes	High	Quick
Potatoes, russet, whole	7 to 10 minutes	High	Natural
Pumpkin, wedges	3 minutes	High	Quick
Spinach	1 minute	High	Quick
Squash, acorn, halved and seeded	6 minutes	High	Quick
Squash, butternut, halved and seeded	4 minutes	High	Quick
Squash, butternut, large chunks	4 minutes	High	Quick
Squash, spaghetti, halved	5 minutes	High	Quick
Sweet potatoes, whole	15 minutes	High	Natural
Swiss chard	2 minutes	High	Quick
Turnips, whole	5 minutes	High	Quick
Zucchini and yellow summer squash, thickly sliced	2 minutes	High	Quick

Index